THE PSYCHO RECORDS

LAURENCE A. RICKELS

WALLFLOWER PRESS
LONDON & NEW YORK

A Wallflower Press Book
Published by
Columbia University Press
Publishers Since 1893
New York • Chichester, West Sussex
cup.columbia.edu

A complete CIP record is available from the Library of Congress

ISBN 978-0-231-18112-9 (cloth : alk. paper)
ISBN 978-0-231-18113-6 (pbk. : alk. paper)
ISBN 978-0-231-54349-1 (e-book)

Columbia University Press books are printed on permanent
and durable acid-free paper.
Printed in the United States of America

Cover image: *Psycho* (1960) © Paramount

THE PSYCHO RECORDS

Contents

Acknowledgements vii

Preface: Late arrival of the 'New Vampire Lectures' ix

Psycho-Historical Introduction 1

Nazi Germany and Ed Gein; death is always murder; mass cultures of preparedness; *The Bad Seed* and Winnicott's allegory of hope

Record One: Playing Catch Up with the Vampire – But with *True Blood* 9

If at first only zombie movies succeed, then eight years later bring back vampirism, the return of hope; integration of the vampire (*Blade*, *Underworld*); *Twilight* and the pre-teen, post-*Buffy* media market; true bloodlines pitch Dracula against Jack the Ripper; by mourning's light we can begin to face our double, the psycho

Record Two: Schauer Scenes 22

Adorno on television; the withdrawal of sublimation and of the transitional object; the shower scene as altar of mass media culture; the public shower in *Carrie*; cutting closer to the screen than *Les Diaboliques*; disrespecting mother; perfect TV in the sound mix; Hitchcock is dead (undead, undead): let the sequels begin

Record Three: Alternate History – 1960 46

Eyes Without a Face and the serial heterograft; *Peeping Tom* and the cinematic horror apparatus of sight unseen; cryptology and *The Gold Bug*; *Raising Cain*; *Frenzy* of diagnosis; the psychotic and the psychopath are in it together (*In Cold Blood*)

Record Four: Epidemics of Mass Murder 62

Fido and zombie fathers as totem pets; virulence of the taboos upon the dead; *I Am Legend* and a vampiric mourner in a world of zombie consumerism; disrespecting the buried dad; the fruit cellar in *Night of the Living Dead* and *Fade to Black*; getting past Ben's murder by the protocols of terrorism (*Dawn of the Dead*, *Day of the Dead*); Romero mixes his favorite *Martin* out of equal parts psycho and vampire; Roland Kuhn on psychopathic fetishism with human material

Record Five: Manuals 81

Hand-to-eye coordination in horror films (*The Crawling Hand*, *Dr. Jekyll and Mr. Hyde*, *The Hand*); Ernst Kapp and the hand-held progress of technology; Hershell Gordon Lewis and the Grand Guignol of special effects (*Blood Feast*, *Two Thousand Maniacs!*, *Color Me Blood Red*); whose hands fulfill my death wishes? (*Mad Love*); dial M (by Fritz Lang) for serial murder

Record Six: Still Working on It 93

Arrest in *Pieces*; grave top publishing in *The Texas Chainsaw Massacre*; haunted Holmes and hotels (*Motel Hell, Hell House*); Texas is only a few hours from the Coast or New York City (*The Hills Have Eyes, The Last House on the Left*)

Record Seven: Phantoms 110

Séance on a Wet Afternoon and *Family Plot*; the double as mask in *William Wilson*; the tomb show of unmasking in *Phantom of the Opera*; Spiritualism, investigative reporting, and detective fiction; envy in *Phantom of the Paradise*

Record Eight: The Turning 124

Maniac and the POV-mask of the dead; killer mascots in *Halloween* and *Friday the 13th*; Kuhn and Elias Canetti on both sides of the mask; the unmasking of Michael Myers and the transvaluation of Laurie's survival

Record Nine: The Crowd and the Couple 140

Incest is best for werecats; Val Lewton and the horror of leaving it blank; Canetti on keeping in touch in groups; the American flirt meets the haunted commitment from Europe (*Cat People*); the *Fatal Attraction* of group or groupie

Record Ten: Getting Into B-Pictures 152

Schizoid, *Don't Answer the Phone*, and transference transgression; do you like Hitchcock, Powell, and Romero? (*Sisters*); the new Norman in *Dressed to Kill*, *Blow Out*, and *Body Double*; the feminist reproach in *Slumber Party Massacre*

Record Eleven: The Emperor's New Closure 169

War trauma besets the next generation (*The Prowler*); on the rebound from the containment of the *Psycho* Effect (*A Nightmare on Elm Street*); we're in the inoculation now (*Freddy vs. Jason*); Freddy Krueger's 'cyberglove' as advance preview of new media falls short; misplaced prospects in *Shocker* and *Wes Craven's New Nightmare*; reckoning with Freud in the 1980s and 90s

Record Twelve: By Rule of Tomb 181

Just Before Dawn; the mirror mother between Lacan and Winnicott; the internal home movie made by psychos, the slasher movie on TV decoded by gadget-loving expertise, and the greater film of Sid's survival (*Scream*, *Scream 2*, *Scream 3*); treating the mother's depression in the child (*Mother's Day* and *Baby*)

Record Thirteen: The Renewal of Psycho Horror by Compact with the Devil 194

Spoiler alert: occupational therapy for academics; *The Sixth Sense* and the ghost of the *Psycho* Effect; *The Blair Witch Project* and the house of leave-taking; therapeutic closure under demonic attack (*The Ring*); turning up the contrast on testimony between *Prom Night* and *I Know What You Did Last Summer*; who, what, how – but why? (*CSI*); the purloined letter or underlying label (*Manhunter*); infernal projective identification; the old *Saw* of torture-teaching; psychopathy's true self is the prize for passing the test of survival

Filmography 214
Bibliography 219
Index 225

Acknowledgements

I spend enough time in the book historicising this project (and myself). Let's just say that it is not surprising that the list of articles that appeared in advance of this book's final cut seems as long as my career. Already in 1990 I applied to *Fatal Attraction* insights into couple and group relations within the psycho-horror milieu which were going into my 1991 study *The Case of California*. A select portion of "Alex" (*The American Journal of Semiotics* 7.3, 1990) is back in the penultimate section of Record 9. The local success of my course offerings on horror at UC Santa Barbara throughout the 1990s, amplified, then, by the appearance of *The Vampire Lectures* at the end of the decade, prompted invitations to update my interpretation of the genre. 'Recognition Values: Seeing *The Sixth Sense* Again for the First Time' (*Other Voices* 2, March 2002) and 'Economies of Leave-Taking in Mark Z. Danielewski's *House of Leaves*' (in *Twenty-First-Century Gothic*, ed. Danel Olson, Scarecrow Press, 2011) contributed to the first section of Record 13. 'By Mourning's Light. Laurence A. Rickels on *True Blood*' (*Artforum*, October 2009), 'Like Squeezing Blood Out of a Zombie: New Directions in the Projection of Undeath' (*The White Review*, online, October 2014), and 'Integration of the Vampire' (in *Carmilla. Der Vampir und wir*, ed. Annette Rainer, Christina Töpfer, and Martina Zerovnik, Passagen Verlag, 2014) preview aspects of the full account I provide in Record 1. 'Integration: Understanding New Mediation via Innovations in Horror Cinema' (*Communication + 1*, vol. 4, article 13, 2015) also addresses the franchise *A Nightmare on Elm Street* and thus looks forward to Record 11. On other occasions contemporary artworks triggered my reflections on slasher and splatter films. What I adduced in commenting on the early paintings of filmmaker Ulrike Ottinger ('Rest in Pieces. On Ulrike Ottinger at the Neuer Berliner Kunstverein', *Texte zur Kunst* 22, 85, March 2012) fits the first section of Record 6. In 'Second Death' (in *between two deaths*, ed. Ellen Blumenstein and Felix Ensslin, Hatje Cantz 2007) my reading around Stephen G. Rhodes' work, which roamed between *Hamlet* and several films that overflowed from Hitchcock's shower scene, summarises my work on the *Psycho* Effect prior to the encounter with D. W. Winnicott's analysis of the antisocial tendency. The theorization that comes complete with Winnicott's input is already in evidence in 'The Other Coast of Terrorism. On Sue de Beer's *Hans & Grete*' (in *Terror and the Roots of Poetics*, ed. Jeffrey Champlin, Atropos Press, 2014) and 'Back to Frankfurt School' (in *A Concise Companion to Psychoanalysis, Literature, and Culture*, ed. Laura Marcus and Ankhi Mukherjee, Wiley Blackwell, 2014). Finally, 'The Emperor's New Closure' (*art / text* 70, 2000), my reckoning with the slasher treatment of Freud in an exhibition of his influence, continues to resound in the final section of Record 11.

William Murphy was responsible for the deal that sealed my first (double) profile as author: in exchange for letting him publish as a book the transcript of my vampire lectures, he brokered a contract for my three-volume work *Nazi Psychoanalysis*. But then he left university press publishing and entered the mainstream. Since that highlight I have relied on the kindness of stranger editors. One stint of mutual estrangement went on for so long you might wonder why I kept trying to make it work. For the children. My thanks to Yoram Allon, Commissioning Editor at Wallflower Press, for including this book in a list pitched equally to US and UK readerships, a targeting opportunity I appreciate given my current expat situation.

Preface: Late arrival of the 'New Vampire Lectures'

You get a break today because we're back in class. At least the first layer of this book dates back to the tape recording of lectures comprising my course on 'The Horror Film'. They reach back to the same era from which I sprung *The Vampire Lectures*. In the longer while between that transcription period and the completion of these 'New Vampire Lectures', I was able, by catching up with the laying and layering on of changes, at once to update and conclude my California chronicles of occult instruction in B-culture.

I adopted the film studies genre course on the horror film in the early 1980s and immediately adapted it to a new focus on the slasher and splatter movies that were in the foreground of the media Sensurround at that time. I fixed the focus of the survey class on 'the *Psycho* Effect', my summary term for those metabolic interrelations (self-evident back then) between the new slasher movies of the 1980s and the shower scene in Alfred Hitchcock's *Psycho* (1960), the traumatic origin of an identification that was being worked through. I rushed into the topical, without yet realising that it was the onset of allegorical reflection. In other words, I kept plugging away at the 'Effect' in the regularly offered course without noting changes in the Sensurround.

While I kept working on the rip and tear line of the shower scene, its re-metabolisation in countless slasher and splatter films, I discovered it was time to wake up out of my Rip van Winkle slumber. Even before Gus Van Sant's remake (1998), one of my students warned me that we were probably no longer in thrall to a reception of the shower scene as traumatic. Her proof was a newspaper clipping, largely the image of the announced 'Psycho doll', the brief report on the latest creation by dollmaker Madame Alexander, who, 'departing from classics like Cinderella and Scarlett O'Hara', was adding to her lineup Marion Crane as 'towel-clad doll in a shower with a silhouette of a killer lurking in the background'.

In the opening season of my investigation of the *Psycho* Effect, students would come up after my lecture and relate their own near misses with serial death. Coeds recalled almost entering the car of a famous killer but then miraculously deciding to let it drive away. I also remember my own close call; the student who told me three weeks into the class that he loved slasher movies but that he had to drop the class because he just didn't know what he would do if he heard another word from Freud, our sponsor. By the 1990s, however, the students no longer shared their near-death experiences but contributed instead anecdotes on the side of fabulation and recovery, like the report that the actor who played Leatherface was running a Santa Barbara souvenir shop called something like Shells O'Barbara.

Now that we are all so over them, it's time to file my *Psycho* lectures away as archival, but yet allegorical. They file down the aisles of the most enigmatic construct of historical understanding and reflection: the recent past. Following Hitchcock's 1960 film, after a post-traumatic delay of three or eight years, until some point in the late 1980s or early 1990s, horror films were all about metabolising, digesting, reversing, remaking the impact of the shower scene. Once it became clear that the wound of the *Psycho* Effect had come to be redressed, it could be readdressed in history.

At some point in the 1990s I began adding to the *Psycho* focus of the horror film class a prehistory, tracking back to Rupert Julian's *The Phantom of the Opera* (1925), on the video track, and to the Leroux novel in a lower tract of melancholia.

Psycho-Historical Introduction

Gaston Leroux's novel *Le Fantôme de l'Opéra* (1911) and its film adaptations occupied the busy intersection of three modern institutions and genres: Spiritualism, investigative journalism and criminal detection. The occult tradition of horror was undergoing renovation according to what Freud termed the secularisation of repression: mediatic transmission and the situation of testing came to occupy the foreground. Upon selecting the setting for its story – melancholic, demonic, Oedipal or psychotic – every horror scenario would continue to bear at least residual traces of all the other selections.

A genealogy of cinema folds out of its horror genre, which is as old as the medium. In any horror film you can watch the medium getting in touch with itself, with its constituent parts and constitutive partings. The horror film is the allegory of its medium beset by inner and outer changes – often in contest with 'new' media.

In 1960 *Psycho* breached the anxiety defence of moviegoers and compelled the horror film genre, after a post-traumatic delay, to repeat or restart in the spot it was in with the shower scene. Hitchcock began developing his signature thriller style while apprenticed to German cinema in the 1920s. German films were steeped in horror: doubling, serial and mass murder, phantom control. They faced one way as haunted screen (the title of Lotte Eisner's study), the other way as projection (forecast and programming) of the rise of National Socialism (the thesis of Siegfried Kracauer). To keep their remarks private when daughter Pat was in earshot, Alfred would converse with his wife Alma in German.

The German word *Schauer* is cognate with the English 'shower', in the sense both words still share of rainstorm or rain shower. As the German word for horror, as we will see presently, *Schauer*, too, derives from the storm advisory. But no meaning of *Schauer* fits in the stall. Instead German borrowed the French *douche* for the proper designation of the shower: *Dusche*. Coming to moviemaking via the horror cinema of

German Expressionism, Hitchcock invited the double that linguistics refers to as 'false friend' to enter the installation of a scene that became primal.

The mascot killers in psycho horror films are Germanic in provenance, either by the token of their own surnames (Myers, Voorhees, Krueger) or by the cargo they bear. Norman is the fictionalised delegate of Ed Gein, who was a close reader of sensationalised accounts of Ilse Koch. The good war had kept it all over there, but through Gein it suddenly broke through in place and time, a blot upon the very heartland of America.

The ability to switch off empathy can be regularly trained into soldiers for the duration of warfare. Nazi Germany counts as the first social order in the civilised world to enjoin the entire population to close ranks in remorselessness before the ongoing prospect of mass destruction and murder. Christopher Bollas draws the equation: 'Genocide is the quintessential crime of the twentieth century, and genocide is exemplified by the serial killer, a genocidal being who swiftly dispatches his victims and converts the human into the inhuman' (2011: 158).

While adolescence was streamlined in Nazi Germany and advanced to the position of cultural superego, a distinction in extinction, the Teen Age was to be continued in the United States as the experiment that was on, but open-endedly imbricated in the mass media of sex and violence. Following Gein's arrest and the release of the details of his designing with dead women, the crime scene became an attraction visited by many as though on a pilgrimage. That those attending the Mass of murder also collected relics is a continuity shot going back to Europe. What was new were the teen-idiomatic correlatives of these relics, the so-called 'geeners' that released the laughter stowaway in the slaughter of identification. 'Ed Gein is traveling on a bus. He walks up behind a woman an' gooses her butt. She says, "Hey, cut that out!" He says, "Why gee, thanks!"' (in Woods 1995: 94). I don't know off hand where the fad of dead baby jokes came from, but I remember that after schoolteacher Christa McAuliffe went down with the space shuttle an epidemic of dead-teacher-in-Space jokes broke out. In addition to what this signifies in the classroom setting, the joking coincided with the rise in the number of schoolchildren at that time declaring the career choice of teacher. Trauma triggers identification. Sometimes a horror scene gets you to identify with one of the players, sometimes the trauma is unbound in an excess of untenable identifications. It then requires the mass media to carry forward the identification.

In *Hostel* (2005) the German language and its world are displaced in the story of the life-and-death struggle for which Americans and Eastern Europeans are enlisted. Its world only appears toward the end as the station stop where the protagonist takes revenge for his friend's torture and murder. But the protagonist's own excellent German, which takes the Eastern European youths who are setting him up by surprise, is his means of interrupting the session of his torture unto death, a break on which he can then build his getaway. Only then does he discover that Americans have also paid to 'hunt' the kidnapped tourists. The *Psycho* Effect that was born in the staple of American popular culture pitched the casting call often enough to veterans of the post-world-war wars, from Vietnam to the wars against terrorism, military engagements that stir up the old good war to the point of reversing sides.

After I spent considerable time in my seminar at European Graduate School elaborating on the *Schauer*, including, for example, Theodor Adorno's reflections on the 'Schauerroman' (Gothic novel), one student, who had to excuse herself, told me she kept hearing 'Shoah'. But we must not be too quick to draw the equation.

The *Psycho* Effect's containment in film therapy by the 1990s breaks direct connection with the WWII-era's traumatic history. What it does document is that film, like psychoanalysis, is a medium in which the 'analytic' dimension (self-reflexivity, doubling, etc.) may be interminable but which of necessity also includes a therapeutic side or inside which is radically cure-driven and finite. Let's call this the truth of B-culture. To study its products is to engage with what Walter Benjamin considered the assignment of modern allegory: the full immersion of transcendence in finitude.

Once upon a time, *Schauer*, in the sense of horror, tracked back to rain and lightning storms that blew in from the North and brought devastation. *Schauer* preserves a splitting off in the meaning of horror and the attendant historical shift in its reception and administration. The rain storms that still regularly go by *Schauer* in German are no longer continuous with *Schauer*'s other meaning of 'horror'. Around this blind spot, then, a concise genealogy can be tracked. In the course of industrialisation, and then through the follow-up treatments of media technologisation and mass psychologisation, all natural causes of dying came to be subsumed by techno accident, the new focus of our ongoing efforts to contain violence. The parallel genealogy of risk calculation and insurance was also ready for this close-up. A reformatting of death as murder followed. The mascot of the new topography of our psychic reality was Jack the Ripper and his surgical cutting the new legend to this map.

As Freud underscored in 'Thoughts for the Times on War and Death', our psychic realisation of the other's death cannot allow for natural causes. Every death is registered as murder. The accidents of industrialisation and transport – for example, down in the mines – went sight unseen. But then the train emerged from the underworld of mining to transport the public across long distances. Accidents were out in the open and the incidence of phobia and hysteria specific to the risks of train travel introduced into psychological treatment or assessment and insurance coverage the prospect of the accident-induced or -triggered symptom pictures of traumatic neurosis. At the same time electricity introduced illumination and technical mediation into the new staging areas of preparedness. Thus we came to adopt and adapt to the group format of techno-catastrophe, and to extend it into the safer zone of preparedness. Every group becomes a group of survivors already prepared for and thus in the grip of impending techno-catastrophe. The theme parking of the insurance bond with the other via risk-as-thrill traversed the close quarters of projected catastrophe (where we're either survivors against all odds or all die together). In the end mass media culture has, bottom line, no other content than violence.

Through the mode of control release, which meets our own anxious preparedness half way, the content remains 'contained'. When, in *Beyond the Pleasure Principle*, Freud re-addressed traumatic neurosis in its WWI-induced mass format he postulated violent shock of a degree capable of penetrating the protective shield of consciousness. Through repetition of the traumatic contact the shell-shocked soldiers, for instance, sought to restore the anxiety defence of preparedness against its devastation. Ever since WWI, when the train of traumatic neurosis arrived in so many stations at once, we have had to immunise ourselves via the media with and against the shocks of the new. To withstand the pressure of massification we form in-groups and out-groups or enter support groups, all of them inoculative replicas of the larger mass that wears us down.

What proves unbearable is the disconnection in the face-to-face in which our nothingness alone is reflected. It's when the hitchhiker turns off the friendliness and stares you down with the look of vacancy, your nonexistence. The unbearable moment of the switch from connectedness to the view to the kill gets massified in the horror film in two ways, either by foregrounding a mass epidemic setting, as in zombie movies, or by making recourse to the duo-dynamic explanations that go back to early childhood. Our entry ticket in the latter case is provided by the inevitable moment in every development when there is a station break in the maternal expression of unconditional mirroring: whether in anger or depression, mother no longer looks back. In the case of the psycho killer we can therefore imagine a childhood in which the mother was not able to contain unattractive feelings of feeling unattractive, and thus did not install in little one a container for affect static. The psycho killer control-releases the turbulence by cultivating over dead bodies the disconnection with mother as another form of connection.

Up to this turning point, my reception of psycho horror cinema was already included in *The Case of California* and reflects the overlaps (I was doing then in my pool of application) between Freudian psychoanalysis and the Frankfurt School. In my running commentary in the series of my teaching I had reached the limit of applying to the *Psycho* Effect and its film therapy the model of the transference neurosis. It was by its inoculative proxy service that Freud sought to dislodge otherwise untreatable disorders by depositing them (or bracketing them out) in the background of a treatable condition or construction, like mourning for the father, which could be contained. I had adopted the model for understanding Freud's pursuit of the father neurosis in the published Ratman case, for example, which diverted attention from his patient's encryptment of his dead sister, the significance of the underworld in the Ratman case that Freud took note of but left behind in the original record. Thus the transference neurosis acts as a 'container' by drawing attention away from the dire legibility of the melancholic loss which, hidden or encrypted, is subsumed inoculation-style by the treatable scenario. In this way a double reading of mournable and unmournable losses and their interrelation was possible. This applies to the more or less neurotic setting. As he sidled up to psychosis, Freud in turn applied the legibility of melancholia as borderline caption to the outer limits of psychoanalytic understanding.

D. W. Winnicott's work on the etiological gap and overlap in developing child 'hoods' between psychosis and psychopathy begins to assemble a profile of the psychopath, at once the great unknown and the ultimate double in our faces. Based on his wartime work with symptomatic charges who had been relocated during the air war to the countryside, Winnicott began making the psycho transitionally identifiable in case studies with children he nipped as budding psychopaths at the onset of their 'antisocial tendencies'. His signature intervention was to characterise the initial 'nuisance behaviour' as expression of 'hope' that illuminates the 'importance of the environment' ('The Antisocial Tendency', 2000: 123–4). The etymology of 'hope' includes in the word's Germanic prehistory (preserved to this day, as *verhoffen*, in the German 'language of hunters') some of the senses Winnicott pursued with his clients at great length. In a word, hope begins as the startle response to a sudden change in our environment, whereby we (humans and animals alike) take the moment of hesitation to try out in our minds a new next move.

Without the allegory of hope, which is basic to what we might reclaim from British orthography as Winnicott's Psycho Analysis, psychopathy is reduced to *The Bad Seed* (1956). The screenplay is immersed in Freudian psychoanalysis, but only as the milieu for falling for the child's false self or, upon recognition of this failure, for abandoning all treatment projections and surrendering to the judgment of inheritance. Through Freudian technique, then, even if only recycled as party game, the mother of the perfect child can lift the repression from her own recollection that she was herself adopted and adapted for the good-object life. But first she was the child of a murderess raised by her adoptive father against her descent. While she was spared the evil influence, the next in her own line grows the seed of ruthlessness. This perfect child, who killed a rival schoolmate and did so, the clincher, without remorse, cannot be cured, let alone stopped, except by the death sentence of divine intervention.

It is because everyone's adolescence is a time-based version of psychopathy that we come so close to the psycho, our near-miss double. In object-relations terms: there but for the grace of the good object go I. The adolescent returns in fundamental ways to the starting block of early childhood. What has changed is the teen's physical ability to act on the wish to kill parents, who in the meantime begin to bear the date mark of expiration. The teen must find room in psychic reality for this death. What also starts over, then, is the delay in onset of the ability to mourn. To catch up with the delay the antisocial child or teen responds to a diffuse sense of deprivation and irreality by acts that call attention to the importance of the environment or container and thereby signal hope. Hope refers to the ability to turn around impingement by balking, starting over, finding a new approach, carrying out reality testing. But hope also refers to the search for the missing onset of the ability to mourn.

The psycho criminal is always the extreme instance of tendencies the prosecutors, bystanders, victims and survivors also share, but at the shallow end of the psychopathology or to the limit of its immunising dosage. Winnicott's understanding of the antisocial tendency applies to the whole milieu and is not mainly focused, in the mode of overkill, on the identified psycho. Before we are immersed in the deep end of Norman's madness we know that everyone 'goes mad' on occasion, as did Marion when she stole the money entrusted to her.

In *Psycho* we identified with the killer and killing at one remove: we entered the performance of containment with the editor's cut, right where the killer entered with the knife. In the tight spot of the *Psycho* Effect we were required to make this cut. In their therapeutic treatment of the *Schauer* scene, slasher and splatter movies began singling out one intended victim to be the delegate of the moviegoer's survival at the end of the projection. Beginning with the survival of Marion's delegates the therapeutic momentum of the horror scenario grows in the scope of hope. But since the psycho didn't stop or go, a continuum of ambiguous survival opened its chapter and worse in the course of the *Psycho* Effect. The slasher and splatter films began to enfold killers and victims alike as fitting in with a norm of adaptation to psychopathy, the environment of survival.

Moving from the allegorical pageant of Philip K. Dick's science fiction in *I Think I Am* and of James Bond in *SPECTRE* to problems of psychopathic violence I shifted from, respectively, Ludwig Binwanger's and Melanie Klein's phantastic, quasi-psychotic re-theorisations of the Oedipal mainstays of mourning, transference and reality testing to Winnicott's analysis of the obstacle course of deprivation that withholds the prospect of the very onset of the ability to mourn. *Germany: A Science Fiction* had to come before this book. Winnicott's rerouting of the psycho path from devastation through reparation and restitution toward mourning as its final frontier is a treatment plan and therefore optimistic. It fits the long history of the integration of 'Germany' in the postwar world, which I found inscribed within science fiction's preoccupation with psychopathy (the failure to pass the empathy test). The history of the *Psycho* Effect, like the span of time in which each projected horror is displayed, is too short to stagger the therapeutic optimism of Winnicott's psycho analysis. Instead for this book we must take from his understanding of the transitional object all that is set to go wrong in the course of development – until the wrong turn into delinquency begins to appear like another norm or Norman.

Did the finite run of the *Psycho* Effect contribute to the therapeutic termination of psychopathic violence? I come not to raise this question, but to bury it. Just the same, the *Psycho* Effect amounted to the longest running accumulation of evidence of film-therapeutic treatment of the effects of trauma. My study reaches back into the recent past to identify, describe, and interpret the remetabolisation and containment of *Psycho*'s traumatic scene in a great many films. Several attempts to counter the uncontainment of traumatic violence backfired – yielding a stricken reception that in turn had to be worked through. The relationship between violent crime and survival became one of the parameters in which subsequent films sought redress for the fatalities of Marion in *Psycho* and Ben in *Night of the Living Dead* (1968).

Since some point in the 1990s the figuration of this violence came to inhabit an unsuspected boundary-blending between zombieism and vampirism and found anew a champion in the Devil. *The Psycho Records* joins my earlier books on the vampire and the Devil to conclude my trilogy on horror. Can the psycho be located on the map of occult and technical mediations I pursued in my classes on the Coast? Even before we unpack the psycho we know he occupies a position between melancholic relations with the unmournably dead (the recycling of the maternal bond in vampirism) and the relationship beyond inhibition to the Devil Dad. Over the course of the *Psycho* Effect the identification of the psycho has been all over this map. It is still possible to read Norman Bates vampirologically. Freddy Krueger might be considered a relative of demons. Of the two bookends of my occult instruction in California it is *The Devil Notebooks*, through the reading it makes possible of the pre-Oedipal father, which opens up both the personalisation of the subject of *Nazi Psychoanalysis* and this outside chance of analysing the psycho. In 2009 a review of *The Devil Notebooks* in an Austrian journal of criminology astutely pointed to the value of understanding the appeal of what I called in that book 'Dad certainty' for students of crime and criminals.

The Psycho Records aims to examine in its full contextualisation within occult and secular horror the inoculum of a concluded film therapy. I am not offering another reading of the movie *Psycho* nor a film study of its reception. I do address Brian De Palma's homage movies, for example, which might be viewed as demanding an exception to this stance. But I take them at face value: I tend to consult them as equally engaged, however ironically, in addressing horror B-pictures at their source as a resource in therapy. While there is a good measure of doubling back to a fresh start in retraumatisation in the first season of the *Psycho* Effect, which yielded new tributaries of and tributes to the *Schauer* scene, overall there is a momentum that progresses to a turning (*Halloween*, 1978) and then toward closure. While a stay to therapeutic termination was offered through a surprise twist in the setting of the horror (*A Nightmare on Elm Street*, 1984), even the extensive self-reflexivity that looped the termination phase through a new rule-driven legibility (*Scream*, 1996) could not really deny that it was over. While it was proceeding, the *Psycho* Effect brought earlier horror films into its orbit. It is possible to say, for instance, that the turn to masking and unmasking pulled the *Phantom of the Opera* film complex into the slasher milieu not only because psycho remakes of the film story were in fact produced, but also because the tendency was already present but not accounted for in Rupert's original adaptation. Of course, the numerous films that upon release were left out of the main momentum of slasher and splatter cinema can in the meantime be entered as exhibits in defence of the seriousness of the film-therapeutic effort. While first and foremost there is the example of *Peeping Tom* (1960), in the meantime, the time in which this genealogy unfolds, quite a few films, including Herschell Gordon Lewis's trilogy, will not be ignored.

Not before I have considered the problem of psychopathic violence within the new-millennial updating of vampirism, and then again in Theodor Adorno's TV reception and its reprieve-revalorisation via Winnicott, do I treat Hitchcock's masterpiece directly. By its late introduction alone, my reading of the film cannot be presented as a model for application to the films that follow. In this genealogy *Psycho* is another station in a process of multiple resolutions, repetitions, reworkings and sublimations of a traumatic effect that neither resides in itself, coming from nowhere, nor belongs in any exclusive or original sense to Hitchcock's film. There is no reading of a single film in this book that I consider final. Of course there can always be more examples, but, in theory, my psychohistory of an effect (or trope), pursued as thematic through generations of film and across a wide range of genres and media, purports to be exhaustive.

Playing Catch Up with the Vampire – But with *True Blood*

1

Whiletouring in 1999 with *The Vampire Lectures* I noted that the fans of undeath had a real problem with John Carpenter's 1998 film *Vampires*. Goth girls shivered with revulsion at that ugly depiction of vampirism as exercise in all-around psychopathic violence. The memory of this in-group resistance to the Carpenter film is all I had to build on when awakening from another bout of Rip van Winkle oblivion that befell me upon closing the book on vampirism in the early 1990s. In 2009 I was invited by *Artforum International* to address the changes that had gone into vampirism according to the TV show *True Blood* (2008–2014). In the process of fulfilling my assignment to catch up with the new vampire, another longstanding project was dragged up in its train, the figuration of psycho horror in slasher and splatter cinema. While vampirism was re-emerging in the place monopolised by zombie projections, the psycho violence specific to slasher and splatter films, which had been therapeutically terminated by 1990, was beginning to find a new delegation under the aegis of the Devil. These reflections on the Undad and the closing reflections on the Devil Dad frame the concise psycho history of the secularisation of occult horror that is this study's content.

It's true that in time for the new millennium the vampires were changing. Whereas bloodsucking was routinely interpreted in the era before as metaphor for genital sexuality (which I always felt missed the points of the encounter), the vampire fictions themselves began to flesh or flush out the pre-Oedipal blood bond with the fully sexual bodies of our undead neighbours (for example, in the TV series *Buffy the Vampire Slayer* (1997–2003)and the film trilogy *Blade* (1998, 2002, 2004). This normativisation of the vampire was attended by narratives of race (and class). Previously werewolves walked in the fine print of undead defence policies issued to protect the vampire during the span of time he spent stuck in the coffin, as utterly unprotected as only the dead can be. To the extent that the werewolf figured at all in vampire fictions in the pre-*Buffy* days he was often a familiar; at times he was the metamorphic mask a vampire could assume to maintain mobility during daytime programming. That was then. In the meantime werewolves could be recognised as belonging to the service industry of the underworld. If you show me a vampire you have to show me the local disgruntled werewolf or shape-shifter, too. Indeed we were soon instructed (in *Underworld* (2003) and its sequels) that the lycanthrope was originally related to the vampire, whose 'purity' was but the guilty assumption whereby the snarliest vampires maintained a false sense of superiority. These new fables came to the point by overcoming the prohibition against intermarriage.

It's true that the werewolf is the other melancholic, indeed emphatically so, since his original name, lycanthrope, issues the diagnosis of melancholic incorporation. But vampirism gets immersed in melancholia to sort out the contents of the crypt it transmits and by which it is transmitted. Only that which was good to go – in other words, the good object – qualifies for undeath. The melancholic werewolf wallows in the death wish. That's why he invariably begs a true love to release him from his sorry state. But the crypt carrier holds the good in storage, not the bad and ugly. As vampire he perpetrates on his victims and their survivors the wounding of the loss of the good but also secures the chosen object's inner-world-like preservation.

Though not conjugated with werewolves, the plot points of *Blade* and its sequels – deregulation of the bloodline (and even of the lust for blood) within vampirism (and, as always, in humankind's relationship to undeath) – are symptomatically in sync with the development of genital sexuality against a backdrop of race relations. The African-American vampire hunter (who is himself half vampire, or 'daywalker') emerges in the late 1990s from a 1973 pocket of superhumanity inside Marvel Comics. He is caught between 'pure-blood' vampire interests and the fascist aspirations of those merely 'turned' (who, as in the case of Frost, would be blood gods). Subsequently Blade is realigned in another reshuffling of interests to meet the advance of 'Reapers', whose bottomless thirst even for vampire blood threatens humans and vampires alike with extinction.

That vampires can be 'vegetarian' in regard to their bloodlust, which is retained in *True Blood* only as hick, I mean hickey accessory of genital sex with mortals, is a hope as old as the era we remember as the 1980s, when the sexual revolution had really spread itself thin. At least in the movies from this era, at least those playing in New York or on the Coast, everyone spoke 'Camp', the idiolect of unprotected experimentation. But then there was AIDS, which changed everything, albeit in stages, like the stages of grief. Because of the changes in vampire sexual mores, Stephenie Meyer's *Twilight* (2005) can fall back on abstinence to promote vegetarian vampirism as the medium of marriage, while *True Blood* scatter-shoots vampiric identification across the all-inclusive topography of survival.

When her vampire boyfriend gets to ask Bella (the protagonist of *Twilight*) 20 teen questions for the first date or love forever we enter the deep end with Bella's release: 'I sighed in relief, and continued with the psychoanalysis' (2005: 230). What keeps *Twilight* cursory as vampire fantasy is, for example, the deeper commitment to something like Mormonism underlying good vampire values, which is as explicit in the management of non-reproductive sex as in Bella's decision to fly in the face of all she values and induce sleep one night by taking what's known on the Coast as the Mormon cocktail: 'unnecessary cold medicine' (2005: 251). If the Cullens, the vegetarian vampires, are Mormons, then do those still drinking human blood qualify as Catholics? The opening of the sequel to *Twilight* (appended inside my copy of *Twilight*) makes explicit the relationship to the dead in Bella's involvement with vampirism: a fixation (which may indeed be age appropriate) preliminary to any consideration of mourning. Bella dreams she sees her deceased grandmother coming toward her for reunion. But then she recognises that she's the old woman in the mirror, which is the affective moment of horror and yearning. Developmentally we might as well be inside a zombie projection.

In *Grammophon, Film, Typewriter* (1986) Friedrich Kittler aligned the historical changes in the itinerary of haunting with the advances in the media sensorium. For a long time ghosts were at home in books, and their range of spooking was analogised with the ins and outs of the volumes of the brain. Following haunting's seat in photography, the range of analogy occupied, within a cascade of mere decades: radio, film, the telephone, the tape recorder and television. Increasingly, haunting was integrated within the media Sensurround as the form, literally, of keeping intact by keeping in touch. Telecommunication is always also communication with ghosts.

But there are also changes in the consumer population that turns to media contact with the departed and, by going to the movies, turning books into bestsellers, pays for the exchange service. The ongoing Chinese cult of offering paper representations to the departed in the meantime specialises in burning copies of commodities, which are continuously updated. By the items reproduced in paper for burnt offering the Chinese signal their new status as consumers. The US became a world power by the early 20th century largely through the number of citizens carrying disposable cash. With the Chinese middle class growing, and the prospect of hundreds of millions of consumers coming to the fore, those seeking profit within the US economy started fracking its layers of reserve.

Innovations in occult horror capitalised on early teen and pre-adolescent girls, who, in alliance with their parents, promoted the *Twilight* phenomenon. *True Blood* is the cable TV syndication of this renewal but made for adults – conceivably for the parents who had to attend with their daughters to the perils of Bella. As good girl, Bella enjoys a relationship to canon works, even in the school setting, but mediated by her favorite film adaptations.

Adaptations make the literary canon more accessible. Symptomatically in sync the trend developed in the book market to remake the canon in similar terms of adaptation but mixed up with B-horror, like *Pride and Prejudice and Zombies* (2009). The teen could now be caught where she reads (for the first time on her own, not as assigned, and thus as true consumer). The introduction of the young teen as target reader of 'mediated' books was the counterpart to the global impact upon all markets of the introduction of the Chinese consumer.

2

In *Dead Until Dark* (2001), the novel by Charlaine Harris on which the first season of *True Blood* was largely based, the narrative loses the momentum of first contact once mortal Sookie and her vampire boyfriend Bill start having regular sex. By the second novel, when Harris starts borrowing elements from the fantasy genre (maenads and dragons), she is already at the last resort of reader stimulation. Now that vampires are real, we are taught, all other fictional figures press for realisation.

Sir Arthur Conan Doyle almost got lost in this diversion when he involved himself in the controversy around the evidential status of the fairies, sprites and elves represented in spirit photographs taken by two teen girls. Doyle didn't see that they failed the proving or testing of the rule that otherwise reserved spirit photography for the ghostly emanations attending communication with the recently departed, which the advent of live media opened up right away as their Spiritualist syndication and advertisement. But he wasn't blinded by the light, the other world of fantasy or Christianity; he was determined (even Hell-bent) to bend and blend the borders of materiality to promote, even if by proxy or displacement, the media link to one's lost loved ones. Regarding the matter of the supernatural existence of the fairies recorded in the controversial photos, Doyle writes from Australia (where he was conducting his 'down under' occult research) to his colleague Gardner, who was giving the photographic phenomenon in question another close look:

> The matter does not bear directly upon the more vital question of our own fate and that of those we have lost, which has brought me out here. But anything which extends man's mental horizon, and proves to him that matter as we have known it is not really the limit of our universe, must have a good effect in breaking down materialism and leading human thought to a broader and more spiritual level... We have had continued messages at séances for some time that a visible sign was coming through – and perhaps this was what was meant. (2006: 98–9)

The occult and fantasy genres are as different as necromancy and Christianity. When the genres are brought together Christianity tends to guide necromancy into the light (the unbearable outcome of most ghost movies, from *Poltergeist* (1982) and *Ghost* (1990) all the way to *The Sixth Sense* (1999)). We found ourselves headed off at this impasse watching *Buffy the Vampire Slayer*. When, in season six, Buffy was in deep despair over her return to life from Heaven, even wearing shades couldn't save the show from its own apocalypse.

The author of the Sookie Stackhouse novels is fundamentally a mystery writer. Indeed in the fictions *True Blood* adapts, every main character at some point is motivated, by coming under suspicion or by appointment or calling, to join as detective in yet another murder investigation. And yet the happy end of crime solution, as Christian as it is Oedipal, can still yield to an occult desire for reanimation (not redemption), as did Doyle when, responding to reader demand, he brought Sherlock Holmes back to life.

What the TV series added to Harris's novels was a far greater development of the African-American contingent, beginning with Sookie's BFF Tara. In her cousin Lafayette, black, gay and vampire identifications and rights met and crossed over. The mortals know that once you go with a vampire there's no going back. For the vampires it's 'out of the coffin' into the desire. 'Fang banging' is as addictive as ingestion of vampire blood (marketed as the drug V). However, vampires who don't integrate or 'mainstream', but remain in 'nests' with their own, become as consumers of sex flamboyant, outrageous and apparently disposable. No one likes a Miami Bitch vampire.

The greatest contribution of the African-American figures is their resistance to the fictional world suspended between occult and fantasy genres, which, paradoxically perhaps, gives that world traction and reality effect. I remember listening to a hip hop station while driving around in LA the day another of the newer *Star Wars* films opened. The host, no doubt preaching to the laugh track, kept asking his phone-in listeners what their plans were for seeing the movie, and he each time drew a blank. Immunity to complete vampirism, which was the big idea behind *Blade*, is rephrased in *True Blood* as a fact of everyday life — reminding me that only the African-American vote was not 'glamoured' by Ronald Reagan. Our mass psychology registers or installs this resistance as dissociation, like that of Tara at the meeting of the Descendents of the Glorious Dead. She bears even in name the burden of dissociation American popular culture maintains by the prominent placement in its canon of *Gone with the Wind* (1939)

In the 1990s the *Candyman* trilogy (1992, 1995, 1999) showed us racism, by hook or by crook, in our mirror reflection, while the *Leprechaun* franchise (which commenced in 1993 but began internally, or so the story goes, in 1983, right around the time 'therapy values' came to dominate the slasher genre) sealed away its pot of gore at the end of a rainbow coalition that this figure of Irish superstition (or of Celtic belief, like the holy day of Halloween) kept on testing. Candyman was an African-American artist whose slave ancestry was variously underscored. In the beginning he is murdered by the racist mob for miscegenation (first they cut off his arm, then introduce the rest of him, rendered sweet, into a tight corner with countless bees). Liberal white kids, who find the study of urban legend 'relevant', come across the belief (specific to the film adaptation of the original story by Clive Barker) that if you call his name five times while looking into the mirror the Candyman (who, as played by Tony Todd, looked like O. J. Simpson) is summoned. He's another bogeyman on call for those who dare doubt his existence. At the end of the trilogy his great-great-granddaughter, who tries to rehabilitate her ancestor as painter of works for sale in her gallery, falls victim to jealous murder but thereby accedes to the role of new incarnation of Candyman.

Though there were several short-lived entries in the past, it was with *Blade* that the African-American body was integrated in the mainstream of vampirism's reception and fabulation. Before the racist phantasm of purity could be addressed or redressed within this reception, vampirism had to undergo the kind of development that admitted full frontal genital sexuality for the undead. Thanks in part to *Buffy the Vampire Slayer*, *True Blood* is more 'integrated' than that, at least in the psychodynamic sense. (The teen therapy that Buffy cheerled into our relationship to occult horror was largely borrowed from the momentum of the slasher genre's turn to serial survival in groups.)

The rerouting of censorship on cable TV into compulsive nudity and sex forced the glamour of vampirism to show its hand in symptom formations of pathogenic identification and desublimation. Our affair with vampirism was indeed conditioned by our trauma survival. The sexual body in our faces during the first year of *True Blood* belonged to Sookie's brother Jason, who, underneath or above it all, was the splitting, I mean spitting image of the young George W. Bush. Tara, who qualified in the terms of family systems therapy as the identified patient of the show's first season, had a thing for him since childhood. But then she started exorcising the demons in her relationship to her mother (the relationship that determined, in her case, the pattern of falling for the wrong man). In the second year, Jason converted from wild 1980s-style hedonism to rigid Christianism – the Christian Right being dedicated in this fictional world to the killing of the dead (or undead).

In *True Blood*, vampires, now lodged in sexual bodies, could be openly integrated as minority members within a socius comprised of countless special interests, including those of every occult figuration imaginable across genres. Integration described neither a happy harmony nor did it admit inimical interests that were equal and opposing. The Christian Right was also admitted: but while dedicated in the show to the destruction of undead integration, its dialectical opposition had lost its footing in the ever expanding crowd of minority interests. The melting pot model was left behind, together with its paranoid variation – the melting plot. Instead there was integration or disintegration of parts held or brought together without opposition.

That vampiric existence would become integrated as sexually embodied in close association with the political integration of the African-American body condenses histories of the touch taboo and its mass psychological dissolution that are legend to the mapping of integration not only in the United States.

3

Whereas the vampire is allegorical in the intermediate way of interpretation, the zombie is allegorical in the topical sense of immediate application. The zombie is the violence in our midst, in our foreign policy, in our racism, in our consumerism – at which point the interchangeability with us begins. The first screen zombies were adapted from the 1954 novel *I Am Legend*, Richard Matheson's conceit of a massification of vampires through an epidemic of undeath.

The vampire's return displaced from the screen the dominance of zombie films we watched throughout the Bush Junior years. A generalised post-9/11 condition of post-traumatic stress disorder, continuing through the second Gulf War, went into these zombie years. In 2009 *Zombieland* was the diminishing return as farce of the tragedy that 'Eight Years Later' we had to recognise: we thrilled to our survival through killing ambulatory corpses. It was this niche market of guilt-free killing of the dead already opened up in 1968 that recommended zombie movies for makeover into video games. It's hard to imagine how adding 'interactive' to the films would make any constitutive difference in the case or face of the living dead.

Once there was hope again with the change in office, we were prepared to project our vampires. The turn to vampirism demonstrates a renewed capacity for affirmation of life in undeath, a relational predicament. Identification with the dead or undead again became possible. (That one doesn't identify with your average zombie is the flash point of our consumption of those films.)

In 2007 *Thirty Days of Night* supplied a transitional objective in the course of switching over from zombies to vampires. It peeled vampirism off the back of the zombie invasion, beginning with the title which smuggles quality time for vampires into the generic countdown to mass contagion (as in *28 Days Later* (2002)). Though they resemble zombies, the vampires are linguistic creatures and thus, like the members of the mass phenomenon in *I Am Legend*, stand between zombies and vampires. They're sloppy drinkers who tear apart body parts with their teeth to get to the blood flow. The title's published schedule counts down to survival. With the first new dawn the vampire invasion is out of there. The transitional state of these vampires is underscored on the human side. The mortal leader of the group of survivors injects himself with vampire blood so he can combat the undead chieftain on a level dying field. After he triumphs he stays put for the sunrise. He turns to ashes while in the grieving embrace of the one he died for. What takes us out of the zombie equation between surviving and killing is this prospect of our dead dying for our survival. Thus the psycho violence that follows the new vampires emerging out of zombieism is countered by mourning.

During the years of vampirism's makeover, new variations on psycho horror also slouched toward the screen to be borne. What remains in the background of the ascent of the vampire is the psycho killer, who fully returned to the screen during the zombie years. The psycho is the problem that even identifications with vampirism can't avoid.

The story that Stoker's *Dracula* (1987) records takes place in a span of time shared with the real crimes of Jack the Ripper. Vampiric affirmation in mourning may displace the zombie milieu but it cannot shake the psycho, who follows the downbeat of a real-life bummer. 2010 saw the publication of the first sequel to Bram Stoker's *Dracula* to be proclaimed authentic on the basis of family ties. *Dracula – The Un-Dead* was co-authored by Dacre Stoker, Bram's great grandnephew, and Ian Holt, a vampire enthusiast who managed over the years to style himself as expert. In the appendix we learn that Holt was given his enabling boost by a distant relative of the historical Count Dracula, Radu Florescu, who claimed to be presenting the definitive interpretation and history of blood sucking in his own co-authored study in 1972. For Dacre Stoker the sequel was a work of reclamation: *Dracula* didn't sell in Stoker's lifetime and his widow fell short – through a loophole in the copyright – of benefiting from its being marketed in Hollywood. Now a piece of the reception will belong to the Stoker family after all. In the end Dacre dedicated the sequel to 'all who carry the Stoker blood' (2010: 423). And yet the blood that's carried forward in *Dracula* is not the authenticating seal of family lineage (it's always only the Count's blood that counts) but instead opens up sending and receiving capacities in his initiates. The relationship to the undead extends in time and place via occult or technological replication – never through reproduction, which secures the future generation's blood ties to the dead.

Baby Quincey, the son of Mina and Jonathan Harker, who in the Note appended at the end of Stoker's *Dracula* bounced on the lap which seven years earlier, as Friedrich Kittler underscored, held his mother's traveling typewriter during the last legs of the chase that led to the staking of the vampire Count, is in the meantime grown up, in time to take up the fight once more. Through the revalorisation of vampirism in the bigger meantime, however, Quincey is in possession of a new prehistory that leaves out the gadget love. In Bram Stoker's narrative Mina makes it to the border between occult and technical media when the Count nurses her at his bleeding breast. At this border and over her own in-between state she asks that the Burial Service for the dead be read out loud. By this mourning, which addresses that part of her that is internally and eternally identified with the vampire, Mina directs the chase unto its successful conclusion: the Count's second death.

Twenty years later according to *Dracula – The Un-Dead* this highpoint in the transference interpretation of vampirism was but a screen memory, which covered by slight displacement Quincey's origin in the sexual intercourse between Mina and the

Count. In the old days a sexological interpretation of the breast-feeding scene would identify a displacement upwards from the significance of genital sexuality. Now this interpretation is no longer a reading against the reign of perversity. The displacement is reversed into a scene of generation no longer psychically defended against at some level, for example in the mode of fantasy, but in fact disguised inside the narrative's reality. That Count Dracula was all along all good annuls the mourning work undertaken by Mina. Her breakthrough insight was that the Count was mixed up between good and bad and therefore available, as available as were Lucy and Mina, for the work of mourning, the sorting out of the good from the bad. Now it is the Blood Countess Báthory who, all bad, fights with her relative the Count for control of the inheritance. That means, however, that the staking of Lucy following her vampirisation by the Count was a gross error; in fact it was murder.

The big problem in Bram Stoker's *Dracula*, the ruthless killing of Lucy, albeit in her vampire incarnation, required that the narrative start up again and repeat the Lucy story with Mina, but the second time around without the appalling outcome. Now it was all a big misunderstanding with grave consequences, which the new narrative admits but cannot repair. That the staking was a mistake leaves the extreme psychopathy in evidence in the scene of Lucy's extinction unaddressed. The sexological correction of scenes of blood lust apparently does not extend to the stake as instrument of murder. *Dracula – The Un-Dead* cannot really find refuge from this problem via the split between all good and all bad in the household of vampirism. The very camouflage the Countess selects for her violent deeds, the serial murder spree of a fabricated Jack the Ripper, is, in contrast to the new interpretation of the blood lust, plain text. The normative reversal of the representation of vampiric acts via sexual repression relies, it seems, on another more fundamental repression, one that goes deep inside our relationship to the psycho, our double.

The older Arthur Holmwood reproaches Professor van Helsing for having kept him, back then, from following his beloved Lucy into undeath. "'Lucy, Lucy, always Lucy", van Helsing said. He reached out and took hold of the cross in Holmwood's hand. Time to teach this fool a lesson. He was not remotely repelled by the cross. By joining the ranks of the un-dead, one did not necessarily ally oneself with the Devil' (2010: 316). In the final phase of combat in alliance with Dracula against the Blood Countess (aka Jack the Ripper) van Helsing himself became a vampire to secure the good in vampirism for himself. The professor, who exchanges his instrumentarium for fangs, enjoys only a brief span of undeath. The incomprehension of his former student is the limit he can't get past. A Faustian second life was granted him but only for a brief respite. When the professor kills his former student, who can no longer follow him, Holmwood, before he goes, takes out van Helsing, too. Van Helsing's ultimate death, which as always follows undeath, closes the circle. The chain of revenance is broken. Now there is no life after the transference, after the analysis. This revisionism also remakes the conclusion of Browning's *Dracula* (1930): the sexual couple of students, who also can't follow, ascend with the readership into the light, but the analyst-teacher no longer stays behind to dispose of the dead vampire. Instead he is another vampire who went ahead of Dracula into double death. That this renewal of vampirism cannot get around the position of the psycho is evident in its handling of the scene of instruction and transference.

4

In the face of the newer developments in the vampire franchise, the question remained: Why admit the vampire as real only to lose him in the crowd of all the other un-majorities? One day not so long ago the copy shop nearest you started offering a new service of super-sizing your photographs. For birthdays, weddings and anniversaries, among any number of special events for friends and family, images of those celebrated began to be presented on large posters. Once deregulated or desublimated, the only size that counts is life size. And it comes as no surprise that these services would be extended, in the end, to remembrance of the dead. 'Flat Daddies' and 'Flat Mommies', the life-size posters of US soldiers deployed in the Iraq War, helped the family members back home reserve a place for and thus cope with a loved one's absence. The simulacrum didn't only sit in front of the TV or at table but accompanied the family in the car and was present at all the station stops of everyday life. It went without saying (literally so on the official product website) that should a condition of long-distance separation more permanent than deployment befall the loved one, the survivors would be in the ready position to carry around their posters like Nosferatu his coffin. I was wondering how *True Blood* would get around to the fact of life that a vampire is dead. But this time *I* was missing the point. In episode 11, when Sookie laments out loud that she really wishes that Bill were here, Terry, the local vet back from Iraq with PTSD, responds that he understands her well: 'There are some dead people I wish were still around too.' Fangs *are* for the memories.

With the introduction of Jason's true love, Amy (a vampire-blood addict who kidnapped an undead local to feed her habit), *True Blood* made an intervention that went beyond the teen or group therapy of *Buffy the Vampire Slayer*. Her vampire victim called Amy a 'psychopath'. In spite of all the paraphernalia of her political correctness, the whole legacy of the 1960s, the identification was apt. But Amy just as aptly rallied to her own defence, pointing out that she rebuilt the economic infrastructure in a third-world village, saving many lives – and that she was vegan (not just vegetarian).

The fantasy of 'vegetarian' containment of a blood lust that can exhaust a victim's supplies unto death rather than undeath found direct application to psychopathic violence in the show *Dexter* that played on the other cable channel. The focus was on serial killer Dexter's acceptance of his violent nature, the first step toward calibrating its release. If it has to be murder, then let him kill off all the other serial killers who, because they are uncontained, are free game for Dexter's unique self-regulation.

Neither vampiric melancholia nor infernal abandonment of inhibition, the psycho position is situated on a sliding scale between psychosis and psychopathy. Within the protocols of psychological treatment the psycho represents a failure of interpretation. Psycho horror films may be metonymic of real crime but they also refer to mutative changes in the norm that were first identified in the lab space of modern war.

'Psycho', a term first popular as nickname for the soldier returning from WWII a psychological casualty, was applied by Robert Bloch and Alfred Hitchcock to hold a gap in understanding as overlap between the psychotic and the psychopathic disorders. Norman Bates and his heirs present as psychotic but it is by dint of their ruthless criminality that they hold mascot positions in mass culture, which compel or admit doubling. In the setting of psycho horror, the diagnosis of psychosis supplies a stopgap in the failure of interpretation of psychopathic violence. But the psychopath remains our double at the close quarters of a near miss.

While a zombie cannot count as psycho, the living dead convey psychopathic violence. Two leading fictions compete to supply metaphorical/metaphysical comfort in the zombie setting: science fiction (living death as radiation fallout, for example) or Devil fiction (the living dead as blanks filled or fulfilled by demonic doubling). That mourning is therefore not a working concept is explicitly thematised at the start of George Romero's *Night of the Living Dead*, which opens in a cemetery. In the course of copping the thrill of killing all zombies together with the cops, the consumer meets psychopathic violence half-way in a new setting of improper burial that looks like successful mourning: the mass murder of the dead. For the span of this encounter we are secure in our place in the succession of living on. To be wrecked by the success of mourning is the condition vampirism addresses.

According to Richard Matheson's 1954 conceit, it was an epidemic spread of undeath that massified the relationality of vampirism unto zombie-like consumerism. But inside the stronghold of the sole survivor in *I Am Legend*, the recent past is recycled melancholically in the mode of vampiric relationality. Mourning becomes the vampire. That in *The Texas Chainsaw Massacre* (1974) the full-blown psychopath who enters the picture as hitchhiker is at first identified by the unaware as Dracula figure showed how unprepared we too were by classic horror entertainment for the violence soon to be served up on a splatter. But it also identified the theme of mourning that psycho horror breaches. The prospect of catastrophe survival takes over where mourning is left off. Vampiric mourning would be, then, a niche market largely hidden but stowaway in the phantasmagoria and suburbia of psycho violence. Since it occupies the pre-massification origin of living death, vampiric mourning is programmed to catch up with the zombie theme park of killing the dead, just as mourning shall overcome and overtake the death wish.

The remetabolisation on the screen of all aspects of horror's representation and history, bringing back the zombie, the vampire, the Devil and the psycho killer, among other figurations, crowded the project of integration like the pack of teenagers in the fifties shoved inside a telephone booth. In the meantime, however, the digital relation could accept all entries, but as returns. Whatever was back was recognisable, to be sure, but now, in sync with the total synthetic accessibility of the digital archive, it was no longer immersed in the aura of the old oppositions, like the opposition between film's final cut and video editing.

A TV show like *True Blood*, therefore, was a syndication of the United States in the news with an African-American president and an insurgent Christian Right, for example, among the many parts that seemed together again in a crowd of return engagements. Barack Obama's election was not so much the realisation of the Civil Rights struggle, the resolution at the end of the opposition for and against integration, as it was the return of that era in the midst of all the other returns.

When Winnicott expanded on the significance of integration in his unfinished summary work *Human Nature*, he underscored that integration was one out of two developmental moments interrelated as 'achievements'. For the first, integration itself, Winnicott liked to turn to Humpty Dumpty ever since his psychotic child patient 'Bob' made it his Dasein-rhyme: 'it is useful to think of the nursery rhyme of Humpty Dumpty and the reasons for its universal appeal. Evidently there is a general feeling, not available to consciousness, that integration is a precarious state. The nursery rhyme perhaps appeals because it acknowledges personal integration as an achievement' (1999: 117–18). The lodging of the psyche in the body is the other achievement.

When we jump out of our skin we reflect a disturbance unsettling integration itself. Achieved integration carries forward the internalisation of respite that the transitional object (or sublimation according to Freud) introduced. The disturbance associated with paranoia, which has its integrative moment in attack as best defence, by and large exemplifies an oppositional momentum of integration from which essential rest has been withdrawn or mutated as arrest. The disturbance is basic, like the reaction or overreaction to environmental changes which do not originate in personal impulsive experience: 'there is an interruption of being, and the place of being is taken by reaction to impingement' (1999: 127). Or again: 'The gathering together of the self constitutes an act of hostility to the NOT-ME, and a return to rest is not a return to a resting place, because the place has been altered, and has become dangerous' (1999: 124). At the other end of the transitional obstacle course there is the double achievement of integration and – or as – the lodging of the psyche in the body. 'The idea of a ghost, a disembodied spirit, derives from this lack of essential anchoring of the psyche in the soma, and the value of the ghost story lies in its drawing attention to the precariousness of psyche-soma coexistence' (1999: 122).

To understand why Winnicott in his day could say that psyche-soma coexistence or integration is so precarious we would have to go directly to Klein's final unfinished essay 'On the Sense of Loneliness', where she argues that the sense or direction of loneliness, of irretrievable loss, must come at the end of the inevitable falling short of integration. Klein introduced integration into the lexicon of psychoanalytic theory in her 1940 essay 'Mourning and Its Relation to Manic-Depressive States'. Given the silent partnership of integration in her mourning work, it is hardly surprising that integration would prove imperfectible. But loneliness, according to Klein's posthumously published essay, is also the new frontier of relationality. The fraying at the edges of psyche-soma coexistence breaks us up among our parts, which however share the sense of loneliness. Klein concludes: 'The lost parts too, are felt to be lonely' (1984: 302). I would want to argue that this relational loneliness that arises in the shortfall of integration can be reclaimed by the revaluation and return of melancholia, a sort of lonely parts club within the digital modalities of integration.

Schauer Scenes

Psycho II (1983) starts with the psychiatrist assuring Norman, now cleared at the court hearing for early release from his in-patient status: 'I had the phone reconnected.' Out of the unexamined transference the new horror of a deregulated mother position emerges on and around the phone connection.

When Norman, back home again, notices the telephone he lifts the receiver and finds a note attached: it's from his mother; he starts hearing her voice at the other end of the line.

At the local diner where his psychiatrist arranged a job for his adjustment, Norman picks up another note from his mother among the orders. A young waitress, Mary, takes up Norman's sublet offer – and proceeds directly to take a shower. The shower upstairs lessens the water pressure down in the kitchen sink. We watch a colour remake of the opening stretch of the shower scene.

Norman assumes the peephole position.

Phone rings: 'What? Who is this? My mother is dead!' From the motel Norman can see his mother in the window just like in the old days. He finds another note, this one in mother's old room, which Mary now occupies: 'Slut!' The sheriff fills in Mary on the old black-and-white prehistory: 'He kept his mother's corpse here. Stole her from the grave. And then he talked to himself in her voice and answered in his own.' It turns out Mary is Marion Crane's niece and in league with her own widowed mother, Lila, of course, to drive Norman back to the asylum where he belongs. But Mary now thinks he deserves his chance. Mary and mother argue: 'Norman needs me.' 'Norman needs you? A psychopath needs you?' 'I'm not living for dead people anymore! I'm not hurting Norman Bates anymore!'

If Mary's surname is Loomis, then the sequel's prehistory begins with the double elimination of Marion. If it's not Mary herself, then it's her mother who must be staging Norman's mother's comeback. 'It's not them. It's mother. She's not dead.' The psychiatrist therefore has the mother's grave opened for Norman's benefit. 'She's not coming back to life, is she?' 'No.' But his real mother is coming back into his life. She told him on the phone. Norma Bates only took care of him.

The psychiatrist assumes the role of mother on the line and tries to issue counter orders. But Norman continues talking to a dead connection. 'No! I won't do that. You can't make me kill her! Why?!' Mary rushes down into the basement and puts on the mummy suit. Now she orders him to put down the phone. Then she rushes to the other extension and tries to reach him by phone. But Norman doesn't answer anymore.

Norma Bates, her sister, agreed to take care of Norman while she went to the mental institution: 'When I got out you already had had your troubles. So I waited for you.' He poisons her tea and, when it begins to take effect, takes a shovel and smashes in the back of her head. At the end Norman talks to and through the corpse he has replaced as receiver back upon the old apparatus of haunting.

When we're back at the Bates Hotel in *Psycho III* (1986), the sequel Perkins himself directed, there's the Help Wanted sign, the telephone book flapping in the wind, and birds in a feeder, soon dropping when the poison kicks in. A recap of the end of *Psycho II* fills us in on the non sequitur of the real mother and Bates's murder of her two. While sewing up another dead bird he hallucinates the arm he stitched in the meantime.

A reporter is in town determined to write the story of cured and then relapsed psycho-killers: 'murderers who can't help themselves are victims too'. A Marion Crane lookalike contestant is also passing through: she even has the same M.C. initials stamped onto her suitcase. 'The past isn't ever really past.' The flashback that follows takes us all the way back inside a replay of Hitchcock's shower scene. Then, when she drops her head to the side, Norman sees Marion staring death in her face. The replay freeze-frames and takes on colour: it's the living girl. Mother and son discuss the prospects for Marion's return. 'The dead don't come back.' 'You came back.' 'I never went away.'

Norman watches the horror movie on TV. When he turns it off, the audio, the portion of the mother inside him, continues. The 'Rape of the Sabine Women' tableau now absorbs the free floating sound as its own audio track. Right below the transmitting picture there's that peephole: he watches the blonde perform the stations of the shower. When mother next tears open the shower curtain we get a view to overkill: the new girl, her wrists already slashed, is taking a blood bath. At the hospital she meets her saviour, the son portion. 'You're the one who found me, Mr. Bates. Thank you.' He offers her a place to stay. 'Why are you so kind to me?' 'You remind me of someone.'

At the motel Norman picks up wig and knife. But then he grabs the knife blade borderline-style and commands M.C.: 'Go to your room and lock the door.' The killing machine is off and running. Someone else, another motel guest who happened to be there at the wrong time, gets the point. While chiding the snoop reporter on Norman's behalf for her misguided vigilance, the police officer sucks and chews real ice to beat the heat. He takes the cubes from the chest behind him without looking. Is that blood on the ice? (My, says the vegetarian, this is really good ice.) After the reporter filled in M.C. on who Norman really is and what he's capable of, M.C. tells Norman she wants to spend some time with her suicides-anonymous sponsor and leaves with the reporter.

When Norman and M.C. are reunited again, mother's voice comes on strong. Norman responds to the murder command by pushing M.C. away: but the push comes to shove since they're at the top of the stairs. The M.C. of this show gets impaled on the arrow of the little cupid statue at the foot of Norman's stare: despair! In the back of the police car, Norman lets slip out and up the severed hand of mummy he's been clasping in his handcuffed pair: he strokes the third limb, the one he had to hand to mummy and now has taken back.

It was suggested at the end of *Psycho III* that Norman got his sexual groove back. But can reproduction replace the missing grave? The conclusion of the series, *Psycho IV: The Beginning* (1990), is a made-for-TV movie organised around a live radio talk show. Tonight the topic is matricide. Norman Bates phones in under the name Ed. 'I've killed before. And now I'm going to have to do it again.' Several women had to go, the first one because she came on to him. 'That was grounds for murder?' 'For my mother it was.'

When he was six his father was stung to death by bees. His mother had ambivalence in her bonnet at the funeral: she tickled little Norman in the front row only to slap him around in public when he started laughing. The primal cabling of long distance and the long distant was first laid across the nonmetabolisation of father, for whose absence no place was set between mother and son. Mother's new boyfriend gladly joined in when it was once again time to abuse Norman: he hears Norman's really a girl, which is a shame because he also hears from his mother that he's really hung. The jury is out on this genesis of his drag. Norman's verdict: 'I have her seed in me.'

This brings up the reason why the next woman who has to go is his wife: she tricked him and went ahead and got pregnant. She doesn't believe it's genetic. At the house he faces the music of compulsion and overcomes the command in the wish to kill the mother inside himself. He sets fire to the house.

Hallucinations of his mother and of all their victims pass before our eyes. The couple embraces in front of the burned-down house. Norman: 'I'm free.' (They're three.) We see the empty rocking chair in the fruit cellar: mother's voice can still be heard behind the scene. The *Psycho* music comes back on. Dark screen. The cry of a newborn baby. The *Psycho* Effect turns in its grave. But this happy ending brings back with the new something old. The posing of new generation as countermeasure that dispels evil is a citation from the Devil complex – as was spelling the end of father with bees.

1

Leading up to the release of *Psycho*, a film that reflected and came out of Hitchcock's involvement with the TV medium, Theodor Adorno offered his interpretation of television as a new norm of adaptation, which was adolescent going on antisocial. Adorno showed how psychoanalysis, stretched to its limit concepts on the small screen, allowed a degree of criminality to come forward as cynical norm in place of compromise. Adorno organises his view of adaptation to the new norm around the small screen's evacuation-packing of sublimation. It is an impasse to which Winnicott responded in giving an update internal to psychoanalysis, which extends the sense or direction of Adorno's genealogy of media.

In 'Prologue to Television' ('Prolog zum Fernsehen') Adorno argues that the culture industry animates that which 'slumbers pre-conceptually' in the audience. But the TV viewer at the same time receives owner's manual instruction in how to adapt to an imposed adaptation (2003: 514). The TV viewer is manipulated to fit in with the status quo by startled stops and starts ('zurechtstutzen'). By folding inside the manipulation he describes as 'zurechtstutzen' the very term, *Stutzen*, signifying the startle response so central, for example, to Gustav Bally's psychoanalytic study of the test situation, Adorno underscores the hope withdrawn. By dint of the images buried inside us – the unconscious to which the culture industry seems to have direct access – we accept as spirit of the times that a controlling interest benefits from our manipulated adaptation. As seen on TV, the mind warp that concludes the culture industry's promotion of acceptance of our manipulation as psychic reality is that 'not the murderer, but rather the murder victim, is guilty' (2003: 514–15). Survival is the norm that the victim transgressed against more than the criminal who unconsciously on purpose tests for the will to survive – to fit in as survivor.

In his follow-up reflections in 'Television as Ideology' ('Fernsehen als Ideologie') Adorno identifies the normalisation of criminality as the moral of the TV show. TV completes the culture industry by techno-doubling our perceptual and libidinal world without apparent gap, like the hierarchical difference between high and low culture, whereby one double might be pried loose from the other one. The kernel of reality in the TV broadcast is this kernel of perfect doubling. 'The initiated viewers may not transfer the scenarios of the TV crime drama to everyday life, but they are encouraged to arrange their experiences in a similarly frozen and mechanical manner' (2003: 522). On TV the trivial romanticism of ill deeds is conjoined with the realism of gadget-loving attention to the properties of techno-external life. 'If the procedure for dialing a phone number did not conform to reality in a TV show, the station would not hear the end of it from an indignant audience, which otherwise is willing to accept with pleasure the fiction that a murderer lurks at every corner' (ibid.).

In Freud's thought, sublimation rests on the uneasy settlement of incorporated or interred melancholic identifications. Adorno picks up the breaking news of psychopathic behaviour on TV in terms of the withdrawal of sublimation, which he registers medium-specifically as the absconded ability to treat actual size and proportion aesthetically. While what was projected large in film could still be interpreted as life-size, Adorno identifies in the receiving area of TV an inability to reformat the miniaturist representations.

TV is the station of withdrawal of sublimation within the culture industry owing to a non-negotiable reduction in image size, which TV's over-reliance on stereotype to reveal the character of a dramatic figure without delay reinforces. Each TV show is a contest in which the component parts of representation must reach their conclusion in record time. Turning up the contrast on the small screen Adorno argues that the recorded voice, already split off from the 2-D image in sound pictures, is the ultimate *Doppelgänger* that always comes life-size and which television's tendency to rely on voice-over as referee seeks to uncanny-proof.

In 'Television as Ideology', Adorno identifies the adaptation as seen on TV as proceeding via an ambivalent acceptance of criminality. Defence mechanisms are valourised and individuality and autonomy discounted in deference to a higher power (2003: 528). By the manipulation of the signifier appeal of psychoanalysis old patriarchal ideas are promoted as new therapy fictions (2003: 525). In one TV show Adorno analyses the conceit of a therapeutic process installed in one's situation, like that organising Jensen's or Freud's *Gradiva*, which leads a narcissistic actress to a dramatist who directs her to take the cure of marrying him. This instrumentalisation of the Freudian understanding of the relationship of transference represents, Adorno underscores, psychoanalysis in reverse, the formulaic diagnosis he applied earlier to the conflation of psychological warfare and mass psychology in Nazi Germany.

In spite of the ongoing idolisation of the strong man on TV, however, the figures of high culture are also held up – ultimately for ridicule as 'introverted', but also, thus lubed, as available for identification. 'The culture industry forgets its moralism at every opportunity to make ambiguous fun of the image of the intellectual it produced' (2003: 524). Valourisation of artifice, deception and cheating would comprise, then, the unofficial norm, which, according to Winnicott, the teen of course exploits but also rejects as compromising, not real. If sane people can be seen to relate to the world by cheating, Winnicott concludes, then sanity spells compromise.

Freud emphasised in his reading of Daniel Paul Schreber's *Memoirs of My Nervous Illness* that even after the paranoid schizophrenic was able by projection of his delusional system to enter recovery of a new world order in lieu of the former world that had succumbed to repression and psychotic breakdown, it was a 'wealth of sublimations' that remained irretrievably lost ('Psychoanalytic Notes on an Autobiographical Account of a Case of Paranoia', 1959: 73). In other words, sublimation is what is first destroyed at or as the breaking point of psychosis and constitutively missing from the ensuing delusional order.

With his notion of the transitional object Winnicott extended Freud's notion of sublimation, which postulated the necessity of a restroom in the midst of nonstop sexualisation, to earliest development. The all-important period of transition, originally enacted and secured between mother and infant, offers and models intermission from the ongoing struggle to relate inner and outer worlds: 'From waking to sleeping the child jumps from a perceived world to a self-created world. In between there is a need for all kinds of transitional phenomena – neutral territory' ('The Deprived Child and How He Can Be Compensated for Loss of Family Life', 1989: 143). The gradation of experience of the object through the transitional object and its border zone of respite is what gives way before the introduction of the antisocial norm. 'If we deprive a child of the transitional objects and disturb the established transitional phenomena, then the child has only one way out, which is a split in the personality with one half related to a subjective world and the other reacting on a compliance basis to the world which impinges' (1989: 144–5).

Basic dealings with absence, like mourning and remembrance, rely, according to Winnicott, on the impossibility of separation as another form of its possibility, and thus on the successful derivation of potential space from play as well as, ultimately, from the transitional object itself. While adding transitions to the time of development, Winnicott at the same time kept the watershed of transition close to the potential for traumatisation.

Winnicott writes into the fine print of the transitional contract, which in his repeated presentation of the transitional object he each time spells out in italics: *'Of the transitional object it can be said that it is a matter of agreement between us and the baby that we will never ask the question 'Did you conceive of this or was it presented to you from without?' The important point is that no decision on this point is expected. The question is not to be formulated'* ('Transitional Objects and Transitional Phenomena', 1992: 239–40). The transitional object, therefore, which is designed to lead us through good-enough mothering to an integrated sense of presence in absence, is the ready occasion for trauma waiting to happen.

At first 'good enough' sounds like we're cutting reality some slack and making room for hit and miss in healthy development. Truth is, parental guidance is never good enough. That the transitional object is the defective cornerstone of development attends Winnicott's shift from what he termed 'neurotic analysis' to his reclamation for analytic understanding of the institutional containment of psychopathy. Winnicott delineates the deprivation in the background of the antisocial tendency that burns transitional bridges. In 'Some Psychological Aspects of Juvenile Delinquency', he points out that the child bereft in this way starts looking for trouble: 'Unless he gets into trouble, the delinquent can only become progressively more and more inhibited in love, and consequently more and more depressed and depersonalised, and eventually unable to feel the reality of things at all, except the reality of violence' (2000: 116).

The antisocial tendency manifested 'in a deprived child who is otherwise hopeless, hapless and harmless' (2000: 103) 'means that there has developed in the child some hopefulness, hope that a way may be found across a gap. This gap is a break in the continuity of environmental provision, experienced at a stage of relative dependence' (2000: 103–4). Winnicott hitches reparation to the delinquent patient's industry consequently withdrawn from the reality or realisation of violence.

The antisocial child was interrupted when his development was already far enough along not to qualify for the options of 'neurotic' analysis: the endless involution of dependency in neurosis or the powered-down condition of safe deposit in psychosis. The antisocial child is riveted instead to a near miss. He doesn't blame himself but he is kept by the intrapsychic scheduling of the onset of his deprivation from blaming the mother. Instead he strikes out by displacement against the environment he relentlessly tests for holding capacity.

That the 'child knows in his bones that it is *hope* that is locked up in the wicked behaviour, and that *despair* is linked with compliance and false socialization' (2000: 104), points the way to the true or spontaneous self the antisocial child carries forward. It has been encoded in the acting out like the mother in the environment. That's why Winnicott sought to revalourise the sentencing of criminality that sends juvenile delinquents through a relay of holding cells in which they are kept (and kept occupied) as therapeutic containment folding out of and meeting half way the very industry of delinquency itself.

At the close of 'Transitional Objects and Transitional Phenomena' Winnicott places psychopathy on one side of the parting of ways at the end of the transitional phase. On the one side we find the development of so-called cultural interests. But if it's not that way it's the path of addiction (fixation on the transitional phenomenon), fetishism (persistence of a specific object or type of object dating from infancy and linked to the 'delusion of a maternal phallus') and pseudologia fantastica and thieving (which follow out the 'unconscious urge to bridge a gap in continuity of experience in respect of a transitional object' [1992: 242]). And then, at the outer limit of the wrong side, there's the psycho path.

2

Last time I visited Universal Studios, in the 1990s, the special-effects pavilion still folded out as its altar piece, its communion of psychic alterations (or alternations), an exhibition run-through, mediated by dissection and lecture, of *Psycho*'s shower scene. The tour guide's lecture demonstration of the making of the scene, which included a diagrammatic display of the many camera angles used, underscored by counting the many pieces of film going into the brief scene and showing in the slow-down that neither the act of murder nor a complete or completely nude body can be seen, abstracted in advance from the scene its constructed nature. The guide was following the demonstration Hitchcock had in mind for getting his scene past the censors and which he built into it. Following its dismantling, the guide then projected the scene as film: in the old days the tourists would still gasp, but in the meantime one could hear in the main the aspiration of admiration for a technical feat. Thus the *Psycho* Effect passes through a concise history of gadget love as wooed and won from our proximity to the psycho.

Following the walking tour of special effects, the visitors entered an amusement park train on wheels to tour actual outdoor sets used and seen in films. What was once functional was allegorical: the outside sights were way stations of the perpetual sightseeing tour of locations and lots from the recent past of film history, like the excavations of Pompeii (updated by a makeshift *Jaws* (1975) surf report at the lake-side setting of a village still being used for TV shows). The wash-out of a bridge under the rain of artifice was another live demo from the no longer functioning past. Then there was the village square last seen on screen already recycling through *Frankenstein* (1931) and *The Wolfman* (1941). But the Bates place on the hill with the motel below had been updated by their doubles from Gus Van Sant's remake.

Alternating with the ancient history props outdoors, the ride passed through a series of internal showcases of filmmaking, which were all generic group-formatted containers of horror pitched to the thrill factor and factory of amusement immunisation. There was a ride through King Kong's disastrous walk through Manhattan, a sci-fi combat zone for the survival of the specious, and a stop at a BART subway station that came under earthquake attack (which meant you also faced drowning). The tour on training wheels encircling the special effects pavilion and its shower-scene services thus followed out the stations of the crossing of the film medium with catastrophe preparedness. They were the external ganglia of a circuit the shower scene had traumatically interrupted and which were then restored to a new orbit – from the traumatic impact of the scene of individual anonymous murder back to the big picture and group portrait of catastrophe preparedness. Passing through this phantasmagoria of faked or dissected and resurrected scenes the visitors passed the test as group.

I remember the confidences of two Germans, brothers and techno-theorists, who, in one case, recalled cycling home hysterically after the first time seeing *Psycho* at the local theatre to see if his mother was still alive. His (younger) brother went with me to see the remake of *Night of the Living Dead* in Santa Barbara. Post-traumatic recollection set in on the morning after, so he told me, with his inability to take a shower. That was the matter with Janet Leigh: 'It's true that I don't take showers. ... It wasn't the shooting of the scene that caused the damage, it was seeing the film in its entirety later' (1995: 131). In networking through the trauma, Leigh collected 'I was there' accounts of first-time viewings of *Psycho*. (Three pages later she will begin recording the collect calling of pranksters asking for the Bates Motel.) The shower scene is up there with the Kennedy assassination and the moon landing. In 'On Some Motifs in Baudelaire', Benjamin assigned to the date-marking of journalism, for instance, the function of repackaging a potentially traumatic experience as souvenir one can also remember to forget (1969: 163). That the film narrative in *Psycho* begins with the date and place marking (down to the minute) of its beginning projects the protective grid of information gathering – another defence that will be breached by the shower scene.

Following a posttraumatic delay of three to eight years until some point in the 1990s, there were hundreds of remakes, retakes, remetabolisations of the shower scene in horror cinema. Did each return of the scene issue the stamp of genre identification or reflect the push and pull of symptomatic syndication? Allow me to select De Palma's 1976 film *Carrie* as the group-psychological and group-therapeutic redistribution of the *Schauer*. After gym class and sports are over, we file into the showers, identifying now with Riefenstahl's Olympic athletes, now with the Jews. Is it time for one's own private cleansing in the group setting of ritual practice or is it the prelude to a sacrifice? Are we in a place of respite from sexualisation, where we rally our hopes and exchange information, or are we at some crisis point of over-stimulation of the same-sexual social bond without timeout or rest (room)?

The shower is a chiasmus: you turn it on and it turns you on. Carrie, otherwise in the abject position, comes alive as self-object in her niche of nurturing at the breast of the group bond. At the same time the rest of the group has already advanced to the drying-off stage of their group ritual. But even alone she partakes of the group bond. But then she is terrified to see that she's bleeding down there. She turns to the group getting dressed for help. But menstruation trauma is taboo. The group of little sisters is founded on non-phobic acknowledgment of the calendar and repro future opening up on each girl's body. The period becomes part of the greater scheduling of the date – on which teens take each other out for sex outside the group but still under group protection.

In the group shower scene the other girls gang up on Carrie for having an unprotected period. At the acme of humiliation a light bulb bursts which diverts her assailants and shows Carrie that she now wields telekinetic powers over the death wish crossing her mind. Before following the group into the shower scene we already witnessed out on the playing field that the group identifies Carrie as loser or scapegoat and 'piece of shit'. By assailing her with all the tampons in the locker room dispenser they mock her but also initiate her: 'Plug it up! Plug it up!'

The confrontation with the group doesn't simply increase her isolation and alienation. In fact she wins a friend or two. Sue is one peer who feels shame for ridiculing Carrie, whose incomprehension of the period that was upon her reflects parental neglect. Sue and Carrie, who are without fathers, each suffer a mother's groupie adoration of her Mass outlet, the TV medium in the first case, Christianity in the latter case. The gym teacher, who may well consider Carrie a likely target of opportunity for recruiting for the other team, becomes her other friend or sponsor.

Toward the end of the film the bleeding or wounding in the shower at the movie's start, like the pinprick of blood in the story of Sleeping Beauty, gets rewarded by the arrival of Prince Charming, who is talked into taking Carrie to the prom. The new best friend is his girlfriend, who plans Carrie's episode of Queen for a Day. Like the menstrual trauma that unleashes it, Carrie's 'power' of telekinesis is her other 'curse'. Carrie's crowning attainment of teen self-esteem – she's the prom queen – sets her up to walk the prank of another shower when a bucket of pig blood is dumped upon her. She was right when she felt that the bleeding in the shower meant that she would die. While the prom crowd is having its fun, Carrie telekinetically brings down the house in flames. She destroys the group to its core when she sends all the kitchen knives into her Christian-yahoo mother, who just before took a knife to her 'demonic' daughter in the bathtub. At the end of this relay of *Schauer* scenes Carrie lights her pyre.

What about the father? As in the case of Norman, Carrie's father beat a retreat from the mother long time ago. Best friend Sue is fatherless, too. The mother is a body of shameful identification. Sole survivor or BFF Sue dreams of atonement which ends in fairytale nightmare: Carrie's bloodstained arm emerges out of the grave in defiance. But then, still screaming, Sue wakes up in the comforting arms of her awakened or reanimated mother.

The French film *Les Diaboliques* (1955) was precursor to the extent that Hitchcock assigned it to his *Psycho* crew to view over and again to get the suspense right. In *Les Diaboliques* the surprise twist is that the man murdered by girlfriend and estranged wife did not die; his demise was faked so that his apparent return from a premature grave would shock his wife to death and thus leave her fortune to the surviving couple. We watch, then, at one inoculative remove the effect of horror on one woman who stands in for us. *Psycho* removed the middleman central to the internal plotting of thrillers and aimed the impact of the horror, the psycho horror, directly at the audience, as though striking at and through the thin defensive screen. The shooting script directions for the shower scene read: 'The slashing. An impression of a knife slashing, as if tearing at the very screen, ripping the film.' In *Scream 2* (1997) (as in *Demons* (1985)) the literal rending of the screen releases the film violence that then afflicts the audience (though at the remove of a staged self-reflexivity that can't get around being internal to the film). By its preparedness, its sojourn in the receiving area of the *Psycho* Effect, the audience as group could meet the breakthrough half way. With *Psycho* in 1960 the moviegoer was alone at the border of the death wish stabbing and being stabbed along the dotted lines, filling in the blank.

In *Psycho* the slashing has a running or flying start in the arc of camera movement that swings low from on high, which, Hitchcock points out in interview, was itself another motivation, implementation and internaliation of the cut.

Psycho is probably one of the most cinematic pictures I've ever made. Because there you had montage in the bathtub killing where the whole thing is purely an illusion. No knife ever touched any woman's body in that scene. Ever. But the rapidity of the shots, it took a week to shoot. The little pieces of film were probably not more than four or five inches long. They were on the screen for a fraction of a second. . . . Now also in *Psycho* you had a scene where the detective was coming up the stairs. Now the audience knew that there was a menace around. A monster. So he came up the stairs and when he got to the top of the stairs, I took the camera very high, extremely high.

So that he was a small figure. And the figure of the woman came out, very small, dashed at him with a knife. And the knife went out, and we're still very high, and as the knife started to come down, I cut to a big head of the man. And the knife went right across the face, and he fell back from that point on. Now the reason for going high – and here we're talking about the juxtaposition of size of image. So the big head came as a shock to the audience, and to the man himself. His surprise was expressed by the *size* of the image. But you couldn't get the emphasis of that size unless you had prepared for it by going high. (Hitchcock in Gottlieb 1997: 288–9)

3

In the novel that inspired Hitchcock, Bloch's *Psycho*, Norman is fat, like Hamlet (like Hitchcock). Bloch's Norman is a kind of Hamburger Hamlet, who cuts off his victim's head to spite their face-to-face. His 'case' is lined up explicitly with the recent past: 'the Gein affair up north' (1959: 209). While Norman undergoes a diet for the screen, the victim's dead eyeballs are left in our court of cutting or putting back together again. Marion's dead eye or ego, that of the other woman on one track, and thus of the mother, but also, on the other track, that of the wannabe wife, the representative of father, goes down the drain. *Psycho* was the first film to show a toilet flush. And yet the flush remaindered and retained a piece of the guilt sheet Marion filled out on herself. A piece of her reckoning of the debt or guilt, the only trace not erased, guides the film to close in on Norman and lock him up, but also to preserve him, the mother inside him. At the end the toilet's flush is again reversed when the dredged swamp releases Marion's getaway car.

Ed Gein decided after his mother's death to redecorate with corpse parts, those of his mother as well as of many others he also dug up in the cemetery. The loss of his mother can thus be seen to organise this interior decoration project at its melancholic core. His mother continued to communicate with him along lines more occult or technical than prayerful. In the closing pages of Bloch's *Psycho* the media portray Norman as guilty practitioner of cannibalism, Satanism, incest and necrophilia (1959:

210). The Bates Motel, advanced to the status of 'house of horror' (ibid.), is, as was the case with the Gein crime scene, a draw for 'morbid curiosity-lovers' (1959: 211). A capitalisation of this tourist attraction is projected, but disallowed by the authorities: 'Quite conceivably, a goodly percentage would have been eager to rent rooms, and a slight raise would compensate for the loss of the towels which undoubtedly would have been filched as souvenirs of the gala occasion' (ibid.). (Last time I was at Universal Studios, 'Bates Motel' guest towels were for sale.) Bloch continued to develop this marketing scheme in *Psycho House* (1990), the third installment in his trilogy. The title refers to a scheme underway in Fairvale to reconstruct the original motel and house as a kind of haunted house attraction. The plan includes the sale of 'Murderburgers' (1990: 76). But then when one of the developers is identified as the psychopathic killer behind a new serial spree the amusement park project is dropped.

It was relatively late in his mortuary practice that Gein committed murder. Did he deplete the local reserve of the recently deceased and interred? How inevitable was his advancement to the position of psycho killer? (When asked whether he practiced cannibalism, Gein replied that his mother would never have approved anything so Catholic in taste [Woods 1995: 81].)

In *Psycho* when Lila, at the end of her scanning of the contents of Norman's room, picks up one leather-bound book we see nothing but her look of horror. But Bloch's novel filled in the blank stare: Lila discovers a reading list that investigating officers tend to find in the background of high school shooters. Norman is well-versed in ethnographic, psychological, S&M, occult and Spiritualist literature. But he applied his reading in the first place not to shooting the gun-dead but to making his mother undead.

> Oh, yes. I brought Mother back home with me. That was the exciting part, you see – going out to the cemetery at night and digging up the grave. She'd been shut up in that coffin for such a long time that at first I thought she really was dead. But she wasn't, of course. She couldn't be. Or else she wouldn't have been able to communicate with me when I was in the hospital all that while. It was only a trance state, really; what we call suspended animation. I knew how to revive her. There are ways, you know, even if some folks call it magic. Magic – that's just a label, you know. Completely meaningless. It wasn't so very long ago that people were saying that electricity was magic. Actually it's a force, a force which can be harnessed if you know the secret. Life is a force, too, a vital force. And like electricity, you can turn it off and on, off and on. I'd turned it off, and I knew how to turn it on again. (1959: 190–1)

Mother is a movie.

Norman sees another movie under his mother's direction whenever he looks into mirrors. He sees reflected back only fragmenting wavy lines (like the lines cutting through the opening titles of Hitchcock's film): mother smacked him hard in the head when she caught him giving the mirror a shot of his full frontal nudity. In Freud's case study of the Ratman, when his patient looked in the mirror at his penis (his 'rat' according to the patient's OCD language) he was, by this reenactment of the masturbation for which he was punished in childhood, summoning his missing father. But Norman's mother stepped in to monopolise this channel (Norman, too, conjures Hamlet's father's ghost [1959: 120]), a disinheritance she completed by allowing another man to step in and assume authority. The motel was his idea. Norman eliminated him, too. He inherited the amalgam of step-relations and faux pas in which all who stopped for the night of nothingness had stepped too close to mother.

Reading up on the Incas, Norman finds in the description of a human drum another screen memory of the die-hard origin of the mother-and-son dyad. That he almost sees the scene with half-closed eyes shows that we're in close proximity to the primal scene.

> When Norman half closed his eyes, he could almost see the scene: this throng of painted, naked warriors wriggling and swaying in unison under a sun-drenched, savage sky, and the old crone crouching before them, throbbing out a relentless rhythm on the swollen, distended belly of a cadaver. The contorted mouth of the corpse would be forced open, probably fixed in a gaping grimace by clamps of bone, and from it the sound emerged. Beating from the belly, rising through the shrunken inner orifices, forced up through the withered windpipe to emerge amplified and in full force from the dead throat. (1959: 11–12)

In hindsight, as already in hide-site, one can't be sure who occupies which end of the skin-taught drum roll. What the novel introduces by following this different drum, the film situates within the process of taxidermy. Is the look the camera identifies backed up against the nothingness of disposal able to create only by stuffing the stiffs of destroyed life?

Marion Crane is one bird who's stuck in Phoenix, the city with the name of the mythic bird that rises up from its ashes. As in Hitchcock's *The Birds* (1963), for example, not only mythic birds, but all of the above do not so much arrive as always return; it is the trajectory on which ghosts book passage. The bird's eye that rises up in *Psycho* out of the slashing of the titles is the camera's force of visibility and judgment, now the all-seeing eye of God the father, now the maternal eye of the early dyad before which the infant lies open to view without concealment. The eye swoops down on Marion's tryst. It swings low sweet harlot: superego tells her this is the last time. She wants respectability. She assures her lover, Sam Loomis, that just as he pays the other's debts so she too pays by meeting him in sleazy hotel rooms during 'stolen' lunch hours. Stealing, being secretive, even deceptive, not respectable – an antisocial trend seems set, which Marion, however, wants to bring to an end before yet another one of those hotels lets her know when her time is up. But she can't, apparently, escape the verdict of places rented by the hour or for the night. When free money is in reach she completes the profile of delinquency.

In the opening hotel room scene she delivers the ultimatum to Sam, that their relationship must be respectable or not at all. She tells him that when they meet again it will be in her home for a family meal with her sister – with the picture of her dead mother on the mantle looking on. Sam jokes about sending the sister to the movies (!) and then turning the picture around against the wall for what will follow. But Marion's slip is showing when she says Sam turns around 'respectability' into something 'disrespectful'. That Marion mistakes respectability, the social relation that fronts for sexuality, for respectfulness shows that the turn against the supervising picture has crossed her mind, too. She issues the 'sentence' that her attempt to marry and attain respectability slips upon the disrespectful substitution for the dead mother, which is basic as backfire. The mother's image and look, from which the infant could never hide, cannot be turned around. This early all-seeing eye or maternal superego, which Slavoj Žižek identifies as active throughout the film, is bound to return, like a bird. In Marion's case it lowers the doom (like the camera POV that swooped down upon the post-coital scene). What weighs Marion down is the dead wait keeping her from being made an honest woman. Sam slaves away in his dead father's hardware store, a place of storage for tools of repair: in this underworld he pays off his father's debts and the alimony owed his divorced wife (another incarnation of his failed relationship to his father, which Hitchcock's film added to Bloch's story). There is no mention in respect of his mother. Down the highway lives Norman Bates: no father, only a mother he loved to death and who now has him under her tomb.

Marion is his fatherless kindred – also under an undead maternal demand, the demand for the respect in respectability.

The exchange in the parlour between Norman and Marion sets us up. Norman is constructed as neurotically repressed in sexual or corporeal matters: while showing her the room, he can't utter the word 'bathroom' in Marion's earshot. When he stammers out 'false' his taxidermy is alert to prosthetic amplification of Marion's breasts through 'falsies'. His sudden move to the office and then into the parlour away from Marion's motel room seems on the same creepy quaint trajectory. The downward or inward plunge of the bird's eye view at the film's opening hits bottom in the stuffed-bird parlour, the underworld of whatever its momentum otherwise signifies.

Just as Klara, in trying the cognitive therapeutic approach with Nathanael (as emphasised in Friedrich Kittler's reading of 'The Sandman'), is overwhelmed by psychotic backfire, so Marion helps Norman to respond in murderous rage when she makes her well-meant suggestions (that he get out of there, that he send his mother some place). Norman has all his birds in a row when he compares the get-well death wishes of those who, like Marion, mean so well to the clucking of hens. Like Nathanael, Norman is justified in striking out against the cold undercurrent of the rational substitute's interventions.

Both parties to the turbulent exchange end up falling, it seems, on both feet. Marion realises that her private island is, as Norman advised, a private trap (a fitting caption for the earlier scenes of Marion's entrapment in the eyes of the policeman and used-car salesman). She thanks him. He in turn seems to have held up under the challenge of experiencing his ambivalence toward his mother. (Although technically we don't know she's missing yet, Norman's eloquent conviction that mother could not survive his abandoning her is already a strong sign that he is serving out a melancholic sentence.) That at the end of their exchange Marion drops the pretence of false name and false hometown and admits the two bird names, Phoenix and Crane, includes Norman in her sense of therapeutic closure. (After Norman, during check-in, uttered some platitude about not letting one's losses get one down, Marion signed in as coming from 'Loss' Angeles.)

When Norman peeps through the painting at Marion preparing for her shower, she not only undresses but also calculates her actual guilt or debt on a piece of paper before flushing it from the book of her life. She first became a criminal when she took the money from the free loot to pay the difference on the new car. That's why she does the math on her debt to society in preparation for the cleansing shower.

But that doesn't wash with Norma, who has her own economy of loss to protect against the losing that substitution introduces. In fact you can watch the split in Norman at that very moment of seeming therapeutic closure and change. Whereas she signed in with an assumed name that's a souvenir of Sam, Marion, now that she's made up her mind to open her trap, simply reverses the deception for Norman to hear and see, not caring that he notices, indeed, no longer noticing that he's there. One can see the change, the changing of the guard, coming over him. Like, don't treat psycho like the furniture.

At the end of the camera's downward arc we encounter the superimposition of all of the above onto the drain and the dead eye. But which is it? When we saw Norman's eyes peeping, they looked as dead as all the other eyes or looks. Does the camera threaten to stuff and then projectively reanimate whatever it comes across, whenever it doubles back onto the eye? Or does the nothing behind the look act as a drain?

It is in the tense relations with the cop wearing impenetrable shades that Marion's mother emerges in the boundary-blending of the police, the force of the law unbound by the laws they enforce. This licence of police work – to engage in improv nightmare – inspired Benjamin, in 'Critique of Violence', to address the police force as phantom-like. The police officer keeps in mind everyone's potential for breaking the law. When Marion asks if she's free to go, the officer wants to know, in exchange, if she's broken any laws. The flexibility of these boundaries is underscored when the officer huddles with the used car salesman. Her only infraction in the eyes of the salesman is that she hurried with her purchase without even letting him give his pitch. It is as though she performs the change of car (whereby she activates her crime) only for these reflecting eyes without boundaries. She becomes what she is: a suspect in the eyes of that guidance she would flee rather than respect. (The willingness to pay the salesman's pitched or projected price rather than engage in bargaining it down to a consensus amounts to another withdrawal of respect.) According to Thomson (2009: 34), the officer, salesman and his assistant form at the end of this preamble a group of three Furies, whose voices pass through the voiceover crossing Marion's mind in the subsequent drive into the storm, the rain shower, the *Schauer*. I would add the caption to this allegorical pageant that the Furies specialised in avenging the crime of matricide.

The money Marion stole belonged to a father who planned on using it, as always, to buy off his little girl's unhappiness. It is in this sense that he can afford to lose it. That she recognises this 'private money' as the maternal provision of free money is both the trigger prompting her theft of hope and the change of heart she will experience in exchange with Norman, the psycho in grief's clothing. But when the buyer's voice enters the voiceover to threaten to get his money back, even if he must take its exchange value out of her soft white flesh, Marion's smile at the thought mirrors the disrespectable/disrespected expression of the maternal superego.

The film shows the ultimate violence – easy substitution without complications – by superimposition of Marion's life or death onto toilet and drain. In the novel, however, this violence is taken interpersonally. Once Mary, Marion's name before she makes it into pictures, is down that drain, Sam only has eyes for her sister Lila. Hitchcock does imply that the disposal services of drain, toilet and swamp are held for Marion in lieu of commemoration. These blanks – the blank stares of mother turned against the wall for lack of respect – are more explicitly filled or fired in Bloch's novel (as in Gus Van Sant's few changes to Hitchcock's shooting script). From the start of the novel Sam wonders if he and Mary aren't rushing things. 'Sometimes he almost wondered if they hadn't made a mistake when they planned ahead. After all, what did they really know about each other? . . . In the letters, Sam had begun to find another Mary – a moody, almost petulant personality, given to likes and dislikes so emphatic they were almost prejudices' (1959: 84).

These second thoughts commence with his guess that Mary didn't like the kind of music he's enjoying. This is tied to his advocacy of the modern means of recording and playing music, which overcomes in 'the age of hi-fi', like the Internet avant la lettre, the very idea of being-stuck-in-the-sticks (1959: 105). Earlier he experienced the sound and power of the music playing on the FM radio station: it was 'annihilating space and time and death itself' (1959: 81). It's at the moment of doubt about Mary ushered in by his solo-and-global experience of music that Lila arrives, whom he takes at first to be Mary but then takes to heart. Now when he reflects on his incompatibility with

Mary he has a good reason to feel guilty: 'He'd never suspected that he could entertain such hidden doubt and disloyalty concerning Mary' (1959: 104). But in the book this substitution guilt cuts Mary more slack than comes Marion's way. Bloch gives Mary an adult profile in mourning. In a film that voids mourning or respect Marion realises instead how easy it was to go psycho.

4

The internal film projected by Norman – the shadow show via his ultimate taxidermy prop cast in the window or against the wall of the fruit cellar – is a simulacrum of the medium reconceived as making the cut of reanimation via mummification, cross dressing and projection. When Lila unmasks the mother as mummy she unmasks her as camera obscura inside this projection booth. Is the focus fixed again on the dead eye or have we moved on to the prosthetic *Gestell* of empty eye sockets? The psycho fulfills the requirement for representation or for any kind of staying power and constancy by the cut through life to afterlife. The cut preserves.

In the book there's just one sorry squirrel Norman stuffed (but he didn't shoot it, he emphasises [1959: 43]). Hitchcock stocks his film with objects of taxidermy, the cinematic counterpart to the literary references Bloch assigns to Norman's psychic makeup. That gives Hitchcock's film room to overlook the stuffed squirrel and address the figure of a trap instead. In the novel Mary gets the message – to give herself a second chance and reverse her misstep to the extent possible – when Norman argues that by living alone 'everything gets bottled up. Bottled up, or stuffed, like that squirrel up there' (1959: 45). Mary is not in danger of being a loner at the bottom of the bottle. (Norman by the book is an alcoholic.) But she shares the deposit on Norman's bottle. The rain that causes her to stop at the motel reminds her of the day her mother was buried, 'the day they lowered her into that little rectangle of darkness. And now the darkness was here, rising all around Mary' (1959: 33). As she continues to wait in the car for the proprietor to come down from the house, she resigns herself to her wrong-turn setback in the rain *Schauer*: 'she'd made her grave now and now she must lie in it. Why did she think that? It wasn't *grave*, it was *bed*' (1959: 33–4). No, the reply resounds within the film and all the films that followed: it's grave, bitch!

Cinema was in transition in 1960 owing to inroads in the receiving area of media representation brought to us by the TV medium, in which Hitchcock had been engaged hands-on with his TV show. What he learned on the set of the small screen he brought to cinema, which he renovated for slasher violence in the relay of compact settings that, interchangeably, could wrap around sessions and sets of TV viewing. When horror films play on TV in *Halloween*, for example, or the split screen introduces a non-cutting juxtaposition in De Palma's horror and thriller pastiches, we recognise an incursion of the small screen inside the home or economy of film that *Psycho* first introduced. The

Psycho crew came from television, from the show *Alfred Hitchcock Presents* (1955–62). Did it bring along the shorter attention span, the feeding timing of TV audiences, the acting out that remains precisely under captivation and surveillance of remote controls? Hitchcock's gimmick, the injunction that latecomers would not be admitted to the screening of his film, is also oddly televisual. Only coming from in front of the tube can one appreciate the force and source of this fantastic demand that no intruder be allowed to interfere with one's viewing. In the era of TV, parental guidance is first experienced as interruption of the continuity of one's being when a domestic sponsor arrives to interject a word or order while one is trying to watch one's favourite show.

Janet Leigh recalls the taking of the close-up of her eye at the end of a stare: the camera then pulled up to contemplate identification with that eye from on high: '(as from a bird's-eye view? A stuffed bird's-eye view?)' (1995: 72). The stuffed bird refers to, one, the delegation of encrypted effects and, two, to the compulsions that get ironised out in sexology. 'And don't you "bait" birds?' Leigh (or her ghost writer) wants to know (1995: 92). But it takes another baiting to get us to the big picture of *Psycho*'s control release: 'Later, when Norman climbs the stairs of the Bates house to bring his mother's remains down to the cellar, his gait as he walks up the staircase is just the slightest bit swishy. Was Tony offering a subtle hint regarding his character's sexuality?' (1995: 113).

There was that Tony and then there was the other Tony, too. Upon nomination for the Academy Award, Janet Leigh received a telegram from Jack Lemmon (*Some Like it Hot* was released the same year): 'Congratulations, your husband is a fag' (Leigh 1995: 125). The ambiguities of sexual identification and orientation so typical for the film medium are bypassed by audio tape technology, which gets the trans- across.

Bloch's psychiatric consensus is briefly stuck on Norman's 'secret' transvestism, which preceded the mother's death. But a distinction can be made between strong identifications with members of the other sex and homosexuality which gets us out of this groove. An early interest in occultism is also thrown into the mix or mess. The trans-, the crossover, which took over suddenly, a surprise development or freebie, in the time it took for Norman to fake his murdered mother's suicide note, realises in letters what Hitchcock projects as spirit and has on tape.

All along the voices of one actor and two actresses were blended to make up the mother's voice (Leigh 1995: 81). The audio-tape technicians removed the bass line from Tony's voice when he shouts 'Mother! Oh God, mother. Blood. Blood!' – which in Janet Leigh's estimation made it sound 'weirdly adolescent' (1995: 83). While the psychiatric epilogue identifies the mother as dominant, we still see that Norman is his mother's dummy in drag. At this living end of Norman's complete takeover by the missing or long-distant ventriloquist only the two women made up the voice's ingredients: 'The voice is softer, more feminine, almost seductive; clearly that of a woman, as opposed to that of a woman being impersonated by a man' (ibid.).

That Norman is more psychotic than psychopathic is evident at the end. The psychotic break consolidates into a delusional system in which a relational reality is recovered. The mother he becomes wouldn't hurt a fly, which also means she won't be swatting any zippers. The castrative cut of the split Norman shared with two or more personalities has been resolved.

A transvestite also came to be known as 'TV' following a shift in style from the camp of careful imperfection to a new perfectibility (by the 1990s) that denied the audience the ability to tell the sexual difference. Hitchcock's awareness of the changes that TV – as a drag on cinema – was channeling through the older medium (which still incorporates the printing press) is one of the hallmarks that De Palma would expand on in his cinema of transference. The small screen can take you global or universal – as the channel turns – while at the same time hunkering down with your circle of family and friends. This is the gadget-loving zone of shock administration, one that Benjamin theorised in 'On Some Motifs in Baudelaire' between the snapping of photos and the dialing of the phone. Among the videocentric themes in De Palma's early features, *Sisters* (1973) and *Phantom of the Paradise* (1974), it is in particular the use of the split screen that reintroduces every kind of channeling. The audio portion transmitted in the occult 'Voice Phenomenon', which followed close upon the introduction of new and improved magnetic audio tape available by the end of WWII, introduced a new sixth sense able to make out, only upon repeated rewind and playback, in the static of whatever is in the air and thus on record, the voices of the dead.

5

1980 was the year in which the slasher genre that *Psycho* spawned commenced by its own momentum to strike a cathartic pose: by the end of the decade at least three hundred slasher films were released. The undertow of this momentum was the therapeutic termination of the Effect, which was already in sight. 1980 was also the year of Hitchcock's death, which meant that his 1960 film would be available for sequelisation. It gave Bloch license to write into the trail of film's *Psycho* Effect his own sequels to *Psycho* (1982 and 1990). Simply put, what the two books and the three films have in common is a fictional world in which Norman is a case and there never was a film *Psycho* (except in Norman's head).

'Crazy Lady' is the film that in Bloch's *Psycho II* a team of troubled individuals attempts to make out of the Bates case along a continuum that includes the asylum that contained the case (and then let it go – and then, via the treating psychiatrist's identification with Norman, let it go on and on). When Bloch takes his Norman Bates story to the movies it's time for Norman to escape after two decades of imprisonment – which is how the serial momentum of slasher and splatter cinema is excluded and implied. Everyone is double on contact in the staging area of the event's first breaking out into cinematic projection. Actress Jan is Mary Crane's 'lookalike' (1982: 58) while Vizzini, the director, looks like Bates looks after all the years of hospitalisation (1982: 228). The psychiatrist Claiborne, who is serving as consultant on the film project, is the one who recognises all the doubles, and does so ultimately *as* Norman. His colleague Dr. Steiner sums it up in the concluding psychiatric frame:

Claiborne had come to identify himself unconsciously with Norman Bates. Both of them were motherless and alone, both confined, each in his own way, by institutional restraint.... 'But there's more to it than identification.... After a time you began to feel that your fate, your future, was bound up in your patient – restoring his reason, writing a book about the case. . . . And when Norman escaped, it meant you had failed, failed him and yourself. He was gone, leaving you a prisoner in his place. It must have started then, with the conviction that the only way you could escape now was to identify with Norman, share the triumph of his freedom. . . . Then, when you found the body in the van and realized who it must be, hope vanished. You blacked out. Norman couldn't let his mother die, so he became her. You couldn't let Norman die, so you became him. And in the same way, during amnesic episodes when the alternate personality took over.' (1982: 312)

At the start of *Psycho II* Norman Bates knows in the meantime that he's not his mother (1982: 10). Claiborne claims his patient no longer denies reality, though he also adds that Norman will never remember (1982: 25). It seems that parts of or fragments from the past do come together whenever there's a re-enactment. In his therapy Norman became interested in 'psychodrama'; when we meet him in the asylum library he's reading a biography of Moreno. Claiborne assures visitors to the hospital, two nuns, one with abnormal psychology classes to her credit (she recognises Norman's book title as referring to the 'Roumanian psychologist'), that he has 'more or less abandoned' the techniques of psychodrama in group therapy. 'Though we still encourage acting out one's fantasies on the verbal level' (1982: 30). But as a test of Norman's graduation from psychosis (or its symptoms) Claiborne arranged for him to play the lead in *Charley's Aunt*. The psychiatrist was completely satisfied. 'But there was something Claiborne didn't realize. . . . The moment when . . . Norman lost himself in the part. The moment when he *was* Charley's Aunt – except that the fan in his hand was no longer a fan but a knife. And Charley's Aunt became a real live woman, an older woman, like Mother. The moment of fear – or the moment of truth?' (1982: 13).

Moreno was another therapist who claimed he could treat the whole psycho-pathological spectrum, especially at the far-gone end (or foregone conclusion), because the intervention was aimed at the beginning of life. In 'Principles of Spontaneity', a section of *Psychodrama* (first volume), Moreno addresses this start position: 'The infant is moving, at birth, into a totally strange set of relationships. He has no model after which he can shape his acts. He is facing, more than at any time during his subsequent life, a novel situation. We have called this response of an individual to a new situation – and the new response to an old situation – *spontaneity*' (1980: 50). This area of delivery, from which creativity and all good things emerge, is the stage of psychodrama. The actors who help the patient stage his scene correspond to the auxiliary egos which form the syntax of dependency according to Moreno. The auxiliary egos can meet the so-called self-starters in the newborn (or in the patient) halfway.

> As we have pointed out, the infant binds its spontaneous energy to the new milieu, via the physical starters of the warming up process. As we know, it would not be successful in this effort, if the mental starters of auxiliary egos – mothers, midwives, and nurses – in this milieu would not come to his rescue, i.e., by caring for and feeding him. Of course, the warming up to the act of birth has been a perpetual drive to the infant for such a long period that any delay on the part of these auxiliary egos once the machinery of delivery is in process cannot but stimulate the self-starting of the infant. (1980: 54)

In the third volume this approach is applied successfully in the treatment of a psychotic. In the course of the psychodrama the patient was encouraged to recommence her disease, but under more favourable conditions than when it all went down in the 'life situation'. The whole mental production this time can be magnified and elaborated. 'It is a reversal of the homeopathic principle – the disease is overcome by extremely *large* doses of the drug, instead of by very small doses of it. The psychosis is produced and staged by the patient like an experiment in association with a number of helpers, auxiliary egos' (1980: 196). Thus the patient gained objectivity in the course of the reenactments: her delusions could be reduced 'by creating them *at will*, by exaggerating or multiplying them *beyond* the dynamic needs of the mental syndrome proper'. The patient thus learned to live psychodramatically in a world of her own making, in which all forms of behaviour and expression are possible.

When Claiborne is advised that there's a call from Hollywood about the film project, 'psychodrama' is what immediately crosses his mind (1982: 31). To take the call he leaves Norman alone with one of the nuns (the other is completing her round of visits). Suddenly a thunderstorm strikes and the nun shows fear: psycho drama! The primal *Schauer* drives home the crisis point of uncanniness. 'All that mumbo-jumbo about psychological insight, all that nonsense about God's will, had vanished with a thunderclap. She was only a frightened woman afraid of her own shadow. . . . "Just remember what you told me. If God sent you here, then He also sent the storm"' (1982: 37). He escapes in one murdered nun's habit. But as Norman departs in the nunnery van the other nun jumps in beside him, alarmed at her colleague's thoughtless behaviour. Only later, when the driving nun pulls over to the side of the road, does the older nun in the passenger seat make out what's wrong. What psychodramatically ups the dose of Norman's disease is that in the drag of one murdered nun and on top of the other nun's fresh corpse he becomes a 'man'.

When he next asks God for a sign he promptly sees a hitchhiker bearing the sign 'Fairvale' (the Loomis hometown). But psycho, who looks like something out of 'one of those Dracula movies' (1982: 64), has picked up a psychopath, who immediately wants to steal the van. What's later found by the police in the burned-out van are two corpses, two sexes. In the debris of the van, Claiborne discovers the hitchhiker's sign: 'There was a third party after all.' The sign gives him direction and a narrative: Norman, still alive, is in Fairvale visiting vengeance on the Loomis couple (Sam and Lila).

The novel ends in Dr. Steiner's psychiatric institution or epilogue: 'He'd failed Claiborne, failed to reach the violence within him, the violence guarded by silence and hidden behind a smile. There were too many of those smiles surrounding him now – not just here in the asylum, but outside in the streets. Smiles that concealed but couldn't cure the secret sickness. Violence was a virus, a disease becoming epidemic everywhere in the world, and maybe there was no cure' (1982: 315).

Bloch's *Psycho II* was about making the one and only film about the Bates case, which is undone together with Hitchcock's film. The movie *Psycho II* opens with the shower scene from the Hitchcock original. When we hear Norman's cry back in the house – 'Mother, Oh God, Mother, blood' – the frame freezes for the new colour film to bleed into its start position. But only the audience recognises this internalization of the 1960 film; it doubles as Norman's flashback to a scene from his sensational case history about which the public is informed. In the off of *Psycho II*, the *Psycho* Effect was exhausting the possibilities in the face-off between the victim Marion, represented and commemorated by the pool of applicants for survival, and Norman, whose psycho violence came to be wielded both (and most regularly) by other individual psychos or their mothers, internal or otherwise, and by criminally insane clans or packs, originally projected or forecast through the massive introduction of living death.

In the series of the film *Psycho*, Norman was psychotic in the original film and has undergone treatment for over twenty years and is sent back home at the start of the first sequel. Now psychopathic violence is projected onto him while figures from his past seek to manipulate him via the well-known maternal triggers to re-release the violence that will either send him back into confinement or make room for derangement á deux. In *Psycho II* and *Psycho III* Norman adapts to his new role as victim looking to survive in alliance with a young woman who stands in for Marion but falls victim not to Norman but to the intrigues surrounding the more or less stabilised former psychotic. In the final installment Norman is married but must confront the prospect of his own fatherhood as the ultimate test of his new-found ability to shift from psycho to survivor.

In the sequels Anthony Perkins continued to play Norman Bates in films that were the stations of his own encryptment in this role. In *Psycho III* he starred and directed. The *Halloween* franchise did not come to a stop in the midst of the metabolisation of its slasher sequels when Donald Pleasance as Dr. Loomis reached the end of his lifeline. That the next *Halloween* was able to cross the line might reflect the greater import of the surviving prospect of Laurie's return (or Nancy's in the serialisation of *A Nightmare on Elm Street*). The real death of the survivor, like that of Heather O'Rourke, the child actress in the *Poltergeist* threesome, comes to bury the momentum of return engagement. The *Psycho* series seemed as big as the life remaining to Perkins. Of course every limit or condition that grows up within the series of a horror film, as when production comes to a stop at movie three and we thus have a trilogy, is there for the transgression. A self-consciously run trilogy like *Scream* couldn't stop *Scream 4* (2001) – and *Psycho* was itself remade in 1998.

In 1990 the writing Bloch was catching up with the closure of the *Psycho* Effect in film. In *Psycho House* a scheme is underway in Fairvale to turn the Bates crime scene into an amusement park. The props from the film that was stopped in its tracks by the murders on the set in *Psycho II* are to be inserted into the reconstructed sites (1990: 74). In this update, violent derangement is no longer a virus but part of a genetic code.

A new series of psycho murders threatens to bring down the house before it can open. Enter Amy Harris, investigative reporter, who recently authored a book on a female serial killer, a prostitute who killed countless johns. Now for her next book she's taking on the Norman Bates story. She can't stop thoughts of Mary Crane crossing her mind. She tosses them away as unidentifiable but not as fast as they keep coming. She takes comfort that Crane and her world are 'dead and gone' (1990: 17). And yet Fairvale is like 'something preserved in a time capsule' (1990: 19). 'Self-preservation, the first law of nature. Norman Bates had gone a step farther – he'd preserved his mother in himself. Which made him a time bomb, not capsule, a bomb that had long since exploded' (ibid.). But the capsule or inoculation that the author who studies psycho killing must swallow in lieu of inspiration or identification doesn't settle with her as yet, not for a stretch of pages. It keeps coming back up.

> No rain, no pain, no Crane. Because Mary Crane was two years older, she'd died before Amy was born, so what was the point in bringing her back to life? Points were for knives and knives were for killing and nothing would happen as long as she remembered that, remembered next time to bring a bigger bag, buy a smaller dryer, stay out of the shower. (1990: 31)

She decides to stop 'this shower-stalling' (ibid.) and enter the stabilisation of the shower effect: 'the room and shower held nothing to be afraid of. Except the nothing itself' (1990: 32). She's afraid that nothing itself is all she brings to the encounter with the Bates case. Then she meets Eric Dunstable, a demonologist who is in town to study or even intervene in the recent murders, and she is immediately tempted to introduce 'demons, ghosts, supernatural powers' into her Norman Bates study (1990: 99). Since the demons Dunstable is looking for cannot be seen except 'through the people whom they possess' (1990: 86), his import is tailored to Amy's emptiness to fill. She is convinced that coming out of the current Zeitgeist the demon angle will lead her new book to the top of the charts. Dunstable is convinced that the demon that once possessed Norman Bates lives on; at one point it entered Dr. Claiborne (in *Psycho II*). 'It left him last week to seek out another instrument for its purpose' (1990: 88).

When Hank Gibbs, the local journalist, admits in a moment of ironic self-deprecation that he only has empathy with himself, something new crosses Amy's mind, which pulls back from the demonic to lift a mask: 'Self-pity is the trait most of us share in common. But we seldom share it openly with others. Why had Hank Gibbs momentarily removed the mask?' (1990: 167).

Amy tries out her new theme of a possible masquerade on Dr. Steiner. While Amy is off again to pursue her investigations, he is left to ponder the masks that people wear, in particular the main players in the local mystery. The mask one wears belongs either to Tragedy or Comedy. Going down the list he can check off Hank Gibbs as bearer of the mask of Comedy. At the end of the list comes Charlie Pitkin, who wears the mask of Tragedy. But then Dr. Steiner pulls up short. It wasn't a mask. He knows because he is the man's psychiatrist. 'Then he knew' (1990: 201).

After Amy has been rescued from Hank Gibbs's attack, Dr. Steiner explains that it was the thought experiment with the masks that made him realise that there had to be one masked partner behind the tourist attraction. The developer in the public eye, Remsbach, always gave credit for the utterly sensational notions to his collaborator Pitkin, who was, as Steiner knew, too stunted by his doomed incestuous relationship to his daughter to contemplate publicity stunts. The close relationship between Pitkin and Gibbs was always an enigma to Steiner. But then he recognised that so unlikely a couple could only be a business partnership. 'But until this notion about the masks came to me I didn't guess it must have to do with Remsbach's plans to turn the Bates property into a tourist attraction' (1990: 215).

Crime as masquerade belongs not to the psychotic brigade of over-identification with Norman, for example, but to the other end of the psycho scale. In contrast to what applied to his former colleague Dr. Claiborne, Dr. Steiner shifts to another profile: 'This type of personality disorder does not involve irrationality or psychotic patterns of behavior' (1990: 195). According to this profile, the killer would not necessarily believe himself to be Norman. 'But it could be someone who wanted us to think he had such a belief' (ibid.). Thus the killer would not fit the model of Claiborne, who at least in part believed he was Norman. Gibbs wasn't insane. Even the attempted murder of Amy fol-lowed a logical procedure. 'His rationale was psychopathic, not psychotic' (1990: 215).

Alternate History
1960

To avert our glance, though not entirely in the wrong direction, the dubbed version for the US market was titled *The Horror Chamber of Dr. Faustus*. In the film more properly titled *Eyes without a Face* (*Les yeux sans visage*) what we're given is science friction, dermabrasion without cease or release. We're at a lecture on the possibilities of renewal in a new era of graft and corruption: whereas transplants used to be restricted to biological identicals now it is possible for foreign tissue to be received when the antibodies are shut down with powerful X-rays and the blood drained and changed. The technical term is heterograft.

The mad scientist is a father with a daughter, who wears the mask over her disfigurement. 'My face scares me; the mask even more. I wish I were blind, blind and dead.' It's the survivor daughter who's riding the father's fault for the car crash that ruined her look. In Paris, Madame, the father's assistant, convinces a girl waiting in line to enter the cinema to look instead at a room for rent at her employer's asylum-estate. But it's her look, the face she looks through, which makes the cut. The masked girl looks at the graft prospect and touches the captive girl's face. With the screaming girl, we see the daughter's face in the raw. Surgeon-father draws cut-out lines for eyes and around the captive girl's face. We watch them lift her face by the skin of her chin. The daughter's face starts healing. Her father has saved face. 'But I have to live for the others now.' She describes her new face: 'Someone who looks like me coming from far away, far away.' But then her face, she has to face it, starts decomposing. Father forever loses face saving. As soon as the 'heterograft' starts decaying, it must be removed.

On the phone the daughter calls out her boyfriend's name. Madame cuts her off: 'Are you mad!' 'I know, the dead are supposed to keep silent. Then let me be really dead! I'm his human guinea pig. Help me die!' The friend reports the spectral voice of the girlfriend he thought dead. The police set up a plant for the murder assembly line. The daughter without face cuts her free and stabs the father's assistant in the throat. Then she releases all the dogs in the lab compound, co-survivors of endless experimentation. Their rapport is with her, one of them, one of them. There's a shot of father, his face; his botched attempt to replace the maternal face-to-face is now in his face too. One bird flies over her and with one in the hand she glides across good grounds for burial.

1

It's time for your alternate history lesson. Neither a precursor nor carrier of the Effect, *Peeping Tom* was made at the same time as *Psycho* but served up a trauma that did not double on contact, did not repetitively reach out to contain itself, but, in shutting itself down, in turning inward, sparked the kind of binding resistance that makes for a quality reception at a later time. It's more than the playing posthumous so desperately familiar to artists. Only Browning's *Freaks* (1932) compares in the annals of reception by repression. And both are highly regarded today as meta-horror films.

Before we can proceed we must go into reverse: according to Freud, voyeurism reverses exhibitionism the way masochism reverses sadism (*Three Essays on the Theory of Sexuality,* 1959: 156–60). Reversal means here: turning an outward tendency inward and against oneself. Internalisation and turning back upon oneself are the foundation of human sexuality and fantasy. Masochism is the fantasising of sadism, voyeurism the fantasising of exhibitionism. Because human sexuality begins as auto-eroticism it is fantasy-dependent: its outward, object-aimed activity is at the same time and in the beginning the reversal of an internal relation. It is in this sense that two gazes can be seen to inhabit Mark, the protagonist who photographs or films and watches the filming internal to Michael Powell's *Peeping Tom*. But divided we understand: in session as in prehistory we are at once aggressor and victim.

People like to specialise, but the force of identification is such that there is a basic instability and interchangeability between active and passive positioning. When you see a bull's eye, like at the start of *Peeping Tom*, you are on a one-way track. To focus on and control the mark as target denies the evil-eye powers, which a dying bull can yet cast upon the hunter. Next we see an eye. But when you look upon an eye there's the look back that can turn it all around.

Mark (he bears in his name his role as bull's eye) tries to contain the look-back powers of the eye with his merger-and-murder camera. Mark or the camera sees and records the female victim, another 'mark', seeing herself in the attached mirror that reflects and redoubles her own fright sight. There is no first or direct contact with the victim, who is, just like Mark but always on another track, thoroughly mediated and processed by the apparatus.

The film tracks two shots or looks, that of camera-killer and that of the masochistic, identificatory consumer. Mark has internalised the star attractions of his father's experiments – himself as child test subject and his father as cameraman. But he can't re-enter the home-movie recording of these experiments. His father's no longer there and he's not that boy any more. Mark, as psycho killer directing his own fear film, can be identified instead as identifying with the women he shoots. What he does to them was in a sense done to him in boyhood. Mark gets his first camera, a wedding gift of his own, upon his father's remarriage. When we see a section of the father's document of Mark's tested childhood (which is a film within or alongside Mark's own snuff film deep inside Powell's film) we find that we are watching the record of the year of Mark's mother's death. Even the mother's death, an occasion for mourning, was subsumed by experimental exhibitionism or voyeurism, sadism or masochism.

While finding his own comfort with ease, the father put 'mother' in closer range by marrying a figure of libidinal access. More than a souvenir and substitute in mourning she appears (in the father's home movie) like a stepping stone or stepladder bringing the boy into asocial proximity to the off-limits bride. It follows that in Mark's fear films, the objects seem so close but remain, in life as in death, far away.

The plain text of the self-reflexive camera, which is also a killing apparatus, is a succinct presentation of the transvaluation of relationality brought about through the new medium, which you can read up on in Benjamin's 'The Work of Art in the Age of Mechanical Reproduction'. But the paternal regime caught on camera is also a historical property that recurs in everyday life. Piaget based his theories of childhood cognitive development on studies of his own children. Analysts Sabina Spielrein and Melanie Klein, too, made their children into research subjects. B. F. Skinner did it, Big Time, watching little one grow up inside one of his theory boxes. But the most stunning model for Mark's childhood from research hell lies in the background story of Daniel Paul Schreber. His father was into the health of growing children and sought to correct posture not only through exercise but even or especially through harness contraptions, which, on or off purpose, kept the strapped-in kids from masturbating. Many of the mediatic devices that control, penetrate and record Schreber within the delusions he documents in *Memoirs of My Nervous Illness* bear a kernel of resemblance to the outfits the father tried out on his two sons. The first son ended up killing himself, the second one eventually became psychotic – not so much gone as going all the way into the recovery phase of delusion formation. WWI took this kind of investigation of developments outside the home into the new lab space of shell shock. But a third degree of archivisation and surveillance can be found recorded in every photo album and home video. The decisions Mark's father makes for inclusion of scenes in the family record are busybody as usual and date back to the rehearsal of Freud's science in the plotting of education or development in the eighteenth-century *Bildungsroman*.

We see Mark peeping only once or twice: it never amounts to much as violation. In fact it's childlike, more like peek-a-boo. When he's at his peek performance in the serial killing, Mark records not what he sees but what the victim sees: her own fear in the mirror as she looks dying. When we first see Mark in action, he is clutching his camera inside his raincoat, like a flasher his aroused organ. The first frightening feature of the camera that the mark or victim recognises is its third limb, the knife, when Mark pulls it up erect and deadly. But each shoot that comes so close to sexual union pulls up short before sex and consummates only murder. In place of a father function (i.e. castration) there is only the p-unitive relation Mark perpetrates on his victims, with whom he identifies. The wish for merger with mother undergoes perpetual near miss: he almost gets off being penetrated by the paternal camera by proxy, via the stepmother figures he (aligned with his father) kills or penetrates.

Mark turns his Oedipus complex into an inside-out film apparatus of destruction and preservation. His traumatic training as test subject in the missing place of mourning pushes him back into the pre-Oedipal precincts of the primal father's controlling interest in women and progeny alike. Since Mark enters his marks from behind (the camera) he can view this transformation of first contact only as trick with mirrors. In the rearview mirroring of the face-to-face of pain and fear he finds reflected his own withheld satisfaction.

Since Mark is filming actual murders he does his editing in the camera. Each take must be worthy of his film. When he watches the scene of Viv's murder it appears that final cut has been taken from him: the ending falls short as filmed and he must re-take the scene with the next victim. It is all along just one scene that he keeps taking over and again unto perfectibility.

As he prepares to merge with the apparatus Mark is guided by his sense that at last at least he will be feeling the fear, which the father's film documentation split off and took away from him. Like *Psycho*, *Peeping Tom* withholds from view the cut it administers. The machine that reduces everything to visibility and death doesn't show itself, not in its entirety, not really to anyone, not to the victim or mark – and not to the viewers of Powell's film. The exception proving the rule of withdrawal of sight from the cinematic stabbing, the fixing of the focus instead on mirrors on mirrors of fear, comes at the film's conclusion. When Mark kills himself we see how it works: the prosthetic knife pierces the victim's throat, cuts off the voice. The apparatus penetrates the catch in Mark's throat, where a child's screams and cries have been held back. What we hear are the father's audio tapes of Mark's collected cries and screams of fear. Is the audio track the secret recess of greatest terror?

Sometimes a great notion enters a phrase or phase of being punned down the corridors of film studies. I'm thinking of Freud's notion of the screen memory ('Deckerinnerung'), which I would like to scramble somewhat as 'scream memory'. This scream, however, via the contamination I have in mind for the pun of it, refers not to the catharsis offered audiences up front in slasher and splatter films. Nor does it refer to the primal scene, which the screen memory represents and represses. Instead my pun refers to screams upon flashbacking to the abyssal horror of yet another shameful moment. These screams are brief and intermittent but each time mark the spot we are in with shame. The operative word is shame not guilt, which belongs instead to a system of circulation and substitution. The screams of horror in slasher films are often re-constructed and subsumed within a larger narrative of guilty pleasures. When another teenage coupling makes the cut, the couple of kids, like Romeo and Juliet, don't die at the same time. One gets to scream first. And then the audience is invited to scream, too. But when in *Friday the 13th* (1980) the arrow goes through Kevin Bacon and its head pops out just ahead of a spurt of blood it is the scream memory of a popping zit that puts through the physical connection to shame, a horror reflex perhaps more basic than guilt.

In *Cutting Class* (1989) Brad Pitt is both a suspect in a serial murder case and former best friend of the other suspect, recently released from imprisonment for murdering his father. The murder was the application of instruction he received from his former best friend in tinkering with the underside of cars. What the psycho remembers out loud — and which he later applies with a vise to Pitt's head — is a mnemonic rhyme: 'Lefty Loosey, Righty Tighty.' When the friend hears it again he is embuddied again, but it is also too much, and he is caught between shame and rage. The film begins with the POV's first (attempted) murder: the DA out hunting is pierced by an arrow. Intermittently throughout the film we watch his abject survival as he inches his way back home. At the end he returns, only to resume his paternal guidance. When he asks reprovingly if the two survivors aren't cutting class, the joke is on him but also goes through him as identification drawing on embarrassment, empathy, guilt and restitution. It stands in contrast to the buddily shame of one teen's prehistory with a psycho, the scream memory of his shameful dependency in latency upon the screwing of a rhyme.

Shame remains stowaway, not throwaway, in guilt. In Freud's case study of Ratman, we learn that the patient had a friend 'of whom he had an extraordinarily high opinion' to whom he would always turn for support when tormented by criminal impulses (1959: 159). His friend assured Ratman that his conduct was irreproachable. Only his dark view of life cast a shadow. This relief organisation of examined guilt bears association with an earlier case of friendship in which 'a similar influence' was exercised over Ratman. As young teen, Ratman was best befriended by an older student who praised his younger bro's 'genius'. But when he next became Ratman's tutor, upon the recommendation of their close association, he began treating his bro like stupid. The last to know, Ratman realised that his friend, upon entering the household, attained his goal of getting close to one of his sisters. 'This had been the first great blow of his life' (1959: 160). The teen setting of mutual admiration was traumatically exploded when

Ratman was taught a lessening of his self-worth: he wasn't a mastermind but just your average sidekick kicked to the side of the older consumer of substitutes. The shame of it is that for Ratman, the carrier of his dead sister's crypt, there can be no substitution.

In the internal film sequence of Mark standing by his mother dead in bed he doesn't make a convincing mourner, the onset of a spiraling shame. He's abjectified before he's fear focused. In the home movie we saw that his father enjoyed setting him up so that while he couldn't help but peep at a couple kissing nearby the father could film it all. Guilt should go with watching, shame comes with being watched by the guilt free or shameless.

One of Mark's day jobs is as photographer of 'artistic pictures'. There's a new model for Mark to shoot in the studio above the tobacco shop that purveys the soft-porn views. But talk of bruises that one model would like to keep out of the pictures diverts us from what's new about the model. She manages to keep her mole-distorted mouth hidden on one side of her mannequin-like silhouette and pose. But when Mark sees the mark he marks it just as it marks him: he records it, while his face (to face) reflects concern, love and excitement. This scene precedes and makes possible the contact with Helen. While the bruising refers to guilt and expiation, the mark the new model bears signals another relationship to trauma. Between a mole or birth mark and the rush of blushing, we find Mark's one spontaneous admission of libidinal interest. Does this contact still belong to the mother, while the fright apparatus passes through the stepmother's happy face of substitution? The birthmark in German is 'mother mark'. While the 'old mole' moving along underground, the ghost of Hamlet's father, carries forward in its motion picture the economy of guilt, Hamlet like Mark is stuck on another mole, the 'blemish' in Hamlet's face-to-face with his mother. The face thus marked is tied to a bodily release or articulation – like the more transitory blush – of a 'shameful' bond with the body, but also of the melancholic residue of corporeal attachment. Shame, like the German *Scham*, is related to one of the more exalted German words for corpse, *Leichnam*.

2

A couple of times *Peeping Tom* brings up the prospect of the psycho's cure, only to dash it according to the logic of near miss that organises Mark's psychic apparatus. Toward the end of the film, the woman who survives, Helen, tells Mark to show her, show the whole thing to her, and then she won't be forever frightened. At their first meeting Mark showed Helen his horror home movies. He wanted to film Helen while she was watching, but she told him to stop. On another occasion she convinced him to leave his camera prosthesis at home for once. Helen, who lives in what was once Mark's mother's room (in the father's house that Mark has inherited and parceled out into apartments he lets out), almost gets past the fixity of his identifications. Helen has written a children's book about a magic camera: she thus holds out the promise of translating phantasm or hallucination into public/published fantasy through the book's fabulation and language. The daughter of a blind woman, Helen comes up with a children's story about the magic camera: it allows the boy, who is frightened of grownups, to see grownups as they were as children. When he can see grownups as children without the camera, then he has grown up. She says Mark inspired her. And she wants him to take the pictures that will illustrate the book.

We recognise the therapeutic momentum. She places the camera prosthesis back upon his body, but also puts the 'extra limb' in its proper place: on the way to dinner to discuss her book and her proposal she convinces him to leave the camera in her bedroom (formerly his mother's room). When they pass a couple making out, he instinctively grabs for his camera, which he finds missing. This is the first time the loop of retraumatisation is interrupted by a felt absence.

She seems on the verge of releasing his body and sexuality from the order of mad science and the techno-phantasmic body, the omnipotence of which she would subsume within a corpus of language. And yet, taking pictures is not only about seeing, in fact or in language. Helen's own blind mother demonstrates the connection when, with her seeing-eye fingers, she traces and reads the features of Mark's face and thus takes his picture. As far as photography is concerned, even the blind, as they depart, will be seeing you. Helen forgets the touch in imaging, which cannot be subsumed or left behind. From Charles Sanders Peirce to Roland Barthes, we know that indexical images, photographs and mirror images, aren't about seeing. They simply point — there it is, I was there, that's it — while touching and absorbing a trace of the object. They are indexical or pointing and vestigial, bearing the trace of the touch.

Helen's blind mother re-introduces the deregulation of the senses that the primal scene fixates within the egoic span of projection. She says that blind people always also live in the rooms that are right above their own. She sees where she's going in Mark's secret darkroom. When she takes his picture she knows that he is going to have to tell someone about his grief. His pain must find a voice. When she makes it the proviso for continuing to see her daughter, Mark attempts to find help. But first or at the same time he must conclude his serial picture.

There is a psychiatrist on the set where Mark works, who happens to be his father's former friend and colleague. His working model would appear to be psychoanalytic: he recommends for treating scoptophilia the transferential talking cure. When Mark asks him on behalf of a third party, the analyst forecasts three sessions per week for a couple of years (the two-year period that, on average, as Freud suggested, the work of mourning requires for stabilisation of the opening season of death-wish-driven turbulence). Before he creates the separation between them of the two-year projection, the analyst and Mark are doubles, both regressed admirers of the father. What is an analyst doing on the movie set? Just like in a session the analyst gets to ask Mark's question of him. Mark is a 'focus puller', the description of his other day job (the third one is that he works for the newspaper *The Observer*), a quaint expression that sounds like slang for beating off while peeping. The analyst comments that he is one, too, in a way.

Powell and Leo Marks were going to make a Freud movie, but news of Huston's project closed that window and opened the other prospect of making *Peeping Tom*. The film story, which Powell came to identify with as his own, was conceived by Marks in the midst of his wartime work in military intelligence, a backstory that signals another cryptological trajectory underlying the film.

The name Leo Marks gave his protagonist, Mark Lewis, was the mirror image of his own. Marks took his interest in code and cipher initially from the back of the books in his father's store. Information about the history and value of a tome, available only to the initiates working at the store, was imprinted on each collectible book. At this time of his own initiation into what was in store for him, Marks became a close admirer of Poe's *The Gold Bug*, which he moreover identified as the inspiration for his encoded film story about serial killing. As Marks recalled in interview:

> About three months before I was born, Father decided that I was to run his rare bookshop. ... One morning he showed me a first edition of Edgar Allan Poe's *The Gold Bug*. ... And I began reading *The Gold Bug*, and it was about codes – the first time I'd ever heard about codes. And when I looked at the back of the book, I found that Marks and Co. had put the cost of the book *in* code . ... And as Dad had told me it cost 6.50, I was able to work out their code. I then decided that one day I wanted to understand codes and write a horror story, like Edgar Allan Poe. ... Because I didn't want to run Father's shop, when war finally started I said to the Ministry of Labour that I wanted to be a cryptographer. ... I ignored the books and inherited the codes. (in *Peeping Tom*, 1998: x–xi)

He also inherited another father figure: 'An interest in Freud was almost instinctive, in an only child destined to run a book shop, hooked on codes. The greatest code of all was the unconscious, and Freud appeared to have deciphered it' (1998: xii). In answer to the question: What fascinated him so much about codes, Marks replies: 'The fact that so much depended on their being safe' (1998: xi). From his position during the war, Marks thus had to project the torture of agents caught in the field. Before he joined the Special Operations Executive (SOE), if an agent sent a message that London couldn't decipher, the agent would be instructed to repeat the message. 'So the agent would re-encode it, and get caught in the process of retransmitting it' (1998: xiii).

> So I made a rule that there should be *no* such thing as an indecipherable message, and got a team of 400 girls, and we would work round the clock to

break a message if it seemed indecipherable. ... The first thing for which an agent would be tortured would be his – or her – code and security check. And it was torture knowing this. So before going to brief an agent for the last time, I tried to develop an 'inner ear'. Because the best communication is unconscious; what the unconscious says to the unconscious. So I would stand outside the briefing room building for ten minutes to try to forget every other anxiety, in order to belong *completely* to the agent, and pick up what I could. ... I set them some exercises. Now, all I had to do during those exercises was to watch them, unobtrusively; to 'photograph' them when they were coding. ... And so the idea of writing *Peeping Tom* was born in the briefing rooms of SOE. (1998: xiii–xiv)

In Poe's story the gold bug, like the skull, is real but is also a hieroglyph or cipher that transmits messages via the plain text of mathematics. At the indexical level of visual media, however, there is another momentum coursing alongside the realness of these items. The bug, for example, is of *'real* gold' – meaning that, when used properly, its owner can 'arrive at the gold of which it is the index' (1992: 242). The decodable message transmits, in the mode of 'a kind of punning or hieroglyphical signature' (1992: 259), a treasure map, 'a lost record of the place of deposit', which can be reconstructed and reclaimed by flashing back through the genealogy of media. The plain text is the legend to the mapping of a space of vision in which 'a telescope' was 'to be used, and a definite point of view, *admitting no variation*, from which to use it' (1992: 267). Once the map has been redrawn through and for this POV (up in a tree) the bug can be dropped from the organising vantage point to find the spot to dig for the treasure (in which two unidentified skeletons also lie). The drop passes through the left eye socket of a human skull that has been nailed to the tree branch. We are left on the edge of a POV, the mother's skull flashing on/in the head of Norman Bates in his concluding drag of denial of mourning, the very logo of psycho horror cinema.

It is the POV that Powell assumed by putting himself in the position of Mark's father in the home movies and his own son (the father inside himself) in the role of Mark as a young boy. The import of the director's crypto-identification was preserved in peristaltic reversal by the immediate reception of the film. A quote pulled from the *London Tribune* review of the film stands for the all-around rejection that ended a career. 'The only really satisfactory way to dispose of *Peeping Tom* would be to shovel it up and flush it swiftly down the sewer. Even then the stench would remain' (in McCarthy 1986: 183). In sync with the non-sequitur nature of the backstory supplied by Marks, Powell responded with the kind of non-recognition that bespeaks a direct hit: '*Peeping Tom* is not a horror film. It's a film of compassion, of observation and of memory, yes! It's a film about the cinema from 1900 to 1960' (in Stein 1979: 58). But then he stumbles over what the industry calls a continuity error, the foreign body of his identification with the psycho: 'I felt very close to the hero, who is an `absolute' director, someone who approaches life like a director, who is conscious of and suffers from it. He is a technician of emotion. And I am someone who is thrilled by technique, always mentally editing the scene in front of me on the street, so I was able to share his anguish' (in Stein 1979: 59).

In 1992 Brian De Palma added a belated station stop to his genealogy of horror movies in the Hitchcock reception or tradition. *Raising Cain* seems right away De Palma's homage to *Peeping Tom* (or to Schreber), although the film adheres to the TV theme and diagnosis of multiple personality disorder, which is not how Mark or Daniel Paul are disorganised. Oddly, the psychiatric frame in Bloch's *Psycho* gestures in this direction: we learn that Norman Bates housed three personalities: Norman, Norma and Normal, the 'unholy trinity' that arose when Norman turned his mother's death or murder into suicide. Notably it is when Norman reads (or hits the books) that he is able to escape his mother's control. But when he faked her handwriting and signature in the suicide note he set up the split-level economy that's an improvement on the shattered apparatus from childhood, which or through which Norman must glimpse whenever he looks in the mirror and sees the wavy lines of slashing.

The overlap between the threesomes inhabiting Norman and Carter, the psycho in *Raising Cain*, grips the edge of the bog in which the car containing a murdered woman has been dumped. The panic from *Psycho* is there still, with the car not wanting to sink all the way right away. But in De Palma's remake the woman was only unconscious. She wakes up to find herself in a backseat bubble ready to burst when the car finally continues to sink. The ruthlessness in the multi pack of personalities is thus underscored. Did the multiple personality disorder, the organising diagnosis, grow out of the messy overlap between the psychotic and the psychopath to introduce order or priority by nominating one of the personalities in the 'psycho' pack a pure psychopath?

Carter is a child psychologist, whose Norwegian father Dr. Nix was a pioneer in their field but also the megalo psycho type one hopes doesn't run (in) the family. Dr. Nix studied the impact of trauma in childhood. But his colleague at the time discovered something behind the data that only Dr. Nix collected. Dr. Nix was studying the effects of trauma on his own son and then, in the course of the multiple personalities born out of traumatisation, his three or more sons. In theory the traumatised child 'splits' in order to leave the trauma behind in the hands of the new personality.

While the in-house case-history data inspired prize-winning theorisation, science required that Dr. Nix establish a control group to test his initial findings. He started buying and kidnapping children. To escape the authorities he feigned death. But now he's back working through Carter and his multiples, notably the evil double Cain, to obtain the control group after all.

Early in the film Carter kidnaps one of his daughter's friends: the boy's mother gives them a lift. After she laughs off his proposal that her son join his daughter at the special school in Norway he blinds her with a sneeze, followed by a swift application of the chloroform gag. But Carter is incapacitated by panic when joggers are about to pass the car. Cain therefore appears, styling with psychopathy, and gives the right survival advice: Carter makes out with the knocked-out woman to divert the attention of the men passing by with a laugh of recognition. That's how Cain originally came to be: he was the new personality suited to handle what Carter could not.

Dr. Nix, nihilism's Old Nick, in fact came to specialise in the study of this psychopathic personality in the setting of its causation through childhood trauma. He wrote up the findings in a successful book (from which a TV movie was adapted). It bore the title De Palma's film also bears.

Father Nix would have been happy to use only Carter, who was suitably competent and expendable for framing as the kidnapper and killer. But Carter's wife Jenny triggers the return of the splits through the drifting apart of their marriage. Carter's focus on their daughter, his subject for study and object of care, is their permanent coitus interruptus. A TV-size monitor in the bedroom keeps the child under watchful supervision and on record. By her husband's focus she is punished: Jenny was capable of ignoring the vital-signs monitor of her dying patient to make out with the grieving husband. But then the one-night stand returns, now a widower, with a proposal to undo their psycho transgression against mourning.

De Palma was the son of an orthopedic surgeon. But he swerved from following in his father's 'Oedipal' footsteps when he saw his first Hitchcock film at age seventeen (it was Vertigo (1958)). He traded in the surgical incision for the cut of editing. In 'The Work of Art in the Age of Mechanical Reproduction', Benjamin associated the new media access to the visible world with the way the surgeon enters the patient's body, skipping the interpersonal relationship.

In making the film within the film Powell (or Mark) put the cuts where the shots are: 'I never discovered what the British critics found so horrendous, because it's not a violent film at all. The film is a psychological study and that's where we put our effort; there's no blood at all until the end' (in McCarthy 1986: 184). While withdrawing the cut of murder into the cutting of the internal film's editing, Powell affirmed via Mark the director's final cut. G. W. Pabst was another European director who fought hard for control of his editing drive. In exile in Hollywood he found out the hard way that control was handed over to the production hell of teamwork. It was easier for him to be pro-reactive, however; he went back to Nazi Germany to reactivate the guarantee that he could have his movie and cut it too. In different ways the Europeans internalised the cuts of their projections within the camera, down the line of the shoot-by-number motion picture. Hitchcock: 'I learned a long time ago – the hard way, I might add – never give the producer and editor too much footage to work with. They then have the capability to alter the thrust of a scene, even determine a performance, by snipping here or lengthening there. There is very little cutting needed on my films. I do as much as possible on the set with my camera' (cited in Leigh 1995: 41).

The *Psycho* Effect folded its metabolisation of the cut made in Hollywood out of the European tradition of genius, control freakishness, and power coupling. Hitchcock, who married the UK's leading film editor, introduced with *Psycho* the ultimate protection of the intactness of his vision: no latecomers would be admitted into the theatre. In *Rope* (1948) Hitchcock treated us to the complete disavowal of the cut: with one break only the camera's take or intake inhabited the film. Hitchcock had to wind *Rope* in a couple of unedited takes around a colossal denial of the film set. The unseen restless activity that switched the sets and props to allow the camera to take in while moving around as though in an intact apartment had to be in sync, like some circus act, in the camera's real time. 'Every time the camera crossed the room the chest had to be rolled off stage just in advance of the camera crane. (We couldn't stop to make new camera setups.) Moving the chest was the assignment of the four prop men crouched on their hands and knees beneath the camera. Not only did they have to move the chest inside on cue but they also had to get it back into the scene again as the camera returned' (in Gottlieb 1997: 281). The highly edited shower scene was the exception or externalisation that proved the rule of internal control over postproduction or reception.

The title, *Rope*, refers to the evidence of psychopathic murder, which wraps up in its noose reference to the actual adolescent psycho crime committed by Leopold and Loeb in 1924 to test their ability to stand beyond good and evil. Freud turned down the commission to act as consultant for the insanity defence, a documented instance just the same of Freud's professional exposure to the problem of psychopathy. The contact confirmed his reservations about Nietzsche's understanding of the superman as coming event, with which new or now generations could claim to be catching up. In *Group Psychology and the Analysis of the Ego*, Freud placed the superman instead in prehistory with the primal father, the only 'individual' both in his theory and in psychohistory – and the model for the psychopath. It is from his crime spree (which ended in his own murder by our ancestral fraternity) that we sought to recover by struggling to find the ability in the need to mourn.

When Hitchcock returned to psycho horror in his 1972 thriller *Frenzy* he fixed his focus on the psychopathic end of the blend. But he also returned to and through the English milieu of the victims and innocent bystanders in *Peeping Tom*. In *Frenzy*, the presence or absence of the view to the killing is internal to the camera, not to the cut of editing.

In Hitchcock's composite picture of the serial killer as psychopath, the killer's only restriction or requirement is sexual: he must strangle his sexual object with his necktie in order to carry his own arousal to term. What prompts him to select a particular woman as the next victim is called a 'trigger'. What pulls the trigger is no longer the deep motivation of psycho Bates or Gein. Like Mark in *Peeping Tom*, the necktie strangler is no doubt immersed in and determined by some specialised and specialising trauma, but as serial killer he seems random in the choices the killing machine makes. The psychopathic killer kills his victims because he can. Killing them is easier than talking to or even thinking of them. Only the consideration of being caught by the law 'inhibits' him.

The first strangling is shown in *Frenzy*. Hitchcock makes it clear that it's actually really hard to strangle someone to death. The first victim is the ex-wife of the protagonist, Blaney, a former RAF officer who's down on his luck. The psychopath, greengrocer Rusk, was a random killer – until now when he stumbles inside the circle of Blaney's friends. By thus forsaking randomness Rusk must construct his new crimes as perfect by handing the murder charge over to Blaney. When the secretary returns to the office of the Blaney's ex, who runs a matchmaking business, she sees the ex-husband leaving the building (he had gone back to see her, but she didn't answer his knock at the door) and of course remembers the row between them the day before. We were in the office just moments before with Rusk, a client with tastes so particular that the ex-wife, as head of the dating emporium, has to ask him to leave and try another agency. Liking the one he's with who is suddenly just his 'type', Rusk turns into the necktie strangler and takes her out. When the secretary, then, returns from lunch and enters the building, we stay behind outside watching the building. We wait for as long it takes her to discover the body. Then, finally, we hear her scream.

Blaney is easily constructed as the criminal, which soon becomes the opportunism the psychopath will take to stage a diversion or cover and win time for his series. But first suspect Blaney's girlfriend Babs, who also knows the charming acquaintance Rusk, is lured by this seeming friend to wait in his apartment for her planned departure with Blaney. Indeed no one will look for her there.

The second killing isn't shown. The girlfriend (Anna Massey, the actress who played Helen in *Peeping Tom*) enters the killer's apartment ahead of him. He gives her his line – she's just his type – and closes the door. The camera, not admitted, backtracks out of the building, slowly, giving the time it takes for the routine we heard the first time around: off-putting remarks that switch around into rape and then the climactic strangling. It's not only the place and time of her murder that counts (down) here but the room that is made for her absence.

In the drop scene that follows, the inspector's wife serves the latest lesson in the French cuisine class she is attending to spice up her marriage. She dismisses the construction of the current suspect's guilt as crime of passion since his marriage to the victim is history. The insight that brings about a crucial shift in the investigation attends the serving of a soup, which, by the measure of the inspector's inability to partake, commands a feeding frenzy of virtually cannibalistic violence. At some point in the 1960s the phrase 'feeding frenzy', which was first formulated to describe how sharks go about it, caught on. Its ellipsis echoes in Hitchcock's title. And yet Hitchcock introduces the cannibalistic dynamic of aberrant identification, which is in our face in splatter films, through the intercutting of scenes in which the meals served illustrate, in the eyes of the English, the primal re-past.

Later on the killer can't find his lapel pin (the one his mother gave him): he plays back 'photographic' recall of the strangling we thus watch after all and recalls how she clutched at him and grabbed his pin. He has to find the corpse he stuffed inside a sack of potatoes and loaded in the delivery truck. Inside the moving truck he plays hot potato with the irrepressible corpse. The scene is a good example of how in this film Hitchcock uses pickup slap sticks to inflict pricks of horror. 'You bitch, where's that bloody pin!' When the killer finds the pin in Mrs. Potato's grasp tightened by rigor mortis he must break the fingers one by one with his penknife to retrieve evidence and maternal souvenir. We know he idealises his mother, who was probably old stranglehold in his early life.

The broken digits supply evidence of a missing or retrieved clue. As the chief inspector recounts what the suspect did to the corpse's fingers, his wife snaps the bread sticks. Those imports are part of yet another feast of French cooking, a fish soup she prepares for her unwilling husband. It's the old 'seafood' joke featuring a cuisine's unblended presentation of food's proximity to death.

We approach the start of the film from the bird's eye view. But the corner insignia of London and the panorama span of expected sights, sweeping across rather than swooping down, introduces a city of tourism. As we get closer to the group gathered together on the Thames embankment beside Parliament we discover that it's not a tour group after all but an official gathering to celebrate progress made in the cleaning up of the river. But when we catch sight of the floater wearing the necktie of her strangling we cross over into journalism, the other tourism.

It's jolly old England: the expatriate looks upon his former home country, which seems slightly miniaturised and silly. In the local pub we overhear that the psychopath, though likeable, is emotionally dangerous. Like a child he can revert to a 'subhuman' level governed by the 'pleasure principle' alone. And yet sex murders, the conversing gents confirm, are good for the tourist trade. The main change from Arthur La Bern's novel (*Goodbye Piccadilly, Farewell Leicester Square*) going into Hitchcock's film was the era selected. The novel, written during the swinging sixties, was set in the immediate post-WWII period. The man falsely suspected walks into it, drunkenly charging himself out loud for the murder of thousands. In fact he was one of the RAF pilots flying over Dresden dropping firebombs. Fifteen to twenty years is the closest you can get to the recent past if psychopathy is to take us by surprise.

In 1965, between the impact of *Psycho* and Hitchcock's own follow-up treatment, Truman Capote offered with his 'journalistic novel' *In Cold Blood* (which proposed a double scoop or capture of the credibility of fact and the immediacy of film) a psycho profile in its separate parts. Of the two killers, Hickcock fits a 'severe character disorder' (2007: 295), psychopathy by any other name, while Smith's 'personality structure' belongs in the vicinity of 'paranoid schizophrenic reaction' (2007: 298). For the psychiatric consensus and conclusion Capote cites the testimony of a 1960 article on the phenomenon of murderers who seem rational, identified in the article as individuals 'predisposed to severe lapses in ego-control which makes possible the open expression of primitive violence, born out of previous, and now unconscious, traumatic experiences' (2007: 299). Another citation from 'Murder without Apparent Motive – A Study in Personality Disorganization' shows how the exploration of trauma and violent symptomatic behavior gives way before the model of the trigger:

> The murderous potential can become activated, especially if some disequilibrium is already present, when the victim-to-be is unconsciously perceived as a key figure in some past traumatic configuration. The behavior, or even the mere presence, of this figure adds a stress to the unstable balance of forces that results in a sudden extreme discharge of violence, similar to the explosion that takes place when a percussion cap ignites a charge of dynamite. (2007: 301)

I remember an interview on German TV with a Foucauldian sociologist of literature who, as is so often the case, was not satisfied with the reputation obtainable in the academy. It was about running amok, the genre of random shootings associated with educational institutions (although first diagnosed – 'going postal' – in the work setting of post office employees). In 2015 I learned from colleagues at European Graduate School that when teaching in the US they regularly issue 'trigger reports' in the classroom; thus they absolve themselves of all responsibility for any slights that students like to take to court (or to the top of the bell tower). The TV interviewee associated the German term for 'trigger' ('Auslöser') with Julius Robert Mayer, one of the founders of thermodynamics. Later in life Mayer published a paper on 'Auslösung'. In the course of addressing phenomena in which a small amount of energy can control the release of a relatively large amount as in an explosion or a chain reaction, he also attended to the neurological process of his own psychotic breakdown two decades earlier. I couldn't share in the German colleague's triumph that Mayer resolved the enigma of his bout of mental illness by recourse to the trigger science of energy. So I looked into his bio and without too much digging saw that two years prior to the outbreak of his illness in 1850 Mayer was up against the loss of three of his children.

The investigating detective in Capote's journalistic novel was also of two minds in his profiling: the 'psychopathic rage' (2007: 82) evident at the crime scene is hard to attribute to two killers at once. Because it took two there is a relationship there floating in various directions. For example: 'at least one of the murderers was emotionally involved with the victims, and felt for them, even as he destroyed them, a certain twisted tenderness' (2007: 103). Mr. Clutter, a father figure, set the scene for

Smith. While it was Smith, the more psychotic psycho, who did the killing, what set him off was the indiscretion Hickock, the psychopathic psycho, had in mind for the father's daughter. When he realized that his partner planned to 'bust' the girl, Smith felt like taking a 'buzzsaw' to him (ibid.). But instead he took the easier way out and started killing the double-plural disposability of the Clutters.

> I don't feel anything about it. ... Maybe we're not human. I'm human enough to feel sorry for myself. ... Soldiers don't lose much sleep. They murder, and get medals for doing it. ... It's easy to kill – a lot easier than passing a bad check. Just remember: I only knew the Clutters maybe an hour. ... But the way it was, it was like picking off targets in a shooting gallery. (2007: 291)

Epidemics of Mass Murder

*F*ido (2006) was one film in the rash of zombie films during the Bush Junior era that paid homage to the hoping end of Romero's trilogy – but as pet project.

According to the short film inside the film it opens, Dr. Hrothgar Geiger's 'domestication collar' has tamed zombie hunger. While the collar, like its dog-training counterpart, can administer shocks, otherwise it somehow transmits meekness to the wearer when the red light is on. Philip K. Dick pointed out that the meek who shall inherit the earth might best be translated as the tame. Zomcom, which Dr. Geiger founded during the zombie wars, sells domesticated zombies to perform menial tasks in the homes and businesses inside gated communities. That opening film, a documentary shown to school children the way the flag is shown to their Pledge of Allegiance, delivers the message that ultimate regulation of society against the threat of the 'wild zone', where the untamed zombies and dissidents roam free, requires properly conclusive mourning: 'Thanks to Zomcom we can all become productive members of society, even after we die. Or, for those who can afford it, a Zomcom funeral, complete with head coffin, guarantees you a burial you won't come back from.' The fact of life under radiation is that everyone who dies comes back as yet another zombie.

During the zombie wars, Bill Robinson was forced to give his own father, who had turned zombie on him, second death. Now Bill is phobic about zombies.

His wife Helen is unsatisfied with her place in society and his son Timmy suffers at the hands of bullies at school. When Helen obtains a Zomcom zombie to save face in the neighbourhood she discovers all the service she needed was the status he signified. But Timmy now has a best friend and protector named Fido.

The totemic system lays claim to the fatherhood it displaces. Fido is the man in the Robinson family after Bill's finite funeral. Helen's satisfaction is kept on the same short leash as Timmy's friendship with Fido. Zomcom's head of security joins the happy end when he is recycled to be his daughter's totem pet.

At the start of his presentation of the defence mechanism of projection, in the section from *Totem and Taboo* titled 'The Taboo upon the Dead', Freud falls back upon analogy with contagion in the course of immersing himself in the materials of the new discipline and discourse of anthropology. 'The taboo upon the dead is – if I may revert to the simile of infection – especially virulent among most primitive peoples. It is manifested, in the first instance, in the consequences that follow contact with the dead and in the treatment of mourners' (1959: 51). He proceeds down the check-off list of on-location examples: the Maoris disallow contact with anyone who has handled a corpse or participated hands-on in burial of the dead body. Anyone thus considered unclean could eat only trough-style with hands tied behind his back. Or someone would serve as feeder who, however, in turn had to be subjected to restrictions, though less severe than those attending direct contact with the dead. When the period of seclusion was concluded, all the items of contact, from clothing to dishes, were trashed. Whoever goes against the ordinances falls ill and dies.

'Essentially the same prohibitions … apply to those who have been in contact with the dead only in a metaphorical sense: the dead person's mourning relations, widowers and widows' (1959: 53). All the measures taken are 'designed to keep the dead person's ghost at a distance' (ibid.). 'This suggests that contact "in a metaphorical sense" is after all understood as being bodily contact, for the dead man's ghost does not leave his relations and does not cease to "hover" round them during the time of mourning' (ibid.).

In British New Guinea the widower is shunned and must in turn lurk in the shadows: 'if he sees or hears anyone coming, especially a woman, he must hide behind a tree or a thicket' (1959: 54). Freud translates:

> This last hint makes it easy to trace the origin of the dangerous character of widowers or widows to the danger of temptation. A man who has lost his wife must resist a desire to find a substitute for her; a widow must fight against the same wish and is moreover liable, being without a lord and master, to arouse the desires of other men. Substitutive satisfactions of such a kind run counter to the sense of mourning and they would inevitably kindle the ghost's wrath. (ibid.)

Certain restrictions are imposed for life and yet the strictness of their observance diminishes over time. When in the time of mourning the conflict grows less acute, the taboo upon the dead loses its charge. (1959: 63)

We are still within the sphere of the metaphorical or anti-metaphorical when it comes to the special handling of the names of the deceased. To disregard the prohibition against naming the dead in the presence of his relatives or survivors is to invite punishment that is, in severity, 'not less than that laid down for murder' (1959: 55). That's the way it is in certain tribes in South America. In East Africa the Masai change the deceased's name immediately after his death, whereby mention of the departed under the new name is still possible. There are tribes in Australia in which care is taken that after a death 'everyone bearing the same name as the dead man's, or a very similar one, changes it for another'. In North-West America we find tribes that carry this one step further: 'all the dead person's relations change their names, irrespective of any similarity in their sound'. Finally, 'among the Guaycurus in Paraguay, when a death had taken place, the chief used to change the name of every member of the tribe; and from that moment everybody remembered his new name just as if he had borne it all his life' (ibid.). With the name thus uncontained (like the corpus that bore it) the extension of the dread of the name of the dead person to everything bound up with the deceased along so many chains of association would appear unstoppable. For example: 'if the name of the dead man happens to be the same as that of an animal or common object, some tribes think it necessary to give these animals or objects new names, so that the use of the former names shall not recall the dead man to memory'(ibid.).

Since proper mourning rituals are also conducted alongside the taboo restrictions, proper observances dedicated to the preservation of the deceased's memory, Freud concludes that the taboos tread in the ambivalent fine print of the services themselves, which commemorate the deceased at the same time as they ensure that he can never return. Every death is a murder, which the victim seeks to avenge. If the dead are angry it's because they found out that we caused them the harm coming our way. But neurotic reactions to objects and objectives of mourning allow for more comprehensive examination of this double harm. Obsessive self-reproaches that the grief-stuck survivor broadcasts – that he, in short order, caused the death of the loved one – are at some level justified, 'and that is why they are proof against contradictions and protests' (1959: 60). Mixed feelings, inevitable death wishes, all the static on the line and crossing the mind, prove untenable when the one we on occasion wished gone indeed (and in death) goes. The negative component gets projected onto the corpse, which is thus reanimated as vengeful being out to get the survivor. Projection means not only that something internal is cast out or that something of one's own is split off and handed over to another: projection also brings about reversal, thereby hiding that which is protected, I mean projected. Up front, the ghoul is not in the mix of contrary feelings, but rather rides the conveyer belting out of open hostility. Unlike the projector, however, at least for the duration of the horror film, the projection has time to develop, and thus it follows, in fact, that, given time, the figure of projection will undertake the work of mourning the projector was unable to take up.

Borrowed from Kleinpaul, the vampire served Freud as model for the transformation the loved one undergoes through the one-on-one projective realignments of mourning's opening season. But it is Freud's turn to infection in his assessment of mourning orders and disorders that is literalised in the first group portrait of the vampire. According to Richard Matheson's origin story in *I Am Legend*, his undead masses supply the missing link between the occult creatures of the night and the secular prospect of what is announced in *Night of the Living Dead* to be an 'epidemic of mass murder'.

Robert Neville, the last man on earth, is also a group-of-one dependent upon the mass media Sensurround. He must keep the undead masses out of his home, out of his mind. He plays records amplified via loudspeakers set up throughout his personal space to outblast the sounds of undead consumerist demand just outside his doors and windows at night. 'He was glad he'd learned early in life, from his mother, to appreciate this kind of music. It helped to fill the terrible void of hours' (1995: 16).

He just wants to be left alone, not lonely. 'Should he watch a movie? No, he didn't feel like setting up the projector. He'd go to bed and put the plugs in his ears. It was what he ended up doing every night, anyway' (1995: 21). Based on my thirty years in California, I'm certain that Matheson, another California anti-body, didn't have too far to reach to compose this post-apocalyptic mood and neighbourhood.

The undead out there seem reduced to the consumerism of their blood lust. Basic needs or supplies fill up places for absence in Neville's household or psychic economy. His fortress home is the columbarium of his recent past. 'Next he moved over to the uneven stacks of cans piled to the ceiling. He took down a can of tomato juice, then left the room that had once belonged to Kathy' (1995: 17). Something else, too, is being conserved between the closet of cans (and cannots) and the canned music of his habitat. Neville's last stand is pitched against his own destruction, but in the first place against the temptation of the undead babes who strip show him all to get to him where they're already crossing his mind.

> He closed his eyes again. It was the women who made it so difficult, he thought, the women posing like lewd puppets in the night on the possibility that he'd see them and decide to come out. A shudder ran through him. Every night it was the same. He'd be reading and listening to music. Then he'd start to think about soundproofing the house, then he'd think about the women. (1995: 19)

Flashback to his burial of his wife Virginia, which he had to conduct in secret, since immediate mass cremation was already emergency law. But then it was two in the morning, two days after he had buried her. 'Two eyes looking at the clock, two ears picking up the hum of its electric chronology, two lips pressed together, two hands lying on the bed. He tried to rid himself of the concept, but everything in the world seemed suddenly to have dropped into a pit of duality' (1995: 75–6). And then he discovered, upon Virginia's return from the grave, that there are two deaths.

During a visit to Virginia's crypt Neville finds undead dead not of his own staking. 'The heart had not been touched, no garlic had been present. ... Of course – the daylight!

... The sun's rays must have done something to their blood! Was it possible, then, that all things bore relations to the blood? ... He had to do a lot of reading, a lot of research. ... Now this new idea started the desire again!' (1995: 38). With the new start of his desire to research and destroy, he can drive-by-test undead subjects, even the women and children, without carrying forward the grief-stuck associations with Virginia and Kathy. 'Usually he felt a twinge when he realized that, but for some affliction he didn't understand, these people were the same as he. But now an experimental fervor had seized him and he could think of nothing else' (1995: 39).

What he feels he has discovered, however, the interchangeability of staking and exposure to sunlight, was already admitted on the pages of *Dracula*, which he has been reading regularly during happy hour. Neville himself realises that an oversight of what already in legend is as broad as daylight indicates an excess of repression undermining conscious thought. Earlier Neville asked himself why the stakes had to be wooden, and why they had to pierce the heart. He couldn't believe that it was the first time he had paused in the automatic course of the process of elimination to question its scientific basis. 'Yeah, yeah, yeah, he thought, shades of old Fritz. That had been his father's name. Neville had loathed his father and fought the acquisition of his father's logic and mechanical facility every inch of the way. His father had died denying the vampire violently to the last' (1995: 27).

The vampire Neville believes in is not that of 'the B-film factories' (1995: 29). The belief is the precondition for fighting the vampire for real: rather than let them lie he tests sleeping vampires with injections of garlic's chemical essence or with the spectacle of the cross. He tries out different ways to penetrate the undead bodies. He reads up on blood, lymph and other bio systems of circulation. He comes around to the conclusion that the same germ that killed the living gave the dead their energy. He dubs the germ he finds on the slide vampiris. 'I guess I got old Fritz's blood in me, after all, he thought once in amusement' (1995: 85). 'Germ' is also an abbreviated reference to his German patrimony.

First a dog, then a woman (not one of the memento mori babes from happy hour) come into view in daylight. The totemic interlude introduces mourning as a cleansing of the metabolism for a better burn of adaptation: 'Burying the dog had not been the agony he had supposed it would be. In a way, it was almost like burying threadbare hopes and false excitements. From that day on he learned to accept the dungeon he existed in. . . . And, thus resigned, he returned to work' (1995: 111).

With the woman, however, he can't help doubting her humanity. He blames it on himself, that is, on his father. 'It's me, he thought. I've been by myself too long. I won't believe anything unless I see it in a microscope. Heredity triumphs again. I'm my father's son, damn his moldering bones' (1995: 135). But father knew best. The woman contacted him under cover of sun block to find out all his test results and then, because he has touched her, to warn him. 'We are infected. But you already know that.

What you don't understand yet is that we're going to stay alive. We've found a way to do that and we're going to set up society again slowly but surely' (1995: 135). The new species, which regulates or defers the course of the infection by taking pills that combine blood with a drug that prevents multiplication of the germ, has singled out the last man as public enemy number one. His total warfare against the vampires claimed too many innocent bystanders. He believes that when he dies, he will become, for the new species, the legendary Devil of a new faith or superstition (1995: 151). Whether or not demonic, Neville was mass murderer to the new genre of survivors. His testing of subjects unto death, the legacy of his German father, can be realigned, within the perspective of the mutating vampires, to fit the profile of the serial killer.

2

In *Night of the Living Dead* a reference to *Psycho* is one feature of the interior decoration of the farmhouse. When we first enter with Barbara we catch sight of the stuffed animals, which the camera then identifies close up against the wall. Stuffed animal stiffs offer one image of film, the image that the shower scene in its more internal course, and the splatter and slasher films that followed in their more external and visible mode, try to inhabit but also try to take apart. Romero aimed to make a film that did not cut away from the violence, did not slip it by us, inside us, but opened to view the metabolism of identification. 'Splatter' was a term Romero first used to describe the genre he claimed for *Night of the Living Dead*. He intended to show what ghouls eat.

But it is the murder of both parents by their infected daughter down in the basement that brings up the shower scene. In *Fade to Black* (1980) the protagonist, who has lived for the movies and has started repeating screen memories, thus crosses over into psychotic delusion. He dresses up as Count Dracula to attend a screening of *Night of the Living Dead*. We watch the basement scene. We see that some association has crossed his mind. An Australian woman who lives for her Marilyn-Monroe-lookalike looks takes a shower. The camera looks straight up at the showerhead. The shadow of the guy in Dracula drag opens the curtain wide to her screaming on cue. But even though he only wanted her autograph, and thus withdraws the knife point of the scene, we have thus followed the association or recognition between the basement murder and the shower scene.

The basement murder is shown in spades. The little girl's murder instrument presumably enters the mother's body just in front of the frame. Editing doesn't interfere and doesn't participate in it. The mother even lies down to take it. But the cut doesn't, after all, show it all. The citation of *Psycho*, therefore, the mother's murder in the cellar by her little girl, is the only scene that doesn't lay bare the violent contact with the body. The reception of *Psycho* in *Night of the Living Dead* is, in sum, a foreign body, intact and undisclosed, a fruit-cellar-installed, embalmed citation. Did Romero position it to wash up and out with the blood flow? We'll never know because then there was one murder that forsook all others, the crime that slipped in and broke the frame and renewed our vows with trauma. If this splatter film was designed to give the inoculative shot, then *Night of the Living Dead* ended up the symptom that was offered as the cure.

In *Night of the Living Dead* we witness a cross-sectioning of society into fragments of relation – nuclear family, couple in love, incestuous family tie, the leader and the pack – which enter the binding media reception and come together in front of the radio and the TV. The film ends on the news, inside the TV broadcast. We watch society in crisis disintegrate and then come back via the media in the mode of survival. Romero's portrayal of society begins as identifiably adolescent – it is the same issue of 'respect' that triggered the aberrant trajectories in *Psycho* which gets raised at the start of *Night of the Living Dead* – but then goes along with political developments that were bringing the Vietnam War home.

Night of the Living Dead begins within a society-wide format: we see a vast cemetery with the American flag waving overhead. What animates the scene is the drive-through sibling duo, two adolescents or 'young adults', who are here to visit their father's grave on their invalid mother's behalf. Brother Johnny invalidates the mother, who wants to remember but sends the wreath with them in her stead. 'Look at this thing: "We still remember". I don't.' Johnny imagines their wreath being picked up, cleaned up and recycled, even sold back to them next year.

Johnny notices his sister Barbara's dread of the dead, of the dad. He teases her just as he did when they were younger: 'They're coming to get you, Barbara. They're coming to get you.' Johnny speaks with the lilt of Boris Karloff. Does he thus liberate the walking dead from the Hollywood horror film tradition (Hervey's suggestion) or is it time for an update on station identification? We are inside the group or teen psychologisation of horror. Imitating Karloff is what teens do in groups. Barbara moves away, chiding her acting-out brother in phrases that can't be heard above the din of denial. And then she passes by an old gentleman who promptly assaults her. Johnny comes to her assistance but is chomped down on in her stead.

When Ben drives to the farmhouse, Barbara is already inside with the taxidermy exhibits. Down in the basement, it turns out, a young couple and a nuclear family have also already taken refuge. Ben, the natural born leader, attempts to build a group out of the refugees in the farmhouse in front of radio and TV sets. Hervey points out that Cooper's choice of the cellar for last stand of survival was probably the strategy to follow. However, Ben acts as leader of the pack and its group psychology when he secures the live-line to the media. Importantly he also keeps us out of *Psycho*'s fruit cellar.

The first news flash announces that it's 'an epidemic of mass murder'. The next flash in the attention span (and flashback to the Ed Gein reception) makes out the mass murderers to be cannibals. 'Victims are partially devoured by their murderers.'

Once the epidemic of murder is further distanced by the science fiction of radiation released by a spaceship to Venus we can bear to hear what we already witnessed in the opening cemetery scene: the returning dead are the unmourned. 'The bereaved will have to forego the dubious comforts that a funeral service will give. They're just dead flesh, and dangerous.' Once the report is in that the zombies can be killed with a shot to the head, that the undead can die again, it is not so much mourning that returns, down the road from where the dead father no longer insured life against annihilation, but it is a new marketing of successful mourning that opens up for the thrill of killing.

But then there is a living victim, doubly charged in and outside the film as political mascot, stowaway in the ranks of the living dead during the open season of elimination that puts the fun back into funeral.

Ben was the sole survivor. Before we let that stand, however, we need to account for Ben's disciplinary action against Mr. Cooper, which does prevent Ben's idealisation. Ben shoots Mr. Cooper. But is the shot fatal? Even the fall down the cellar stairs seems not to have killed him. When we catch his daughter in the act of eating him, the pledge of freshness that reinforces the zombie taboo suggests that he died in the course of the meal, just as his daughter was getting to gnaw him better. Both Mr. and Mrs. Cooper come back as zombies. This time Ben shoots them both dead-dead. Thus, to reformulate Ben's solo status, we might note that he is the only one to die without first coming back for second death.

The conflict with Mr. Cooper also prepares the way for the theme Romero will address explicitly in the subsequent installments of the 'Trilogy of the Dead': the terrorism of survival. The family fragments that Ben has to work with are too dysfunctional to enter the group bond of survival. The nuclear parents with the sick daughter think they're in a safe place when they're in fact close up and interpersonal with infection. Barbara, who's shell-shocked, makes one regressed demand: she has to go back out there and look for her brother. Then there's the young couple of sweet kids in love who prove a liability to the group getaway plan.

The sheriff, crossing the site of the young couple's demise, cracks the joke that somebody had a cookout here: sweet indeed, they sure made good barbecue. The news flashes have also released shitkicker peace officers and vigilante volunteers. They enjoy rounding up and killing the zombies, for which they borrow the term 'mopping up' from the lexicon of the Vietnam War. The heightened affect of the Anti-War protest goes into these scenes. It was on Oedipal grounds that the protesters, whether the heirs of the victims or of the perpetrators and silent partners in the recent past, were convinced that another fascist takeover loomed behind US foreign policy. We don't see the protesters. Instead we witness the posse of redneck police and volunteers arguably from the protest-perspective.

In time, the zombies will consume the posse too. The zombies are us, right down to the hick reactionaries who in time will have contributed to our makeup, our metabolism. Contrary to the reception of the film folding out of the 'socio-political implications of Ben's being black', what was in fact new about *Night of the Living Dead* was that a black man played 'the lead role regardless of, rather than because of, his color' (Romero & Sparrow 1978: 11). Romero underscores that he 'did not calculate that this would be an attention-grabber'. (What's more, Jones, the actor playing Ben, remembered that the ending was his idea. In the scripted version, Ben's shooting is a mistake, an instance of friendly fire, and is deeply regretted.)

> We backed into it. Our own relaxed, honest, uninhibited, naive attitudes as we approached the production ultimately read-out as unconscious elements in the picture which added to its realism, offhandedness and uniqueness. (ibid.)

> These factors all elevated the film from the ordinary, and because of its realistic presentation, an allegorical interpretation becomes reasonable. (Romero & Sparrow 1978: 12)

It was the backfire and crash of coincidence that fired up the allegory drive. In the film the breaking news of the zombie epidemic and the attending novelty of proscription of the rites of burial and mourning were transmitted out of the static on the car radio. The night Romero and Streiner drove the first print of *Night of the Living Dead* to New York City in search of a distributor the radio announced the assassination of Martin Luther King. At this gunpoint, the allegorical presentation proved compulsory, administered as antidote to the accidental or unconscious nature of history in the making. A black mandate would survive in each of the allegorical sequels.

When the vigilante mob shoots Ben down as just another zombie, and the epidemic or phantasm thus covers up the real murder of an African-American, the film exceeds itself and strikes us with something it doesn't really show: we're in a new trauma spot. The novelisation underscores the impasse by cutting the film's loss of Ben. Karen Cooper, the little girl zombie, attacks Ben. Her bite numbers his time and numbs the film's intervention in the politics of selection in life as in death. The movie's social and political reformatting of the family scene of psycho horror along mass psychological lines convicts the audience of racist murder by association. Just to live in a racist society means, individual views notwithstanding, to be racist, that is, adapted to societal racism.

To appreciate just how uncontained the spill was that the Ben conclusion slipped on in 1968, one might consider the 1990 remake, written and produced by Romero but directed by Tom Savini, who was better known for his special-effects work in splatter and slasher films under someone else's direction. The update downplays one syndication of racism but slips primal racist murder like a subliminal inside the affirmative action of the newly energised leading lady. In the remake Ben is betrayed, is already zombie when he dies, and the only one left to be killed under the cover of cleanup is a stock caricature out of the archive of religious-ethnic intolerance. But he's not killed by the posse. Barbara, who is now destined to survive, the strong young woman in the slasher-therapy tradition, shoots Cooper knowing full well that he's not one of us. She tells the posse: 'Another one for the fire.'

3

By the 1980s, the living dead had crossed over into Camp science fiction. Romero's shot to the brain, which kills the ghoul, keeps zombieism in range of the minds of the beholders. In *Return of the Living Dead* (1985) nothing kills the zombies: when the twice-dead corpses burn up, the smoke soaks back down to earth in the rain and reanimates the contents of yet another cemetery. These ghouls can't be stopped by a shot to the brain. What's more, they feed on human brains. The sci-fi image of indestructible nuclear waste places us in a bigger picture of survival or annihilation of the species. *Night of the Living Dead* is referred to as the virtual documentary of a toxic-spill crisis that marked the beginning for all the Returns.

In *Dawn of the Dead* (1978) and *Day of the Dead* (1985) (each part corresponds in turn to a new decade of topical frame of reference), Romero resituated the story arc of *Night of the Living Dead* within the socio-political allegory of survival of the new or renewable. To reinstall *Night of the Living Dead* as the first part of a trilogy Romero reached back into its prehistory, the story 'Anubis' he rolled off the impressed with Matheson's *I Am Legend*. It, too, was about vampires replacing every human on earth but one. Romero: 'Anubis was about what happens when an incoming revolutionary society – in this case, the mass return from the grave of the recently dead, whose sole purpose is to feast on the flesh and blood of the living – replaces an existing social order' (in Gagne 1987: 24–5).

In *The Omega Man* (1971), the second film adaptation of Matheson's novel, the living dead are staged as the heirs to the counterculture that went down with the final world war. They target the sole survivor as incarnation of the machine era that destroyed the world. The new beginning in mutation that concludes Matheson's narrative models the alternative community of survivors in *The Omega Man*. With a vial of the last man's immune blood this group seeks a place of its own in the countryside for starting over. Earlier the man alone in the world goes regularly to the movie theatre to watch *Woodstock* (1970) (a fitting scenario from Hell for the actor Charlton Heston). This is the point to which survival returns to begin again beyond the impasse of the sole survivor's repeated viewing. Prior to positing the goal of recovery the film fills the blank of survival with scenes of one-stop shopping in an empty city of open sores, I mean stores.

Early in *Dawn of the Dead*, we are inside a TV studio, the transit hub of survival. From here a couple, Fran and Stephen, proceeds by helicopter together with the two soldiers they pick up on the way (Peter and Roger) toward the outskirts of the epidemic where they discover a shopping mall. Once the mall can be cleared of the zombie shoppers, they inhabit it like the pharaoh his tomb of supplies. At first the small group seems organised around the couple. Fran is already pregnant with the future. She sets the selection process going toward survival, the new frontier. In the midst of the group's hypnotised adaptation to the mall she laments: what has become of us! Fran demands that from now on she be included as equal: she wants a gun of her own and flying lessons.

In the end her partner in survival isn't Stephen, however, but Peter, the African-American soldier, who must first work his way through and out of his buddy film of longing and suicide. He alone undertakes the work of mourning. When Roger prepares to die of his zombie-inflicted wounds he begs his buddy Peter to wait before shooting him dead in the head. Wait until he sees that Roger is coming back as one of them. Don't shoot if you see the wait in his eyes. Roger is determined to try and not come back. He spares no one the pain of hoping. The scene of Roger's return and double departure is a show of mourning and closure. But it also fulfills the most difficult requirement in this struggle for survival: you must kill even the undead 'memory' of your former buddy. He belonged with you to the in-group bent on survival but didn't pass the selection test. The one size that's fit for survival also prohibits in the zombie setting the bite sighs of remembrance (still available inside vampirism).

When the TV news refers to the zombies in terms of 'pure motorised instinct' and 'remembered behaviour from normal life', Peter fills in the blanks from his depressed position: 'They're us, that's all.' He also cites the dictum or prophecy he heard his grandfather foretell that when Hell freezes over or otherwise shuts down as overcrowded, then the dead will walk the earth. (What's implied, of course, is that the dead are evil and that in psychic reality there's no room for absence.)

Peter gives Stephen a chance at macho-tender bonding. When his second buddy is infected too, Peter decides to kill himself and let the pregnant woman fly off alone into the outside chance of survival. But the combat shock of another zombie going for him triggers Peter's drive to survive. In order to make the last step into the getaway vehicle he fires up his weapon and then throws it at the zombies to distract them with this prize. Playing with guns is another primal pastime that zombies 'remember'.

The last minute changing of his guard pulls and straightens him out once more from the suicidal impasse of his buddy film. He joins Fran. Romero held in reserve an alternate ending: Peter kills himself after all and Fran jumps up into the rotating helicopter blades to get it over with already. In the survivalist ending of *Dawn of the Dead* the murders of both Marion Crane and Ben are reversed through the survivorship of Fran and Peter. But the survivorship of catastrophe proved selective.

The emphasis on the check-off list leading to survival and to the future tips the scales (from our eyes) from horror to terror and terrorism. Stephen falls for the mall fortress, calls it their world. Stephen's possessiveness, which was the cause of his wounding and zombiefication, also endangered the group. He dies protecting the 'great stuff' in the mall. When they first arrived to find the zombies shopping without dropping, Stephen held the inside view: zombies are drawn to the mall by 'some kind of instinct, memory of what they used to do. This was an important place in their lives.' He ends up another zombie shopper.

Peter's buddy, Roger, the first of the foursome to succumb to zombieism and second death, endangered the group by his risk-taking, thrill-seeking relationship to violence. In the novelisation co-written by Romero and Susan Sparrow, Fran and Roger enter the narrative two years after their respective divorces. While she has been making great strides, giving her a lead in the running start to the future of survival, Roger succumbs to the grounds for the divorce, his traumatic fixation on the Vietnam War.

When it comes time to secure the mall, all the old systems of Vietnam combat are go. What we can see on the screen the novelisation spells out: 'Roger, clutching his walkie-talkie, disappeared among the aisles. As if he were running across a mine field in Nam, he crouched, going deeper into the store' (1978: 100). This combat is more horrible since the antagonists, though they are only zombies, are also recognisably former fellow citizens and not 'gooks'. But the prize is that much greater: it's the American Dream realised for the in-group, although vacuum-packed by absence of life. The name of the mall they conquer: Shoppers' Paradise.

While the zombies can be removed, it's a mall world after all (with the dead-dead kept in deep freeze storage). The real danger would be posed by the first primal band of marauders to identify their hideout a looting paradise. Since looting and shopping are proximate impulses, it is just a matter of time before this station stop must end in motorbike gang bang-bang. Once again two aspects of psychopathic violence pose the threat to survival, consumerism of life and murder of the dead and alive.

While Peter waits to kill his dead pal Roger, and thus find his own release from typecasting as interracial member of the military buddy system, Stephen and Fran are watching a TV show in which the experts discuss survival plans. One can escape to a safe place in order to start over, Adam and Eve style, while waiting out the epidemic, which will exhaust itself like capitalism in the Marxist view. The other option is to live with the epidemic, recreating society to make our cohabitation with the new species livable. There is a theme of domestication in this plan, as in Dr. Logan's long-term plan for the zombies in *Day of the Dead*, the conclusion of Romero's trilogy.

The doctor's plan is still based on the insight that the zombies are us. Taken together with Matheson's *I Am Legend*, the plan to live with the epidemic comes down to living with it as though it were a chronic condition that also affects one's own mutating life or body. In *Dawn of the Dead* the countdown to survival of those who pass the check-off list of traits that don't belong to the future streamlines the mass failure at the end of

Night of the Living Dead and rescues its survival momentum. But it ends up being cruel to be humankind.

Day of the Dead focuses on a post-catastrophic period of transition and adjustment during which society, including the living, the dead and the undead, wobbles along into some steady state. The zombies have replaced the masses. Inside the fortified underworld, human survivors have established a test site for the control of the zombies through basic training. Zombies can gain or regain basic skills. To control them, however, the new survivor elite must face the new fact of life that there is only one thing that zombies like to eat.

The underworld is divided between science and the military. In *Dawn of the Dead* the TV control centre and the shopping mall were the two temples of mass media society. In *Day of the Dead*, the laboratory is the tomb or womb of the 'new' social order in which scientific and military complexes interface or face each other off.

Dr. Logan (or 'Dr. Frankenstein' as he is also known to all) kills off soldiers to feed his new pets. 'I needed him, Sarah', the mad scientist explains to his assistant when she discovers one of the military corpses; 'He's helping us more now than he ever did when he was alive.' Logan has discovered that the zombies are sheer instinct, instinct without organs: they eat without any body to nourish. 'They are us. They are extensions of us. They are the same animal just functioning less perfectly.'

In *Day of the Dead*, Sarah alone fits the profile of survivor. Sarah's partner, though Hispanic, has to go: he's a whining envious spoiler of her capacity to advance all the way to the top of the mourning. To secure an outside chance for his remaining an accessory to her survival, she cuts off the limb the zombie chomped down on. But then he makes restitution by taking himself out in such a way that he brings down the house of the military complex. He goes up above on the elevator platform as bait for attracting the zombies; when they commence feasting on him he presses the descend button and the living dead invasion enters the stronghold. It was even nice to gnaw the soldier named Rickles.

Sarah and her ex were in double-couple or in-group formation with two outsiders associated with the military camp, an Afro-Jamaican pilot and his dusty Anglo sidekick, who doesn't believe in drinking as a problem. On the outskirts of the underworld, these two managed to set up a simulation of the vacation spot they'd rather be in. It turns out they were rehearsing for their next stop. The threesome ends up on an island that brings two of them closer to slacker paradise. Scientist Sarah, who is woman, alone bears the stamp of terrorist approval. The other two seem to be there by multiple choice. In this film, however, the future belongs not to human survival but to the mutation of the zombies, who are us.

At the close of Romero and Susan Sparrow's novel version of *Dawn of the Dead*, the puppy the four in the mall found and named Adam is along for the helicopter ride into the uncertain future. At the end of the movie *Day of the Dead*, pet zombie 'Bub' becomes the one and only being, just like Frankenstein's monster in Shelley's novel, who gives way to grief and mourning. After exacting vengeance for the murder of his master, he fires the ritual shot of salute to his 'father'. Dr. Logan gave his surgeon father's nickname to his top test subject.

Bub is domesticated by turning his food into a contained, control-released commodity, something served up at mealtime. He's on a schedule. He's fed bite-size portions of human flesh. 'Fresh' does not mean 'still alive' but is a condition of timing and preparation. Dr. Logan is thus able to contain the violence of the zombie appetite. But just as important is his instinctual attachment to background music. Listening to it is also on a schedule.

Remember the mother's legacy of music that Robert turns up full blast to block out the zombie sounds in *I Am Legend*. When it's not feeding time, Bub becomes a consumer of the background-music Sensurround of violence control. In *Noise*, Jacques Attali provided the succinct genealogy of music that I plug into here. If music has always, at least from the beginning, had the function first of covering up the sounds of human sacrifice, then of sublimating that sacrificial relation, packing it into its medium and into the communal reception of that medium in groups, by the 1980s it was keeping us going individually, each of us a group-of-one between earphones on top of the stockpiling of sociality in musical recordings. The collars the zombies wear in *Fido* to become, totemically, the fathers one wouldn't have wanted to kill, are not the shock collars of dog training. The ring of Bub's music is around this collar. Dr. Logan's 'pet' belongs to the affirmation of the time to come – and not only as placeholder.

4

Romero had to wrap up the unresolved issue of Ben's murder. While grief can still be experienced over a partner's death in *Dawn of the Dead*, the overriding frame of survival (of the politically correct) discounts loss as the inevitable metabolic elimination of dysfunctional relationality from our best chances for survival. While a great deal of unexamined tension attends the staking of a vampire, the elimination of the living dead, including the massified vampires in Matheson's narrative, couldn't be easier. Romero had something more singular to bury in or with *Martin* (1977).

Romero hesitated before picking up after *Night of the Living Dead*. Even after a successful venture for TV alleviated the flopping of his subsequent films (only one of which, *The Crazies* [1973], bordered thematically on *Night of the Living Dead*) and thus cleared the way for making the sequel he had already thought through and written up by 1974, Romero introduced yet another postponement. He decided to film *Martin* first. *Dawn of the Dead* was held back for the four-year period *Martin* came to occupy.

Romero's inspiration was his passing thought that by now a vampire would have a hard time getting attention. Translation: a vampire movie would have a hard time eliciting serious horror in the era already showing a predilection for Camp. But what if the protagonist was a psycho killer? Romero came across a series of 'vampire' murders committed in LA. The killer drank his victims' blood from a special goblet he carried with him at all times, just in case.

In *Martin*, the eponymous teen protagonist is either a serial killer who drinks blood vampire-style or a vampire who adopts the methods of serial killing to secure his supply. Romero introjects into psychopathic violence vampirism as a mourning scenario that's forever off schedule. Highlighting through the vampire-identification the mix in this psycho of melancholic psychosis, Romero also builds up the prospect of a cure for Martin along two tracks, media therapy and couples therapy. The media already make him think there's a way out. Martin is a teenager who turns to the group outlet – in his case a local phone-in radio talk show – for acceptance as group mascot: 'the Count'. In Romero and Susan Sparrow's novelisation of the film, the radio show is the *Gestell* of the serial killer/vampire's narrative. Martin maps loss or deprivation in the local urban-escape along the route of adolescent insight and brooding: 'People go away so they can forget where they were' (1980: 174).

Martin's serial compulsion is caught between alienation or disappointment and the other shore of sexual coupling, which he achieves only under the conditions of his 'vampirism', for which he now enjoys mascot status on the air.

> People . . . don't say what they mean. They just kind of use each other the same way I use my blood people. But then, they have the other. They have the sexy stuff. Whenever they want it. . . . I've been much too shy to ever do the sexy stuff. I mean . . . do it with somebody who was awake. . . . Someday maybe I'll get to do it . . . awake . . . and without the blood part. Just do it with somebody and then be together and talk all night. (1980: 119)

While Martin is thus not your typical vampire, he still turns up a fundamental contrast with zombieism. The living death of ghouls or zombies is not decay-proof, nor does it lend itself to hierarchical organisations of mastery (except via the mutation that facilitates a new rule of posthumanity). In 'The Delay of the Machine Age', Hanns Sachs tied the machinic mediations of life and death to the outgrowth of narcissism, which survives itself by being staggered into a progression from primary narcissism to secondary narcissism. Whereas the former is body-based, the latter breaks open the corporeal limits and transmutes self-love into the struggle for mastery between ego and superego or, in other words, into self-criticism. Those stuck on the body are stuck in life as in death. The failure to graduate from the primaries of narcissism and win election into the secondary reformatting of self-love (via a new standard and momentum for self-aggrandisement and Faustian striving) cannot but end in the crisis of uncanniness. To pull the emergency break out of this crisis at close quarters, the psychotic, if fortunate (like Faust), projects a technological new world order that affirms the machine. But the endopsychic recovery that inheres in certain delusional systems is two track. The brave new book of Schreber's techno-delusions also packed away an underworld, a place for absence. His older brother, who committed suicide, went ahead to secure it. The vampire is a cut above the zombie's arrest. He carries forward an object relation, which means that he hearkens to the show and *Gestell* of an inner world. The psychopathic violence stowaway in both undeath and living death still bears in the vampiric variant a residual charge of mourning.

Family curse or dysfunctional family system: the family member who took care of Martin died and his uncle must now assume responsibility. Martin is constructed as challenged in some way, a perpetual dependent. But Martin is a vampire, by virtue of illness, which is how he himself sees it, or through the tradition and transmission of some old magic (his uncle's view).

He finds he is able to do 'the sexy stuff' with a living woman. She's one of the midlife-crisis housewives for whom Martin, working for his uncle, delivers the meat. They would be perfect victims if they weren't on his uncle's schedule. But sex is then something else. Martin lifts her depression, too. Though he still needs to suck blood on the side, it seems that he now targets underworld males, the uncanny outcasts of society. But his heroic economising of the lust can no longer be supported by his sexual partner, who couldn't keep the abyss at bay. One day when he drops by for a visit he finds her dead in the bloody bathtub. Her suicide fits the staging of his serial crimes.

Martin makes it further out of the crypt than Norman Bates. His sexual partner's suicide is the only crime that sticks to Martin, the one he didn't commit. Still it is the primal scene that committed him to his double career as psycho killer and vampire. What looks like a blood crime made to look like suicide makes the uncle conclude that his customer succumbed to the nephew's delivery of blood lust. He takes a stake to his undead relation.

Martin folds out of Romero's story 'Clay', in which a severely disturbed young man named Tippy is tracked, supported, treated by his parish priest. The Father's faith is on the line after years of watching Tippy grow up the rank disorders of dysfunctional family life into a lonely kid who brings to weekly confession the stories about the clay people he makes and lives with, lives or dies for. While the priest can only imagine that Tippy continues to play, even as a young man, with small clay figures, the truth is as large as life. Tippy's apartment is crowded with life-size clay sculptures:

Tippy was quite content upstairs with his pals. He'd play with them and mold them differently to suit his moods and purposes. He'd sit them at table and push food into the openings that were their mouths. At night he'd sit with them and hold them and comfort them and tell them stories of the things he'd done when he'd gone beyond where the front window could see. Other times, he'd pretend to be drunk and angry, and he'd throw things about the room and scream and pull the figures apart brutally. (1982: 80)

The story reaches its living end when Tippy murders a young woman to give a harder body or skeleton to his clay fuck dolly, which otherwise comes apart at what seems like sex. But the horror of verisimilitude in low-level or underrated art industries (like cinema) is the measure of withdrawal of sublimation from the representation or repression of sexuality. Consider some of Tippy's possible fantasies or inserts.

In my archaeological excavation of analytic studies of the psycho I found the treasure of two texts authored by Roland Kuhn. The second text I reserve later on for the task of interpreting the POV as mask. (Kuhn conducted these studies as proponent of Existential Analysis, an amalgam of Freud and Heidegger that Ludwig Binswanger composed for therapy of psychotics. But stranger still is that Kuhn was responsible for the first medication to manage depression, subsequently named Imipramine, which opened the doors to out-patient treatment. Kuhn observed that the new drug in the ward, though lacking in the treatment of psychotics for which it was intended, did seem to alleviate symptoms of depression. The eulogies at his death in 2005 were fixated on his lucky observation of the first modern antidepressant. Psychopharmacology was his death mask.)

In 'The Attempted Murder of a Prostitute', Kuhn presents the case study of Rudolf, who lost his mother at age four. Rudolf identified her loss as the loss of her body for which he commenced searching. 'A small boy is searching the house looking for his dead mother. After having found the body he speaks to it and touches it. Later, after the body is lost to him through the funeral, he rummages through the entire house – around all its furniture and into all its corners. In all these instances Rudolf is acting, behaving in a peculiarly active fashion which already reveals a certain industry. There is nothing contemplative to be found in his early memories' (1958: 397). Thus he inaugurated his active life, the life of suspense and survival that henceforth demarcated his reality. He brought back her clothes, her buttons, suspending a gleaming surface in place of the missing body.

At puberty he learns about dead bodies and sex. Thus when masturbating in the bathroom 'he felt a strong fear of being seized by a skeleton hand through the window or of falling through the toilet pan into the sewage. He then imagined he might get stuck in the pipe, get a view of female genitals, and get his face smeared with feces and menstrual blood. He would go through terrible anxiety, tinged with sexual excitement, and imagined feeling the touch of ghosts in various bodily sensations, particularly that of chill on his skin' (1958: 370). Whatever his official activities or day job, he alternated them with time spent, almost 'manically', watching cheap movies on crime (three on Sunday) and reading trashy detective literature (1958: 372, 366).

The inner world of fantasies and dreams occupied closed spaces, butcher shops (he was a butcher's apprentice), movie houses, bars, or the woods. The only props are occasional tools, money, corpses. 'If human beings are present, they act brutally or obscenely or in measured rituals; no words are heard, only screams of men and animals' (1958: 415). In contrast to this 'world of the has-been', Rudolf inhabits an external world of action or practical life dedicated to 'the New:' 'There is an actual greed for the New, a definite curiosity (*Neugierde*), and the forward-rushing movement seeks ever-new impressions and encounters. The new, in general, is also likely to shine' (1958: 416).

Rudolf was able to keep inner and outer worlds, the fantasy world of sex and violence and the real world of action and suspense, physically or corporeally separate. He could have sex with streetwalkers who however had to remain clothed. It was over his father's dead body that the worlds met and crossed over. Not the body was the trigger but its removal for burial. The fresh body brought back the mother's sought-after body which, split between gleaming surface and inner or lost absence, was the model for his functioning between worlds.

There is proximity between forgetting and corporeality at the limit: 'we look for the lost word in our mouth; we say, "it is on the tip of my tongue;" we seek it there where it got lost, and that seems to be somehow in the periphery of the body. Rudolf, too, searches for the lost and the forgotten in the periphery of the body, namely in the luster of eyes and garments. On the other hand, in his world of phantasies, he skips the periphery, avoids the surface and penetrates directly into the inside where nothing lost or forgotten can ever be found' (1958: 422–23).

The impulse to murder a prostitute he first felt on the day after his father's funeral. On the day of the funeral he watched the coffin being brought out of the inside of the house: 'And with this, the contents of the dream existence, until then confined to the inside of the house, poured out, too; the borderline between the two worlds was broken and the phantasy world superimposed itself, as it were, upon the everyday world' (1958: 418). The fantasy world hits the streets, covers all of existence.

Earlier he had been able to check the impulse to murder the women who came out of their houses to accept the meat he was delivering from the butcher shop. Now under the influence of the mourning affect, 'every sexually exciting woman now stimulates this murderous impulse, as the world of phantasies covers the whole of existence' (ibid.). We must underscore with Kuhn that 'Rudolf's mourning affect was touched off not by the loss of a beloved living person but by the loss of a body' (1958: 412). For Rudolf the mourning affect is linked with sexual desire, 'for it is precisely the piercing of the inside which is sought in the sexual act. Since the day of his father's funeral Rudolf is, so to speak, much closer to that inside' (ibid.).

The first targeted prostitute he visited after his father's funeral refused to get undressed and so was saved by the resulting diminution of the murderous impulse.

What's new, of course, is that he now asks for nudity, the full frontal encounter with his fantasy world of sex and violence. 'The dreams of female bodies could be traced to memories of films about the wax figures of Mme. Tussaud and about a sadistic murderer who turned his victims into wax figures' (1958: 379). The street no longer protects the prostitutes. 'A counter-drive against the murderous impulse could not come about because Rudolf no longer stood on the border of his two world-designs and so could no longer view one from the angle of the other, as he had done earlier, whenever the murder impulse emerged' (1958: 418).

Where he stood before was before the clothed/closed body which held the place of that saving line of separation between above and below, the line passing through the orifices. 'In the sphere of the body, outside and inside are connected through the body openings. Rudolf sees in the female genitals the point of transition of the two worlds. Undressing represents an approach to the inside world and is feared to the degree to which an approach to the world of phantasies is avoided in reality' (1958: 416). The investment in concrete material objects, which alone have a real outside and inside, is only momentarily embodied, but significantly so. A body is essentially matter. While a butcher's apprentice he discovered that man and animal are proximate. Also living and dead bodies are not so different. Materiality is more fully represented by the dead body. 'We may add that concrete matter is also the basic material from which machines are made, those machines which so predominantly and recurrently pervaded Rudolf's life, daydreams, and dreams, either in the form of a wish to become a mechanic, or more or less complicated instruments which permit their master to awaken the dead. . . . And only a material substance can be cut up, can be eaten, digested, and make its appearance again; only something that consists of matter can be killed' (1958: 414).

Before he is enrolled in treatment, Rudolf at the point of crisis projects the crux of his defence and assumes it as POV. The knife point of view finds the saving distinction between inside and outside in the body as materiality, the body that sits still for the distinction between inside and outside. Rudolf's relationship to the corpse, the body he must keep fresh, controllable, but undecidable would enter into literalising synchronisation with the fabrication of 'corpses' in pulp literature and film. His failed murder attempt sends him to Kuhn for treatment and wins him time outside the scenarios of suspense. Kuhn observed his patient's progress in his dreams: 'in various dreams . . . he occupied himself, mostly with the help of complicated machines, with the body of his father or of people unknown to him, predominantly of the female sex.' (1958: 373). By bringing bodies that matter back to life under the aegis of the identifiable father the dream machinery makes first steps toward secondary narcissism, steps preliminary to the onset of the ability (indeed even the need) to mourn.

Manuals

In *The Crawling Hand* (1963) an astronaut's limb drops from outer space. Soon it attracts the conflicted attentions of a college couple on the beach in California. The Swedish exchange student is horrified. But her Californian boyfriend is fascinated just the same. He goes back for it. He stores it in the home of his landlady and mother figure. The severed hand can act on its own; it also can possess the college boy's own appendage. These tensions are a magnet for tensions pre-existing in the couple: the hand offered in matrimony cannot be the hand job of the group bond.

Like one of the media explanations for the zombie epidemic in *Night of the Living Dead*, it comes from outer space. The astronaut was possessed by an alien life form. Ground control is surprised that he's still alive even after the oxygen is gone. He raves murderously, only interrupting his derangement to ask them to push the red button. The alien maintains control of what's left after the crash on the beach. At the malt shop the coeds gossiping about a cute boy are served by an old weirdo who announces: 'Eat, drink, and be merry, for tomorrow you die.' The cute boy, the Californian boyfriend Paul, arrives to take one of the girls, Marta, the Swedie, to the beach, He asks for her hand in marriage. She runs off laughing, inciting him to pursue her. Where they embrace the twitching hand was waiting.

Paul's landlady, a widow whose warm gun belonged to her husband, is the hand's only murder victim. Her cat survives her. When the hand attacks Paul next, it stops short of killing him. But now he regularly has fits during which he repeats the attack he suffered on others, pulling up short before murder. This is how sex buffers violence. Paul tries to take back control of the hand, which keeps getting away. Then we see that two cats, delegates of the landlady's totem pet, are devouring the appendage. Paul collapses. But now he's free of the alien cosmic rays. He's also declared guilt-free. When one of the ambulance drivers, curious like a cat, opens the steel box they are transporting to the airport, we know it contains what's left of the hand, but what we see is an empty box instead and 'The End' inside it like a simulacrum of the Happy End of the resurrection.

1

At the time he composed his essay on 'The Uncanny', at the close of World War I, Freud was doubling his science into two systems. The second system was devoted, among other things, to the extension of transferential contact with psychopathology to include psychosis at the borderline between neurosis and psychosis. Nathanael in 'The Sandman', the identified patient of Freud's essay, is not your typical normal-to-neurotic Everyman with an Oedipus complex. In fact he's most likely psychotic, which means the fracture in his psyche took shape already within the original dyad with mother. The father is just the outer rim of the mother's uncontainment of dread of the Sandman. The Sandman, like the bogeyman, is the lullaby figure that's the enforcer. Lights out is when childhood and adulthood are forcibly separated over the issue of sex. What do parental couples do? We know what the primal groups or groups-of-one do when the master bedroom door shuts them out. They masturbate – until sand gets in their eyes.

Rather than pursue sexual research (or just get married already), Nathanael is stuck on the track of Popeye the Sandman. Nathanael thinks he's on the right track because his mother's rational explanation is so unbelievable. It does not correspond, for example, to the mother's own anxious and depressed state each time the lawyer Coppelius, soon to be merged with the Sandman in Nathanael's mind, pays a visit. His mother cannot contain Nathanael's anxious sense of disintegration. That's why he is much more impressed by the primal material he gets from the nursemaid. Even though he's old enough to see through the fairytale, it confirms the mother's uncontrolled reservations. Klara has been raised in one household by Nathanael's mother as the near-miss, the substitute. The clarity that's even in her name belongs to common no nonsense or reasonableness. It cannot contain Nathanael's anxieties. The Sandman recollections from early childhood are stuck in the cracks of the mother as broken mirror and container. Instead of finding reflective clarity in the mother's substitute, Nathanael regresses to the best relationship he never had, which he finds (and loses) in the robot Olympia. She's the blowup dolly, the body you must control completely in lieu of its never having contained you. Nathanael's suicide measures in the negative or in reverse the unattainability of self-replication or union with the robot Olympia. The Sandman returning as castration in the real, the father function unmediated by substitution, is a figure of psychosis. That Nathanael, before killing himself, attempts the murder of his bride-to-be Klara at the border between reality and delusion fits the psycho profile.

If serial killers have sex with their dead victims it's not just necrophilia. It's often a round-about way of finding at least a trace of life left in the dolly. What is being preserved as next best to the best thing you never had is the disconnection from mother. It is less a question of such a diagnosis being correct. What we know is that it is the history (the case history) that our mass media culture constructed and delivered prefab in so many cases of psycho killing. Because lifelike lifelessness is even shorter-lived than life itself, the scene has to be repeated. Hence Nathanael tries at the end to have this fling with his human bride. But in attacking Klara, he comes closer than ever before to identifying his mother as the source of deprivation and hating her for it.

In Michael Powell's film adaptation in *The Tales of Hoffmann* (1951), we watch Nathanael's fling with Olympia take controlling interest in the lifelike corpus and forsake all uncontrollable others. Romero's inspiration from adolescence for the scene his film crew christened 'The Last Supper' was the scene of Olympia's destruction in *The Tales of Hoffmann*, which culminates in one of the suitors fondling lovingly the severed hand of the robot dolly.

In close association with the myth of Osiris, the horror film genre cuts apart the body and puts all the parts back together again that fit into a stiff to be reanimated. But this body can be brought back into the future only by the prosthesis Isis fashions in lieu of the sexual organ and uses to impregnate herself with Osiris's succession. This is all done by hand. The myth sets off the tradition of the 'phallus' against a relationship to the dead that castration and supplementation carry forward. It also offers yet another myth addressing mourning at its foundation. In the Oedipus complex, Freud underscored in his reading of 'The Sandman', eyes and the phallus are grafted together, as in the Roman phalloi. The interchange between these prized body parts thematises either substitution or castration. But in the recovery phase, the myth also defines this visual field in terms of hand-to-eye coordination.

It was up to horror to explore in its mediatic re-settings the coordination that is aligned each time we sign our names but which opens wide and wobbly when we see ourselves at a loss of boundaries. That's why in horror cinema the hand maintains our connection to the body (to be sure a fragmentary connection, though at the same time more real than the mirror whole). In *The Strange Case of Dr. Jekyll and Mr. Hyde*, Stevenson uses the hand as first site of the metamorphosis that crosses (and crosses out) the 'and', but ultimately, in the aligned mode, as last and lasting piece of evidence: Dr. Jekyll's unmistakable hand or handwriting. In Rouben Mamoulian's film adaptation (1931), focus on the hand belongs to the regressed experience of losing it, but as fact of life under media-directed conditions of division and doubling. The film opens with a scene of organ playing in which the player goes unseen while his hands do the showing. We see him first – as Dr. Jekyll – in the mirror on his way out to give a lecture. For today's lecture Professor Jekyll addresses the incursion of visibility – via separating or cutting – into invisible realms. The two souls, the noble one and the evil one, must be separated so each can fulfill itself without disturbing and compromising the other. For mankind this separation is not far off: 'certain chemicals' will get us there. When Dr. Jekyll proceeds on his own with the experiment of separating pure from base elements, he goes to the mirror before which he takes the drink. The screen darkens and the camera spins about: accompanied by flashbacks of superegoical remonstrance we watch him turn into a kind of ape man. The horror begins, however, once 'he' realises that he cannot control the splitting, which now afflicts him on the spot. Any sign of suffering serves as trigger. With focus on his hand turned hirsute we know: there he goes again.

When we first meet the cartoonist, comic strip artist or animator – the protagonist of Oliver Stone's *The Hand* (1981) – he's in midlife crisis. His animation style is legend; but that means it's also by now dated. His wife feels she needs to become her own person. He becomes her own despot, demanding of her the price of submission. Then there's the car wreck. He loses his hand (he can't even find it by the side of the road). She was driving and it's her fault. Thus he's able to have his wife by his side and hate her too, torturing her with his depression. Her departure has been postponed for as long as feeling sorry for him exceeds feeling sorry for herself.

He finally agrees to enter psychiatric treatment. He scoffs that after $1,000 the expert will tell him that he has a 'penis complex' because he lost his hand. His severed hand, which is that part of him that fulfills death wishes in double time, attacks the wife on the eve of her final departure. He sees himself, instead, attacking the hand that doesn't obey his good intentions. In closing we attend a session of the psychiatric treatment he now keeps, following the attempt on his wife's life, by court appointment. The clinician tries to make him own up to his rage and stop splitting it off onto the range of the hallucinated hand. It's time for the transference interpretation: No, it's not the hand that would like to strangle me, it's you, you, you. But then he and we see the hand terminate the therapeutic alliance.

The survival of the loss of limbs was the first progress made in modern medical treatment (notably on the battlefields of the American Civil War). While the prosthesis was being fitted upon survivor bodies, it served as model for our ongoing rapport with technologisation as early as 1877, the date of publication of Ernst Kapp's treatise *Grundlinien einer Philosophie der Technik* (*Foundations of a Philosophy of Technology*). Kapp forged ahead with links that we can place between Aristotle and Heidegger or between the early nineteenth-century studies of visual bio-machinic culture (which are the immediate setting of Kapp's study and can be characterised, one and all, as Hegelian in reception) and Freud and McLuhan's hypothesis of prosthetic relations between the bodily sensorium and its media extensions.

The tool, co-produced by hand and mind, both extends our contact with the world beyond sense perception and externalizes our inner world (1877: 25–6). Kapp has to hand it to Aristotle who called the hand the tool of tools (1877: 41). 'The hammer is like all primitive tools an organ projection or the mechanical copy of an organic form' (1877: 42). The projective fit of the ax can be observed that much more closely by turning up the contrast between two different kinds and kin. 'I was once witness to the demonstration by an old backwoodsman in west Texas of what he called the *philosophy of the ax*' (1877: 241). The ax of Texas, just ask Kapp, accomplishes two-times, maybe three-times more in a day's work than the German ax, all on account of the more perfect affinity between the former and the arm in motion.

From the grasp of the hand to the grasp of understanding (1877: 250), the hand counts as the externalized brain (1877: 151). The very word for act, story, or action (in German) shakes its origin in the *Hand*: '*Hand-lung*' (1877: 237). 'Man can twist and turn as much as he likes, his hand remains part of whatever he thinks and does' (1877: 252). Even though the body supplies image-units of measure – the foot, which is self-explanatory, or the pentagram, which can be seen as the image of a stretched-out hand (1877: 274) – it also introduces ultimately non-corporeal units or digits. 'At the same time as the tool, the hand projected the measure given it by Nature and its numerical values. The hand, the organ that grasps and concerns itself with bodily things, is at the same time the organ that essentially supports the release of ideas and their mental grasp and donates the whole world of culture out of the endless wealth of its organization' (1877: 71).

In its fine print or infrastructure, Kapp's theory of *Kinematik* turns out to be about the pairs constituting the techno prosthesis, one surrounding the other, one moving while the other doesn't, and the different contact variants thus produced and required. 'The basic trait of the machine is its constitution not out of discrete elements but rather out of bodies that belong in pairs or elementary pairs. Of these one serves as the enveloping form of the other so that when you hold onto one, the other remains flexible, but only in the one way that is unique to the pair, as is evident, for example, in the screw and the nut' (1877: 175–6).

The German word for the 'nut' in Kapp's example of coupling is *Schraubenmutter*, literally 'screw mother'. *Kinematik* leads us into a group psychology of coupling versus brute force, a span of tension internal to machine development. The perfection of the machine consists in the replacement of 'energy contact' (*Kraftschluss*) with 'couple contact' (*Paarschluss*) (1877: 184) – exemplifed by the screw's fit with its mother. While *Kraftschluss* is on the side of unconscious discovery, *Paarschluss* comes up on the side of conscious invention (1877: 187). But the tension between the two types of contact – or, according to the other meaning of *Schluss*, two types of 'closure' – is never completely resolved, not even in the machine.

The way the trains and telegraphs form an uninterrupted context and network exceeds the term or notion of prosthesis. 'The nerves are the cabling of the animal body, just as one can call the telegraph wires the nerves of humanity' (1877: 140). The comparisons that can be made, according to Kapp, are not passing correspondences: 'it is the material and representative relationship of projection, which is absolutely available only once' (1877: 136). 'Accordingly all playing in fantasy with arbitrarily introduced comparisons via "just as", "in like manner", "in a certain sense", must make room for the fact of organ projection' (1877: 91). For example: thoughts have the form of telegrams (1877: 146).

In the closing lines of Kapp's study man steps out of the machines he has made and stands before himself as *Deus ex Machina*. Freud's mascot, the prosthesis god, admits what Kapp would prefer to discard as too uncanny, the arm's length of Götz von Berlichingen's legendary iron prosthesis. We come full circle from the inside view of technology as organ projection to the literal prosthesis that models this view, the constitutive interchange (in McLuhan's more popular terms) between amputation and amplification. In contrast to the iron hammer or ax which represents and enacts 'unmitigated vital activity', the iron hand of Götz von Berlichingen is 'the abject refuge of weakness' and 'the isolated mask of a handicap:' 'How imposing the analogue of the organic formation as working tool for engendering work appears in comparison with the unfruitful patchwork of artificial limbs and whole automata displaying the uncanniness of wax museum figures!' (1877: 103–4). Between the assembly lines of organ projection there is violence that Kapp doesn't declare, except to reject any relation with the uncanny medical prosthesis or to pack it away inside military formations.

In *Crowds and Power* Elias Canetti takes a detail of behaviour like our unthinking crumpling of paper, breaking matches, twigs or tearing off leaves to project another layer of legibility onto the hand as our first contact with techno fragmentation and aggrandisement. 'There is thus a separate destructiveness of the hand, not immediately connected with prey and killing. It is of a purely mechanical nature and mechanical inventions are extensions of it. Precisely because of its innocence it has become particularly dangerous. ... It is this mechanical destructiveness of the hands, now grown to a complex system of technology, which, whenever it is linked with a real intention to kill, supplies the automatic element of the resulting process, that empty mindlessness which is so particularly disquieting' (1988: 218).

2

While I stand by my reading of George Romero's *Night of the Living Dead* as the first film to 'treat' the shower scene, Herschell Gordon Lewis's 1963 film *Blood Feast* was in fact the first to refer to the scene. Although the *Schauer* victim decides on a bath instead, as if herself recovering from watching Hitchcock's scene, it was this earlier gore or splatter film bent on exploitation that packed the scene inside its rage of reference. The psycho Fuad Ramses is high priest of the cult of Ishtar. He not only murders women in the serial style but takes away fresh body parts to replace or renew those of the ancient goddess. The fragments are not stitched in time to keep a mummy fresh, but are in turn to be consumed (Ramses runs a catering business) and thus internalised/eternalised as the goddess incarnate. In the end Ramses is disposed of with the trash.

Lewis began his film work at the age of early retirement or midlife crisis. He had been an English professor, but soon took an interest in local media and their national networks. He worked in radio, then in television. But what he learned from the media was marketing, the first American science or industry of mass psychology. Between his film career and the remakes in which he was involved over thirty years later, Lewis established himself in the advertising business as a well-published marketing specialist. What he learned from radio and TV he first applied to the marketing and distribution of his own B-pictures. *Blood Feast* turned out to be a blockbuster in the new teen date culture of drive-in theatres.

John Waters discovered his precursor on location: 'I discovered his monstrous trilogy, *Blood Feast*, *Two Thousand Maniacs*, and *Color Me Blood Red*, at my local drive-in. And when I saw teenage couples hopping from their cars to vomit, I knew I had found a director after my own heart' (in McCarthy 1984: 55). The 'Blood Trilogy' Waters cites came about when the series of gore films Lewis projected as interminable suddenly seemed exhausted by the third film, *Color Me Blood Red*. That the first horror trilogy emerged allegorically from the condemned site of a series gone finite is another advance preview of horror cinema developments still to come within the span of the *Psycho* Effect.

As Romero recounts in his Preface to the novelisation of *Night of the Living Dead*, film in the 1960s was losing out to the 'communications industry'. B-pictures had always offered one film archive or graveyard haunted by occult figureheads of classic horror. B-pictures extended their range via the independent low-low-budget fare admitted by the deregulation of mainstream reception. Psychopathy was the equally spreadable theme that caught the adolescent public where it bred on dates and in groups. The depth charge of neurosis-to-psychosis was given up for the flat land of violence. Psychosis was split off and applied as the continuity shot from the former regime of treatment that gave a safer distance to the psychopathy theme. Mass and serial murder began running the narrative. The dead bodies in the B-picture cemetery were disinterred, recycled as taxidermic props, or they themselves now returned without occult mediation as the living dead. What was abandoned was the distance between the audience and the other audience on screen.

Hitchcock introduced the theme of psychopathy in the first place via Marion Crane's impulsive theft of free money. It was his invitation to the new 'adolescent' consumer to enter the film. From his use of the newly disposable *Playboy* bunnies, whose recognition value addressed a more realistic and more abject chance at stardom, to the police officers brought onto the screen off the streets as amateur extras, Lewis made the adults identifiable from the perspective of high school. While *Two Thousand Maniacs* is pitched to the alternation between making out in the cars and attention-grabbing gross-out on the screen, *Color Me Blood Red* borrows the high school stage of assembly and the annual play to present the artist's agony. He is a big shot in the provinces. His only chance to reach a wider audience and a more legitimate fame is through the influential art critic, who is invited by the small town's leading gallerist to inspect the artist's latest work. The gallery is a hall with a small stage at one end on which the new works are displayed, before which artist, gallerist and the local collectors assemble to hear the critic's verdict.

But the artist is a psycho interacting with his adolescent environs at the extreme end of midlife criticism. After running up against the limits of his own blood supply or that of his girlfriend (whose accidental spurt of blood on a canvas first alerted him to the unique way of countering the critic's claim that his use of colour wasn't compelling) he harvests gore from teens on dates. But he can't get away with trying to turn the daughter of the town's leading collector into gore supplies. At the end the witnesses to his greatness on the high school stage now gather outside around one of the bloody canvases set aflame. The gallerist declares this the proper burial of the artist.

Lewis allows neither madness nor therapy to frame and subsume his exhibition of horror's special effects. The audience, both on screen and parked in front of the screen, simply passes through like the peristaltic reversal of the identification in consumer projection. Lewis remembered that the actress he used in the murder scene from which Ramses walks away with the brain didn't have a brain (in Libbitz 2002: 26). This would be the only double meaning ascribed by the director to a special effect.

The second film in the trilogy, *Two Thousand Maniacs*, was pitched directly to the newly discovered audience Lewis began to incorporate in his films: we spend considerable time in the beginning with and in cars just like those that drove to the screening but which on screen are brought by the ruse of detour signs to a Southern ghost town. Drivers and passengers, all together now, are going to attend the spectacle of the town's centennial celebration. But these waylaid Northerners are to be sacrificed to the ghoulish delight of the townspeople, who in the end have vanished into the past. That the South's gonna rise again is among the many sung lines in the music heard during the drive-through opening – but then seen and heard again in the medley of melodies played by the band that introduces each torture pageant. When the music stops, it doesn't take that long for a barrel of laughs – a barrel of nails driven inward with a woman inside, for example – to tumble downhill.

The focus on special effects raises the question of the special effect beyond its deception or consumption. That is the proximity of Lewis's 'Blood Trilogy' to art, which the third film, *Color Me Blood Red*, thematises. This film belongs to a subset of horror films about making successful artistic representations through incorporation of the murder victim for internal support (the plotline of Romero's story 'Clay'): consider *House of Wax* (1953), *A Bucket of Blood* (1959), but also *Snow White and the Seven Dwarfs* (1937) by dint of its own rotoscoping technique for getting under our skin. However, Lewis's film departs from the sculptural-funereal *Gestell* and instead extracts the blood, which is used for its power in an abstract field of representation.

Blood was the special effect Lewis found missing in the movies. Scenes of gangland slayings were largely cleansed of blood. It was the blood he brought back, but as special effect. Openly declared, a special effect is the sketch of a thought. In Lewis's films, a handful of thoughts are tried out. They forego the condensation or *Verdichtung* of most films, including most B-pictures, which is their proximity to *Dichtung* or poetry. The presentation of a special effect in one of Lewis's films is not time consuming, but raises other standards of reception. In contrast, Kenneth Anger's films subsumed special effects within a condensity of the surface, its deep aesthetic inscription. Anger's films take their time to project a world from nothingness – from the scratch of starting over and over again. In Lewis's films we proceed at measured pace, really a pretty fast clip, from one exhibition of a special effect to the next one, each the sketch or trial application of a thought.

Lewis's 'Blood Trilogy', as the exhibition-pageant of special splatter effects of murder and mutilation, was rehearsed on the stage of the Paris theatre Grand Guignol. The theatre spanned the prehistory of the introduction of the *Psycho* Effect, namely from 1897 to 1961. It would be fitting to imagine that *Psycho* put it out of business. The secret ingredient in its staging of psycho horror, however, was laughter. In an evening the horror play might be surrounded by slapstick, comedy and farce. The technique, which was referred to now as 'laughter and tears', now as 'hot and cold showers', was applied not only through the alternation of genres but also came up as undercurrent when the exhibition value of the special effects proved cheap. An over-the-top production of blood and gore that one could see through down to the effects, if not right away then upon seeing it again, could provoke laughter, which is how many of the films going into the *Psycho* Effect came out again laughably dated upon later re-viewing.

On the stage of Grand Guignol the focus on some brand new gadget, the telephone, surgical devices, the latest equipment for transfusion of blood, introduced the still uncanny device not only to great effect but also to aid the immunising adjustment to its prosthetic insertion into the sensorium. In one 1902 play, 'On the Telephone', a husband on stage speaking on the phone to his wife must hear how at the other end of the line she and the children are attacked, brutalised and murdered.

The Grand Guignol staged rape, execution, infanticide (including a baby's crucifixion and, in another skit, the feeding of dead baby to pigs), drowning, strangling of children, incest, patricide, suicide, surgery, deliberate surgical mutilation and train wrecks, among other stations of the crossing of sex and violence with technology. Recurrent themes or fixations included bodily mutilation and death (and fascination with the same), aberrant authority and the hatred authority provokes, and insanity or the fear of going mad without warning. The actors ignored the audience, often keeping their backs to the fourth wall throughout. It was voyeurism to the max, a peep showing of slices of life or, as the theatre advertised its special fare, slices of death.

Between 1901 and 1926 André de Lorde wrote countless terror plays for Grand Guignol. He often collaborated with medical doctors. The boy who would be known as 'the Prince of Terror' started out the son of a physician. His father saw to it that 'son of' would forever be fascinated with the terrifying and morbid. To overcome little André's fearfulness he took him along on house visits to the dying and dead. The boy's dread began to take shape when he heard sobs and screams emanating from his father's office. He was the first dramatist to set plays in operating rooms and insane asylums. For special effects on stage he used electrical devices, new surgical techniques, hypnosis, and psychotherapy. One play that concluded with a realistic blood transfusion set the record: fifteen members of the audience fainted, while the alley outside was packed with hyperventilating and vomiting playgoers.

3

The animated violence of EC Comics was Romero's declared influence going into his invention of the splatter film. In the therapy setting children's drawings always present as plain or clear text. The special idiom for transcription of phantasy that Melanie Klein developed runs commentary equally plain on child's play and drawings. This gore becomes for the first time allegorical in adolescence. Yes, the teenager can fulfill all his death wishes. The suffer zone of representing the wish fulfilled in childhood becomes skewed as buffer zone in adolescence between one's second nature as daydreamer and the inroads of mass psychologisation and technologisation. Going down the aisles of Grand Guignol we were following the flashlight of Lewis's emphasis on the exhibition value of the gory special effect. We are also following the severed hand in Powell's *The Tales of Hoffmann*, which we already counted among the influences on *Night of the Living Dead*, in considering the first Hollywood horror film to make reference to its prehistory in the Paris theatre in the foreground of its Oedipal film story.

In the 1920 novel by Maurice Renard, *Les Mains d'Orlac*, which was filmed three times, the culture of Spiritualism occupied the foreground that the Grand Guignol assumed in its stead in *Mad Love*, Karl Freund's 1934 adaptation. Before the novel made it into pictures, however, it was re-formatted for the stage and performed at the London franchise of Grand Guignol. London's Madame Tussauds Wax Museum was also originally the more proper franchise of what opened up in Paris as syndication of the guillotine, which serialised execution between the industrialisation of corpses and the mediatic animation of talking heads.

In *Mad Love*, Dr. Gogol is a surgeon-scientist who never misses a guillotining – or a show at the Theatre of Horrors. He attends the executions in his capacity as scientist. But he goes to the Theatre of Horrors as psycho. On stage, Yvonne, the star attraction, is subjected to torture by a great many devices exhibited on stage. But in Gogol's eyes she is at the same time being tested or cleansed. By the time he has screwed up the courage to address her, Gogol discovers that Yvonne has been married for one year and, now that the career of her pianist husband, Stephen Orlac, is taking off, will leave the stage and take up the role of wife. That night her husband's piano concert will be broadcast live. On the ride home by train his hands are injured in a terrible wreck.

When Gogol was rejected by Yvonne, he bought her publicity statue from the horror theatre foyer. He thus keeps his own relationship to Yvonne safe in effigy. He plays his organ as a way of animating the statue. Gogol is stuck on a double feature: organ playing and reanimation (as nonphysical/nonsexual rebirth).

When the publicity statue's model appeals to the scientist to save her husband's hands, the regular visitor of guillotine executions gets the idea of grafting the hands of a recently executed murderer onto his double and rival. The artistic fingers of the rival must be replaced by the efficient, surgeon-like hands of the knife thrower and murderer. It's the death wish one double shares with the other one. And the floodlights of Grand Guignol become the lights of Dr. Gogol's operating theatre.

Because the post-op treatments are so costly, Yvonne must sell her jewels and Orlac must approach his jeweller father with a fateful request. Father refuses to lend support, berates the son, suggests that he become his wife's pimp to earn the extra bucks (the sign in front of the father's jewellry store shows et fils crossed out). By the reflex of his rage Orlac throws a knife against the shop window and departs. But then father is found murdered.

Yvonne and the pianist have not yet consummated their marriage (a staggering of the step from the ceremony to the wedding night that fits the child's I perspective of Hollywood horror movies of this period). It's on the pianist's mind. On the way to his virgin bride, he shares his train compartment with a killer, who is being transferred under police custody to prison and death sentence. The killer's hands already seem to lead an independent existence. There's something sexualised about them – at least in the perspective of the pianist, who is libidinally invested in his own hands. When an autograph hunter (someone fixated on handwriting) approaches, his questions enrage the convict who breaches his containment to throw the pen the collector borrowed from the pianist into the wall.

Orlac's former hands are commemorated in a sculpture, which via the caption's bold print refers to the precursor silent film. The pianist with his murderer's hands cannot reanimate – cannot turn back into the instrument of music and sublimation – this counterpart to Gogol's mannequin. He cannot play the piano but can only throw knives. What's left is the recording of the music he once made or played in his former state. 'Sometimes I feel that these records are all that's left of Stephen Orlac.' The recording, Orlac says, is the only way of overcoming death. But not the death wish, the reality of which he must face.

Dr. Gogol, played by Peter Lorre, counts as one of the first Hollywood psychos. *M* (1931), Fritz Lang's first sound picture, saw the screen debut of Lorre, who abandoned his first pursuit of a medical career, or rather applied it when he made it into pictures. The slasher sentiment of *M*'s original subtitle, 'Murderers among Us', was, ultimately, misapplied to what turned out to be a thriller in Brechtian closing. That's why it was replaced by 'A City Looks for a Murderer'. Like Lang's *Dr. Mabuse* films it followed out the work of detection through a doubling momentum binding the agency of investigation, that of the police inspector and the film director, to the underworld. When Lang arrived on the Coast he was offered the funds to remake *M* for Hollywood, but he refused on account of the unique fit between this film and its historical setting that could not be updated. It wasn't until the profiling thrillers that came at the end of the *Psycho* Effect – most spectacularly *The Silence of the Lambs* (1991) – that Hollywood supplied a link to *M*.

Lorre played the first psycho killer in pictures, a child murderer whose case bore resemblance to what were then current events. Although Lang claimed not to have been inspired by any particular case he couldn't deny his knowledge of Haarmann, Grossmann, Kürten and Denke, serial killers in the German news at that time. In the film's receiving area the affinity with Kürten, known as the 'Vampire of Düsseldorf', sparked a host of aka titles. The children playing in the street cite this case from the recent past in a jingle that echoed also outside the film. The momentum of slasher cinema, which is perfectly realised in the scenes in which the killer stalks his next victim, as well as in the prolonged absence that brings the news home that this mother's child was the latest victim, is displaced by Oedipal or theatrical release when the local criminals move to catch the killer and thus stop the wide-focus police crackdown that's cramping their life-in-crime style. Through operations that are under-cover by being out in the open (like homelessness, the daily repressed evidence begging the question of the uncanny in our midst) they identify Lorre as the murderer among us. To keep track of him singled-out in the crowd they mark him with a chalk stamp that impresses the film's title on his back. The members of the underworld rise up from the drop-out position to turn a signifier of schooling to the child's best defence. The stamping, marking, outlining, dialing M for murder, murderer, or mother, though largely displaced by the Oedipal police work that subsumes the underworld, is nevertheless allegorically etched on the screen already in 1930 in advance of the cuts to come.

Still Working on It

In *Pieces* (1982) psycho violence takes shape and aim between the jigsaw puzzle of a pin-up girl that mother won't allow in the house – whack! – and what the boy then grows up into over the mother's murdered body. The psycho is building a pinup body out of the body parts of his victims. The desublimated but collectible pieces of the puzzle fit the blanks his work of murder preserves and fulfills. The mad scientist professor – specialisation in anatomy – who in 1982 is also a closet homosexual is our best suspect. But it's the dean of the college who was once that little boy. A famous tennis player holds a day job working for the police. She goes undercover as tennis instructor at the college. When she stops by at the dean's place to ask some questions – about the anatomy professor – she gets slipped a drug that paralyses her motility, including the ability to speak. While the jigsaw puzzler prepares to cut her off at the knees, his riveted contemplation of the best cut while she looks on helpless is our only view of the psycho's operation, his slice of life. Following the police operation that shoots the dean and saves his latest victim, whose traumatisation is the *Psycho* Effect upon the moviegoer, one officer discovers the old pinup puzzles. But then as he leans against the bookcase to reflect on the oddities discovered at crime scenes, a secret compartment is triggered to open and the pieced-together body that was the psycho's jigsaw puzzle in the flesh falls on the college student. He was aiding the police operation motivated by his love interest in the tennis player. Psycho horror films pack surprises at the end which are supernatural, hallucinatory or otherwise come from nowhere. The parting shot of *Pieces* shows the psycho's corpse woman grab the college boy by the crotch and castrate him.

1

If the soldiers of Cadmus were sprung from dragon's teeth planted in the soil, then, Canetti concludes, it is the mouth that is the model for imprisonment, with the teeth the armed guardians of the mouth, the strait place (1988: 208–9). Cannibal killers appear driven by a hunger that leads them in part to destroy and in part to mummify. While a large portion of the leftovers gets body-bagged and dumped, liquefied and flushed, the cannibal murderers also regularly keep pieces of the body around, not just in Tupperware for the late-night snack, but also as relics to collect. *The Texas Chainsaw Massacre* refers to the Ed Gein case. The film opens with news of graveyard robbery and desecration in Texas. Grave robbing initially supported Ed Gein's production line; but then, they say, he started eating; and then he started murdering to complete his collection.

There's one *Psycho*-mediated Gein reference: but the fruit cellar is upstairs now. Grandmother is mummified and the grandfather is undead, but hangs out with mummy. We're out of the mother-and-son bond of psycho murder – and deep inside another dysfunctional setting, that of the family system. The van of kids taking the trip down memory lane to this encounter is also neither dyadic nor mass-psychological. It is the family sizing of the group that emerged after WWII to wrap around the TV set for better viewing (and which fits inside a van). In *Night of the Living Dead* the in-group in front of the set was in the first place an outpost of mass culture. In *The Texas Chainsaw Massacre* the two parties to the encounter cannot be further reduced or extended.

What *The Texas Chainsaw Massacre* realigns itself with in the more recent past is *Night of the Living Dead*. The open wounding at the end of Romero's film was that we were consumed and recycled as shitkickers going on zombies. In *The Texas Chainsaw Massacre* Tobe Hooper gives relief, first, in making the shitkickers cannibal killers and the victims college kids who are coded as socially and politically progressive, and, second, by letting one young woman escape. It is important that Sally, the survivor at the end of *The Texas Chainsaw Massacre*, is also a sister, like Barbara in *Night of the Living Dead*, and that both their brothers reflect the draw of regression.

What cuts out future work for the film is that while Sally escapes and survives she ends up a basket case, and the cannibal family disappears without a trace. The slaughter is not contained – only shunted to the side by the big truck that runs over one of the cannibals and gives Sally her chance to get away. However, the conclusion follows an arc of legibility that commenced with the doomed psycho, whom we first encountered when he hitched a ride with the college kids early in the film. We don't know yet that he belongs to a family of cannibals. But what we do recognise is that it was a mistake to give him a ride. Less because he's a psychopath, more because he's psychotic. He suddenly starts cutting himself, a telltale sign or technique of borderline-psychotic self-tranquilisation. Before he's thrown out of the van he cuts the arm of Franklin, too, the boy in the wheelchair who, though heavy, is Sally's brother.

Preliminary to this acting out, Franklin immediately struck up an understanding with the psycho (it's his knife the hitchhiker borrows to sign in as aberrant and violent). Through their initial exchange we learn that both come from family lines assembled in the precincts of professional animal slaughter. While the van was driving into town Franklin recognised the first souvenir from childhood: the old slaughterhouse where his grandfather brought his cattle. Appreciation of the head cheese that psycho extols stops with Franklin: the other group members gag on it.

The grandfather of Sally and Franklin, we learn in the van, was a pro when it came to slaughtering animals. Before the family skipped the sticks, grandfather used the old method, death by sledgehammer. Now their uncle uses air guns (this is the sole reference to an intermediary generation). The hitchhiker is up in arms – putting on heirs – about this degenerative innovation. The old ways are the best, at least when it comes to meat. Franklin thought the new technique guaranteed painless death, but he is willing to be instructed otherwise by the hitchhiker.

Sally and Franklin take their friends to the abandoned house of their grandparents. It happens to be right next door to the farm where the psycho-hitchhiker lives with his cannibal brothers presided over by the grandfather. Grandparents and grandchildren often enjoy an Oedipal-static-free trans-parent bond of doubling. In the double absence of parental guidance we encounter in the cannibal family a bond of regression that has split off psychic functioning until the three brothers each represent just one aspect of a psychic whole. They're a lot like the Three Stooges. The older brother, who doesn't like to do the murdering and is 'just a cook', but who chews out the other two nonstop is, just like Moe, the superego. The brother we first encountered as hitchhiker, who enjoys everything, even cutting into himself, represents, like Curly, the id. Leatherface, like Larry, is the ego, reduced, in his case of prosthetic seeing or sawing, to the activities of killing, eating and collecting.

Sally recalls last visiting the house when she was eight years old, at the time of her grandmother's death. How was Franklin able to go up and down the hilly property back then? He was carried, we are informed. When it's time for each couple to leave the in-group or circle of family and friends for 'about an hour or so' we find Franklin still being left behind as odd child out. One couple takes its time-out across property lines and ends up in the cannibal farmhouse. Their murders are conducted like the professional slaughter of animals. A burden that's hard to handle outside in the dark while the two of them search for the missing members of their party, Franklin nevertheless serves Sally like Perseus's mirror-shield. Sally is saved when Leatherface, transfixed by his double, goes first for her brother, another big baby or ego probe whose attachments are at once regressed and prosthetic.

All tied up at table, Sally sees that the whole decor is made of bones. She screams, she begs. They mimic her screaming fear; it's a laugh a mimic. Her face is ground up into and by countless close-ups. It is a variation on the close-up of Marion's dead eye. The eyes of Sally, however, are gouged out of context but alive to the terror. The camera conveys a torment that the daily meat grinder is imagined to inflict. It's a laugh a minute steak.

But the cannibals are professionals. They humanely advise that they are not going to torture her. Grandpa will deliver the fatal blow to her head. 'It won't hurt none, grandpa's the best.' But the grandfather can barely hold the hammer, let alone aim it. In the fumbling to realise the family fantasy of grandpa's legendary slaughtering skills (this is about her grandfather and her family, too), Sally is able to break free from being held over the blood trough, and jump out the window and get away. The brothers could have caught up with her while she headed toward the open road dragging a limp. I guess they take their time because they like playing with their food. Plus what could save her or stop them?

The hitchhiker is run over by a truck. We make out the truck's name – 'Black Maria', also the name of Thomas Edison's movie studio or lab. Then Sally hitches her survival to a pickup truck driving through. (Though the African-American driver of the 'Black Maria' makes it to the end of the film, a co-survivor and tribute to Ben, he most likely gets slaughtered in the off.) Sally survives. But how can she recover from the chaining of seeing? To be chained to or to be changed by what one saw is the question of survival, which never gets past the torture in Sally's case. She suffers what the cannibals enjoy, being chained to what they see or saw, while they saw away in the absence of burial or mourning. In the film's parting shot Leatherface still wields the saw, the apparatus, and inflicts the chaining of seeing. Whenever the shouting and chain-sawing die down at the cannibal farm we hear the whirring sound that comes from some generator, but sounds like a projector.

The Polaroid the hitchhiker takes of Franklin and identifies as good is an internal simulacrum of the film. When its goodness is not recognised by Franklin, the psycho takes out his portable tinfoil pyre and burns the image with explosive powder. The fire in the magnifier of photography, as Derrida underscored in *Droits des regards*, has the significance of preservation that also captions cremation, which alone can secure a tomb against desecration.

The sculptures made of bones and other bit or bite parts expand on the psycho's photographic praxis in which intake is conjoined through destruction with preservation. He is reproached by his brother the cook for the risks he takes robbing graves. The opening titles pull up short before the gelatinous face of a corpse in decomposition, which appears animated by light flashes. It's an opening image of celluloid. On the news, which is how the film story opens, we learn all about the recent grave robbing craze in Texas. Coverage focuses on one example of sculptures being raised up out of the graves and over dead bodies. The opening voiceover during our flash-punctuated glimpses of the remaindering refers to 'a grisly work of art'.

The van's first stop was the local graveyard. Sally wants to determine that her grandfather's grave has not been compromised. (Isn't her grandmother buried there, too?) One in-group member (who ends up on a hook like a slab of beef) spouts the discourse of astrological forecast and keeps at it like the running news commentary on grave desecrations. The proximity of Saturn signals that fortune is crossing over to the dark side. The boyfriend of the student of astrology sums up the stricken world inside and around the van: 'Everything means something I guess.'

Grave desecration can be seen as the bottom line of the urge to annihilate the other. It addresses the psychopathic core – the death wish – of the mourning enterprise. To mourn the dead successfully we must kill them, make them die a second time, and thus secure our succession. While some are wrecked by this success, others take the psycho path to lose losing. No doubt if there is a distinction to be made here it is really the contrast turned up on one process we can identify in phases. That we mourn at all in excess of disposal was, Freud emphasised in 'Mourning and Melancholia', an enigma. Why is it painful, he asked? Is mourning more difficult than killing and eating people?

2

The 1986 sequel, also directed by Hooper, but with way more consummate special effects by Tom Savini, the gore Meister of so many Romero films, seems more a Mannerist display of Vanitas imagery. Is it, twelve years later, a sequel required for therapeutic working through of the look of trauma? The film may be 'tongue in cheek', but maybe because we don't want to swallow the tasty morsel right away.

In the belated sequel mourning is in progress on the survival track, stumbling over obstacles in its course, but progressing toward an end in sight. The cannibals have taken their rejection of the exogamy of substitution and mourning into an underworld that subtends the local abandoned amusement park, the old thrill factory of cinema. Here they maintain their family values among the refuse of the refusal that cannibalism carries forward (all the way into its commodification, a new form and forum for the allegory).

The sequel opens with the warning that while it's sad if it's the young who are attacked, what awaits even the very old down the cannibalism tract is simply the worst, the worst imaginable. The untraceable horror that took place in 1973 'haunts Texas. It seems to have no end.' The film, however, is intent on making us see the unseen that we feared. The sheriff, known as Lefty, stumbles upon the wheelchair still carrying Franklin, now a skeleton. 'Don't you cry, my brother.' Lefty would unchain us from what we saw or thought we saw, what we imagined we saw. He must put to rest the 'fear' that walks beside him like a 'stranger'. He has been on a long-term quest for justice for his murdered nephew Franklin and his profoundly traumatised niece Sally, who succumbed to what she saw. When Lefty locates the new lair of the cannibals (inside the park that featured simulated Texas battles but which now houses the factory and warehouse for the family's prize-winning, money-making meat supply business), he proclaims that he must see what he fears so he need no longer fear it.

And then he enters the underworld (where the very walls leak the awful offal deposited inside them).

Lefty found the lair by putting Stretch, the woman marked for survival, out there as bait. She's the local disc jockey who one night is ear-witness to a chainsaw slaying of two victims in their car. They called in to her radio show right before they were attacked by the drive-by cannibals. She comes forward with the evidence on tape in response to a newspaper report of the sheriff's investigations. He convinces her to keep playing the tape on her show to enlist the audience to help uncover all the other murders hidden away in incidents the police write up and off as traffic accidents. LG, her sidekick at the station, is suspicious of the other man's special request. And he's right: Lefty was all along counting on what happens next: those responsible pay her a visitation.

She survives Leatherface's chainsaw when he, under her guidance, reinterprets it as a prop of sexual repression. She lies spread-eagled before him inviting his advances with the saw. After stating 'You're not really mad at me', she asks 'How good are you?' and improvises a sexual relationship. He caresses her, slowly moving his prosthesis up her thighs to X marks the spot, and thus experiences, I guess, what he really wants, something corrective. 'You're really good!' It's not that easy, however. The impulse to kill returns; but before Leatherface revs up the saw, Stretch drops from sex therapist to the underlying mom transference. 'No', she says distinctly. Then after a pause she adds 'Good', and then repeats the complete message: 'No good.' The good she gives she can take away. At the end of the scene Leatherface lies for her, telling his brother he killed her, and the boys leave the murder scene with LG in tow as extra side of beef. Stretch follows them – and gets trapped – this time through the bungling, well-meaning assistance of Lefty the sheriff on a mission. This back and forth between the sexualisation or personalisation of Leatherface's relationship to her meat and the unwitting undermining of her efforts through her male rescuer get repeated throughout the film.

After dropping into the cannibals' lair, Stretch soon finds herself and Leatherface reunited. During their first encounter she sexualised his prosthesis; then she interrupted his slaughter drive with the ultimate two-part message from mother. The utterance of command and reward takes apart the rebuke that one is 'no good' (the kind of running commentary Leatherface gets from the older brother). When Leatherface now catches her trespassing, she again says 'No!' Then when he hesitates to kill her: 'Good!'

He takes the face peeled off the victim he was just flaying and puts it on her. He holds it in place with the man's cowboy hat. Then he dances with her. The scene is a mirror reflex: like his name declares, Leatherface wears not a mask but the relic of the face-to-face. When Leatherface is summoned to another part of the underworld, Stretch finds next to her the victim whose face she still wears. There's more missing than the skin off his nose. She recognises her friend LG. He's really all cut up over their reunion. 'Oops, I guess I'm falling apart on you, honey.' He frees her and dies. She performs the mourning service of covering him up and placing the flesh mask back upon his face of gore. This is the first service soon to be followed by Lefty's identification of the remains of Franklin in his chair.

The incompetence of the cannibals is the continuity shot with survival in the first film. Stretch is caught and brought tied up to table. It's the replay of Sally's thousand eyes of fear scene. Presiding at table is the grandfather. At 137 years old, his liquid diet keeps him fresh as a rose. Into this replay the sheriff enters as one capable after all of providing rescue.

Even before the busting of this underworld, the meat processing business was going bust. Private interests are being subsumed by corporate interests. The processing of secret ingredients cannot expand beyond family size. The id brother, identified as Vietnam vet with a plate in his head, nominates 'Namland' as the next incarnation of the family undertaking, an amusement park that could go public. The frame of reference, at once global and topical, fits the sequel's advance into socio-political allegory following in the zombie re-shuffling of *Dawn of the Dead* and *Day of the Dead*.

Stretch enters the family encryptment of the grandmother, her chainsaw forever cradled in her mummified lap. The chainsaw can also serve as funerary emblem. Stretch takes the grandmother's chainsaw from the leathery corpse, reminiscent of Norman's mummy, and wields it at the end, wildly affirming her power over it and through it. She also takes back the consequence of Sally's post-traumatic survival.

But first Stretch interrupted the horror career of the chainsaw by turning it into a prop of sex therapy. That the lead cannibal brother rails against Leatherface's betrayal of their family values indicates that it's too late. 'Turned traitor for a piece of tail! Sex or the saw. Sex? Nobody knows. But the saw is family. Wait till granddad hears about this.' The dysfunctional family identifies its patient and opens for treatment.

3

Motel Hell (1980) prepared the way for Tobe Hooper's sequel. At least it offered a business model for the family to follow in its efforts to maintain its pure community in a world of immunity. In 1980, the onset of the termination phase of slasher therapy, *Motel Hell* doubled the splatter service back onto the slasher motel, the original site of serial killing. Hooper's own attempt in 1977 to set up his s-laughter hotel in place of the Bates Motel, even restaging the shower scene in one of the upstairs hotel rooms (the killer wraps up the victim's body in the shower curtain), was stuck in the slap sticks. In his *Chainsaw* operation Hooper struck a balance between laugh track and torture rack worthy of Grand Guignol. But in *Eaten Alive* (1977; aka *Death Trap*, aka *Horror Hotel*, aka

Starlight Slaughter) there is no respite from the running gags. At the same time every once and future star of psycho horror cinema has a role in this rundown of the Effect. It opens with Englund as the John who whispers to the new hooker what he wants. 'I'm not going to do that.' She's thrown out and proceeds directly to Starlight Hotel. But when the hotelkeeper realises the new guest was once an applicant for a career in prostitution he attacks her, kills her with his hoe and feeds the body to the crocodile in the pond by the veranda. When another hotel guest takes off her wig right before she has her shower scene, we recognise Sally from *The Texas Chainsaw Massacre*.

A short in just one of the letters on the neon sign of welcome respells the greeting and spells out the title of the splatter movie *Motel Hell*. A full stop is introduced and the mouthful the O would have let out retained. If some of the guests never check out it's because the overnight enterprise is the frame within which a family of cannibals sets its traps. It's a family business selling cured breakfast meats to those clients not yet selected for processing. The first step in the process of the cure is live burial of the selected motel guests (as well as victims of local accidents that happen or are staged and, when necessary, local snoops).

A local health inspector makes a spot check of the motel pigs, but leaves, it seems, dissatisfied. Like Arbogast in *Psycho*, the inspector returns unannounced that night. He stumbles through a thicket onto a garden patch. Some vegetables are covered with bags, like when you want all your asparagus to be white. But just as he's about to move on, one of the bags rustles and makes low animal noises. When he lifts the bag we see the head of a man sticking out of the ground. His body is presumably buried like roots and his vocal cords have been severed. He's probably zombie-insane.

While checking out, a couple of parents buy up cured, smoked, dried sides or strips of meat for consumption at home. In the meantime their kids dare each other to explore the inside of the slaughter shed. It all looks like pork. But then a figure pops out wearing the butcher's smock and a pig's head. The girls jump into the car screaming and the family leaves sure to come back now you hear. This enigmatic figure from the start of the film returns at the end. For the final showdown that concludes the meat processing enterprise the butcher/motel keeper wears the pig's head while wielding a chainsaw. It is a souvenir or relic of the 'inverted world' in which folklore metabolised the problem of food and death by entertaining scenarios in which the animals hunt and cook up human quarry. Pigs are often seen to benefit from the reversal. That the dinner table might turn and humans appear on the menu for the change was in the realm of possibility in *The Texas Chainsaw Massacre*.

The rationalisation for the motel keeper's industry is that it serves disposal of social outcasts. But when a choice young woman survives one of his staged accidents he selects her to satisfy another appetite as his object of rescue. He saves her from further association with her boyfriend, an outcast, who dies in the motorcycle wreck. The local sheriff, who is also almost a member of the family and collaborated, without really knowing or wishing to know, with the secret undertaking, is alerted to greater responsibilities by the same young woman. He too falls for the woman the motel owner picked up on the side of his disposal service.

When the motel keeper first tells his sister – she's maybe younger than he is but still too old to be wearing pigtails – to fix her up, she looks at him as though to say Why bother? To acclimate the newcomer to her new home, the still intact family threesome recalls with laughing gusto the time a hungry relation had to be fed her dog. But the two men recognise tail they don't want to go the way of all food.

Because the local sheriff's interest in the world of exogamous choice has been awakened, he becomes an Oedipal detective. The object of rescue is ready to walk down the aisle with the motel owner. When the sheriff presents to the bride-to-be the proof that the accident that claimed her partner was staged by her betrothed, the sister in pigtails listens in, knocks him out and restores the near miss to her place in the family business. In the showdown that follows she's strapped to the butcher's block. It's the tight spot where sexual life finds itself with cannibalistic identification in *The Texas Chainsaw Massacre 2*.

The duel with chainsaws introduces Oedipal conflict and mediation into the regressed family system. The dying grandfather figure dressed as butcher-pig bequeaths the motel and secret garden to the sheriff. However, he brings the reversed world to a full stop with his dying words. The terrible secret he reveals is not that he was a cannibal cook, nor that he mixed in pork with the human flesh, but that he used preservatives.

In 1977 Jacques Attali imagined chains of 'Bates Motels' opening worldwide for consumers of music who, unable to catch up with the stockpiling of recordings, would take the shortcut of suicide (1985: 126–7) – the negative theology that since the late eighteenth century has offered an alternative to the mere impossibility of merger with the machine. Failing replication, suicides were noted, in exchange, most likely to succeed in returning from their graves. It's common practice to check into a hotel to commit suicide. *Be My Ghost* is the variation one overhears in the title of the Conrad N. Hilton autobiography. In the novel *Ring*, the motel cottage, identified as reminiscent of the cabins in *Friday the 13th*, was built on top of the deep well in which the abused psychic girl, dying slowly in a moist place, was able to bend the TV medium to her will and transmit dead but live a demonic curse upon random viewers of her broadcast.

What he added to his fabulation of the Ed Gein history, Robert Bloch found readymade in the historical case of Mudgett (best known as H. H. Holmes, his original alias), on which he based his 1974 *American Gothic*. Holmes, who counts as America's first serial killer, was most famous for his 'Horror Hotel'. In *American Gothic*, Bloch combines two trends from the late Gothic novel, the first from Stoker's *Dracula*, the second from such French fare as *Le Fantôme de l'Opéra* and *Les Mains d'Orlac*. In the late nineteenth century the protagonist, Crystal, counts, like Mina Harker, as a 'New Woman', among the first of her sex to enter the work force by dint of typing and stenography. Thus she is qualified to work as a secretary for the suspected criminal (Gregg in Bloch's novel). But she is also a reporter, the only woman in such a position in Chicago, and her employment serves her undercover investigation. Bloch portrays Gregg as an imposing figure who takes libidinal control of his female marks in some sense by their inclination or invitation, but overtly through mesmerism, drugged drinks and the whole masquerade from his attire to the castle.

Towering above his pharmacy and private practice the castle is not only his home but also a hotel which he built right across from the 1893 Colombian Exhibition to cater to women travelling alone who for decorum's sake would prefer lodgings so close to the fair. That he woos the willing and profits from their disposable cash, jewellry or inheritance is not what makes him a psycho. It's that just as love and marriage are best for obtaining the goods, so murder is the most convenient means of concluding each swindle. Bloch further aligns Gregg with the psycho admixture of psychosis. When we see through Gregg's masquerade we discover behind a closet door the proof of his love: row after row of bell jars each filled with yet another woman's heart (1975: 204). Taken interpersonally as charming, Gregg bears a relation to Uncle Charlie in Hitchcock's 1947 *Shadow of a Doubt*. When Hitchcock's psychopath drops his masquerade during a discussion of the Merry Widow Murderer in the news he pronounces the victims 'fat, wheezing animals' suitable for slaughter. Since 1865 the Union Stock Yards in Chicago were the railroad terminus for the first industrial slaughter of animals.

At the time of H. H. Holmes's conviction a Chicago journalist had to coin a term for him: 'multimurderer' (Schechter 1996: 285). Holmes started out a proper graduate of training in medicine and surgery. But he was soon distracted by the fresh bodies in the lab. For his first scheme, he stole bodies, disfigured them and then collected insurance money from policies he took out on each dead person. From that point onward Holmes specialised in the swindle of collecting. He amassed several fortunes and the estates to match without investment or repayment. When the time came for repossession he sold the goods and split for another location and into another alias. He married several wives; some he left alone, in unwitting bigamous survival; others he killed for the money. His last 'marriage' was one more act he kept balancing in the final acts of insurance swindle and murder. Whenever he needed to go where the wife must never follow or understand, he told her he was once again negotiating patent rights for his invention of the ABC Copying Machine. The fiction of this serialising machine became bigger than life.

His formidable 'Castle' was built all on credit he never paid back. In 1893 Holmes rented out rooms in the Castle to visitors to the Chicago Exposition, the world's fair that modelled the modern amusement park. The Exposition even introduced the first Ferris wheel. For several years — from the very moment that Congress selected Chicago as the Exposition site — Holmes had been laying plans and making renovations. From his private quarters Holmes could turn the control valves to fill via a network of special pipes any of the bedrooms on the second and third floors with asphyxiating gas. After a long day at the fair – and a few turns in the fun-house hallways of the hotel before finding your room that could be locked only from the outside – it was time never to wake again nor ever to be found and buried: the bodies were dropped down a greased chute to the basement laboratory. It was here that Holmes kept his acid tank, quicklime vats, dissecting table and surgeon's cabinet. But to mark the other milieu of the psycho – the psy-fi setting – it should be noted that Holmes also invented and tested his 'elasticity determinator', with which he stretched his experimental subjects to twice their size so that in time he would be able to fabricate a race of giants (1996: 36).

As soon as the Castle came under investigation and excavation, the work of the police had to compete with one-stop-collecting by curiosity seekers. 'On Sunday, July 28, nearly five thousand people had swarmed to Sixty-third and Wallace, hoping for a glimpse of the Castle's ghastly interior – its "torture dungeon" and "suffocation vault" and "corpse chambers"' (1996: 293).

One investor recognised a good thing and turned the site to behold into the Murder Museum, which offered, for the price of admission, guided tours conducted by the Detective who had been in charge of the investigation. In Philadelphia, where Holmes was on trial for murder, another investor turned the already profitable Dime Museum, which featured sideshow oddities or wonders, into the Holmes Museum, where visitors could contemplate a replica of the Castle, phrenological chartings of Holmes's cranial abnormalities, and a skull that was identical to one found by the police and attributed to another one of Holmes's murder victims. The case generated similar collections of sensationalisms between book covers. One bestseller, *Sold to Satan: A Poor Wife's Sad Story*, was quickly translated into many languages, including German (Schechter 1996: 309).

Holmes spent final days on death row arranging for the fulfillment of his lasting wish. The condemned man, who had produced all his special effects of invention, progress, success only through interminable collection, fragmentation and recycling, right down to the skeletons of his victims he sold to medical colleges for mad money, just did not see his own corpus being in turn metabolised somewhere between collection and disappearance. Safer even than a mummy's encryptment, Holmes's burial plan was to have his executed body encased in several tons of cement from which his body, in parts or in whole, could never be collected and put on display. That the structure of collection folding out of or into multimurder was not neutral but hell-bent on extending torment beyond the grave, rests its case.

Although never involved with modern Spiritualism, the dead psycho swindler and collector attracted several mediumistic attempts, including one by his great-great-grandson, Jeff Mudgett, to bust the ghosts he left behind in the basement among the ruins of the Chicago hotel – or to exorcise the demon that possessed him to begin with.

In *Hell House* by Richard Matheson, Spiritualism, which is linked and limited to its compatibility with Christianity, and the scientific outlook (specifically the revaluation of parapsychology between biology and technology), are put to the test of putting to rest the malevolent spirit of the man who in life was a psycho.

To ascertain the reality of the ghosts or ghost-effects of his hot haunted property the current owner of Hell House, Mr. Deutsch, convenes not only two Spiritualist mediums (Florence Tanner and Benjamin Franklin Fischer) but also a parapsychological researcher, Dr. Barrett, who intends to keep haunting on an empirical basis. Deutsch is dying old, but still wants to know, ASAP, if there is truth to the continuous afterlife that haunting implies. The first working hypothesis advanced in group is that they are exploring 'a case of multiple haunting' (2004: 26), which gives way to that of 'controlled multiple haunting', a unique form of haunting by 'a surviving will so powerful that he can use that power to dominate every other surviving personality in the house' (2004: 174). The surviving will was bequeathed by Eric Belasco who built the house in 1919. 'He safeguards the haunting of his house by reinforcing it as a hidden aide for every other haunting force' (ibid.). What is ultimately revealed behind the special effects is a unified ghostly personality.

Belasco's Hell House externalised a mind that was 'a storehouse of information', 'a powerhouse of energy', 'a *charnelhouse of fancies*' (2004: 57). What went down in Hell House? The whole Grand Guignol: mutilation, murder, necrophilia and cannibalism (2004: 61). Under Belasco's direction drug-addicted doctors experimented on animals and humans to test pain thresholds, exchange organs and create monsters. Belasco, a psychopath in his lifetime, wanted, not unlike Mr. Deutsch, an afterlife in the material world. To protect the source of his projected continued existence he even lined his crypt in lead. And he set up many of the ghost effects via mediatic props during the prep work for his post-alive career.

The defective foundation of Belasco's reign of will power was his stature, the bodily shame that he could only cut away and then prosthetically project on a larger scale. When Adler argued that we owed the Great War to the Kaiser's withered arm, Freud corrected his former student (in *New Introductory Lectures* 1959: 66): it was the mother's horror over her child's deformity that was the secret wound the Kaiser hid or denied in the world war. Belasco's screen identity was gigantic, but inside the lead-lined projection booth he was sawed off.

Florence Tanner, the Christian-Spiritualist medium, is directed to view a psycho slasher film, to which she falls victim. She wants to heal the in-house evil with love. It is the long-suffering soul of Belasco's son she seeks to redeem. But then we discover that she is caught in another deferred action: her dying brother mourned his missed chances at intimate relations and on his deathbed hallucinated that she was his girlfriend. Thus her heightened yet unfulfilled incestuous inclination is stowaway in the Christian love she offers her correspondents from the other side.

A former actress, Tanner recognises in her declaration of love the words she once learned for her role in a TV show: 'There was no Daniel Belasco. There was only the memory of her brother, and the way he'd died, the loss he'd felt, the need he'd carried to his grave' (2004: 196). On her way out, she must face the untenable death wish, the legacy of the primal killer and psychopath in every psyche, which she has been skirting with her pulp fantasy of love among the entombed, but which alone determined her relations with her deceased brother.

Dr. Barrett, the scientist of the occult, holds that the mind's power over matter is subject to scientific analysis. In comparison, the concept of ghosts is prosaic (2004: 95). The secular bottom line he occupies with the Spiritualists is that 'man overflows and is greater than the organism which he inhabits' (2004: 224). There's more to life, in other words, than lifetime, a conclusion that doesn't require belief in the immortal soul. The overflow is a form of energy, a psychic fluid: 'This energy surrounds the body with an unseen sheath; what has been called the 'aura'' (ibid.). The psychic discharge is a 'field of electromagnetic radiation' (2004: 226). This is where his machine fits in: 'Man controls electricity without understanding its true nature. What the details are of the energy inside this house is not as vital as the fact that that machine has the power of life and death over it' (2004: 201).

In the film adaptation, The Legend of Hell House (1973), the ghost-busting machine, the construction of which Dr. Barrett brokered for in his initial dealings with the owner of Hell House, arrives in a van that occupies the foreground like Scapinelli's carriage early on in The Student of Prague. The van is the size of the machine and the size of the letters on its side: Deutsch Industries. It signals that the ultimate fantasy is about to begin.

When the efficacy of his machine is in turn reversed Dr. Barrett also goes. And yet just before, the machine he named 'the Reversor' had succeeded in curtailing the psycho's screen of operations. Now it's up to the surviving medium, Fischer (who was initiated into mediumship while still a suicidal teenager), to figure out that the projections began already in the psycho's lifetime and can still be reversed by touching on his shame. Fischer, who was the odd man out, a medium against his own will, whose ability afflicted him like a traumatic condition, identifies the psycho and routs him by reciting the bullying that hardened the psycho's case to begin with between mother and school. He calls him Evil Emeric – a sawed-off little bastard. The withdrawing figment falls into an echoing abyss (2004: 298).

4

Films Wes Craven wrote and directed during the era of the Psycho Effect pursued an independent agenda out of sync with some of the phases we've explored. Though his separate piece of horror had a following of its own, the pre-A Nightmare on Elm Street films never really joined in the mix of the Effect. That Craven was aware of this, if only after the fact, after his first mainlining success within the genre in 1984, is clear by the way he attempted to rewire his 1977 *The Hills Have Eyes* via the 1985 sequel.

The ending of the prequel brings home the doubling between the victim who strikes back, in self-defence or in retaliation, and the psycho killer at the moment of his destruction. At the start of *The Hills Have Eyes 2*, the closing sequence is incorporated in the memory not of the protagonist on his way to the doubling impasse, but of another survivor, whose role in the original film is incidental, a byproduct of the abridged family's survival. She's the teenager of the cannibal family pack who wants to leave home and move to Hollywood. She rescues the baby her people stole for dinner. Once the baby is safe the protagonist survivor is free to join in the overkill, the culmination of the first film's momentum. The second time around, then, the ex-cannibal is reinserted as victim and survivor of the horror that's over the Hills.

Beginning in the prehistory of the *Psycho* Effect, the projected body was in its various aspects being rewired, reshaped, redistributed – both as techno body, for example, and as body of the group. Thus the horror film medium brought us back to basics – and to the mother-and-infant reunion that the relationship to the body, even or especially to one's own body, implies. The psycho inhabits and wields the cut to preserve the disconnection from the mother's body as another form of connection. For the horror protagonists there is always the tight spot they are in with this disconnection. In Wes Craven's horror cinema the relationship to the body folds in and out of a trap. My free association is with the Disney film *The Parent Trap* (1961). Then there's the trap that Marion thought she was escaping while it was being sprung on her and us as the shower scene.

The Hills Have Eyes appeared in 1977, with time to spare for the influence of *The Texas Chainsaw Massacre* to be metabolised and sent in other directions. To use traps in conflict suggests a mobility and diversity of fronts reminiscent of war itself. In the life-and-death struggle that follows, there are three operations underway at any time. The use of walkie-talkies appears to keep these different missions and fronts in (highly vulnerable) alignment. There are two extended family systems facing off here, one passing-through, the other local. The family pack on the trip – the parents, three children, one of whom has brought along husband and baby, and the two dogs – is off to California. The younger generation looks forward to drinks by the ocean, in other words the Coast. But the parents, whose silver wedding anniversary is the occasion for this trek, are also invested in the Wild West aspect of California, which is psychologically further away from the Coast than a theme-park diversion. At least the father, a retired cop from Cleveland, wants to visit a silver mine to mine the associations. On this quick side trip they get lost and stuck.

When high-powered jets fly low to the ground, they realise they shouldn't be in an area reserved for military training manoeuvres. The immediate environs also served as a nuclear test site in the recent past. The local family primalised by radioactivity enjoys human flesh, when available, as a special treat.

The car skids off the desert road and crashes. Father walks back to the gas station they passed miles up the road while the in-law goes in the other direction to reconnoiter. At the end of the day father's not back yet. We know he's been captured and tortured. But back on the mobile home front we're surprised by a sudden burst of light and fire. We hear the father screaming. They rush to put out the fire in time to attend father's dying. During the diversion two primal men take over the trailer, where the blonde daughter looks after her sister's baby. They have their way with her while looking forward to making a meal of the baby. While getting away with their food in store, the more functional member of primal society (even, apparently, in the matter of raping the blonde) shoots both the baby's mother and her mother. The first one was shot dead, the other mother will die on those caring for her. With the father's death the family's will to survive rallies. The family line that now counts the father as ancestor and the baby as the future will be saved.

Totemically represented by the dogs, father still enters into the attack. Brother and sister triumph in league with the dead and killed-again mother. The paternal transmission goes through, cleared of static.

In reversal of *Psycho*, the mother's dead body is treated not to mummification but to utility or disposability in the fight for survival. Once the mother dies her surviving children build a trap of their own with her as bait in a chair in front of the slipknot in the sand. Once the cannibal steps into it to get a closer look and take a whiff, the slipknot can be pulled tight and yanked by car power over the spinning axle dragging the captive to his death. Sister and brother prop her up in the chair in the trap, all the while sobbing, resisting this impossible task. 'It's the only way to be sure.' Dead mother stares straight ahead but otherwise is sitting pretty (for a dusty old gal).

Though there will be setbacks and surprises this act marks the beginning of the reversal of the cannibal attack. The two siblings, their in-law brother, and the baby make it out of there (with the inside help of the young primal woman who is eager to get out of the sticks – and the hicks out of her – and besides, when it's time to prepare the special meal, instinctively protects the baby). But still the hills are alive with the threat of primal people. Craven, influenced no doubt by his experience as academic instructor of American students, replaces the us versus Texas line in the sand with a more mobile or displaced sense of the difference between modernity and shitkicker land: if you stray even slightly inland from the literal coast you could be in trouble out west. In *I Spit on Your Grave* (1978), which was inspired by Craven's *The Last House on the Left* (1972), the implication played out in the Craven original with regard to police protection, is made explicit concerning the locals. Drive out into the country with Manhattan still just behind you and you risk terrible consequences like travelling back in time, into primal time. This near-miss topography of where the violence is suits up well the psyche open both to defence and the best offense.

Before *A Nightmare on Elm Street* Craven's horror films ended with adults surviving as the doubles of murderous psychopaths or cannibal killers. They belonged, in a sense, to the repressed prehistory of Freddy Krueger, which in 1984 is on a return trajectory shaping and shattering the dreams of the next generation, the teenagers. In 1972 Craven finished *The Last House on the Left*, which followed *Night of the Living Dead* in showing the violence inside and out, but under conditions of an isolated event of 'true crime'. To celebrate one girl's birthday, two girls go to a rock concert. On the way there they are kidnapped, raped and murdered by two prison escapees and the two friends who assisted in the break. The presentation of the crime reached a height of screen excess with the infamous pulling out of a piece of the girl's intestine. Craven was a thirty-three-year-old ex-humanities professor at the time he decided to make *The Last House on the Left*. Like Christ, who at age 33 was the ultimate perpetual – protracted or postponed – adolescent, Craven preserved in his film the idealist/ terrorist aim of shaking up the American public's casual reception of violence by making the public another casualty. By all accounts 'choking' was the most common symptom befalling the audiences watching the gruesome scenes.

The girls are kidnapped and raped and then, out in the country, raped again and murdered. The element of comedy or slapstick thrown into this psycho horror film, often through musical accompaniment and editing technique, but also withdrawn abruptly from the scenes in which violence predominates, is particularly disturbing. That Craven initially trained in filmmaking in the porno industry might explain the handling of comedy. It also underscores the basic difference between these B-genres: a porn film might go away upon being consumed, but violence which irrupts within the art span of foreplay can't be used up in quite the same way. It stays with you. Craven's comment on the demise of Phyllis, the birthday girl's friend, captures the out-of-control quality of these scenes.

> The killing of Phyllis is very sexual in feeling, and ended with her being stabbed not only by the men but by the woman repeatedly. Then she fell to the ground and Sadie bent down and pulled out a loop of her intestines. They looked at it and that's where it all stopped. That's when they realized what they had done, and they looked at each other and walked away. They were disgusted at what they had done. It was as if they had been playing with a doll, or a prisoner they thought was a doll, and it had broken and come apart and they did not know how to put it back together again. (in Clover 1992: 137–8, n. 26)

The disgust is kept at harm's length. After the rape, the next victim, the birthday girl, throws up and then wanders into the lake for cleansing or suicide. Her rapist shoots her dead.

The film that has been up to this point a hot-and-cold *Schauer* of splatter porn next enters the concluding portion, which, like ex-prof Craven's inspiration, Ingmar

Bergman's *The Virgin Spring* (1960), is organised around revenge. When the two escapees with their sidekicks transport the girls (in the trunk of their car) to the sticks for the seclusion of their entertainment and its evidence, the spot they choose because the car breaks down happens to be right next to the birthday girl's home. After the murders, the killers present themselves as travellers in trouble to the local residents, who happen to be the parents of their victim. The murdered girl's parents generously and unwittingly host them on the spot. But the bizarre behavior of the guests at dinner leads the mother to go through one of the suitcases in the middle of the night and discover evidence that her missing daughter died at their hands. She and her husband find their daughter's corpse by the side of the lake behind their home. We thus enter the revenge plot of doubling.

The Last House on the Left placed the violence on the turntable. While recto and verso, zombie and shitkicker, played as equally inimical to the future in Romero's film, what turns against the killers in Craven's horror picture is the flip-off side of revenge. Under its label, violent sentencing takes out the killers, who were planning on spreading around some more violence. But the lady of the house is so forthcoming. She really wants to eat the big guy who's all excited. They're outside by the lake. Chomp! She punctuates the literalisation by spitting it out on the site of her daughter's murder. The killer is left with a blood gusher that will only stop with his life. Back inside it is the father's traps that help bring down his talion share of the murder pack.

Phantoms

In *Séance on a Wet Afternoon* (1964), Spiritualism as a kind of method acting is so proximate to criminal deception that a medium and her husband slide psychopathically or psychotically into the recognisable crime of kidnapping. By helping the police track the child's whereabouts with her psychic gift the medium aims to give herself unparalleled PR. Her purpose, however, is to improve in her mediumship by coming into contact, by dint of her fame, with the most accomplished mediums. Her gift is basic telepathy, which she can enlarge upon only if someone else in her séance circle also has the gift. When the child dies on their watch, and the medium keeps reporting the now sorry state of the victim, a leading Spiritualist comes with the child's father and the police to seek her counsel. The little ghost communicates with the medium and gives her away.

In *Family Plot* (1976), Hitchcock's parting shot, the medium's husband, an out-of-work actor, does the research that feeds the Spirit Guide his lines, while the medium is committed to her talent's recognition as real, even or especially by her partner. She doesn't slide into crime of her own but she and her husband cross the path of a psychopath and his partners in crime when she takes on an assignment to use her psychic powers to locate an heir for her séance client. With only a pharmacist's indiscretion to go on – namely that the sleeping draughts he provides cannot stop the client's nightmares – the medium was able to raise from the depths of a session the client's dead sister Harriet and prompt the revelation of the secret of Harriet's illegitimate child given up for adoption forty years ago. It doesn't cross the medium's mind to find a faux candidate for the inheritance – like her husband. Instead the husband as detective tracks down the real heir whose itinerary is obscured by a death claim that wasn't accepted. The gravestone bearing his name set up alongside the real graves of his foster parents at a later date marks an empty spot.

As teenager the adopted child and his best buddy, like two psychos in a pod, plotted the demise of the parents, who died in a fire set by the friend. In the meantime the heir has constructed the persona of a successfully self-made

San Francisco jeweller in which he hides out. Now he executes perfect crimes of kidnapping in which no one gets hurt or implicated while he and his girlfriend collect diamonds for ransom. The lower-class psycho buddy who was left behind to guard the secret of the heir's succession is first alerted to the investigations of the medium and her husband. He set up the false stone some time ago; now he volunteers to kill the meddling medium and her partner. If they reveal the jeweller's true identity the shared secret could be identified. The jeweller also has other exploits to hide. The psycho buddy goes off the road and catches the fire of retribution, while the jeweller and his girlfriend are caught in the cell of their kidnapping victims. The medium and her husband will earn the big reward but must disappoint the client with the news of her heir's descent.

The novel Hitchcock adapted, Victor Canning's *The Rainbird Pattern*, tells the story of a family's concealed psychopathic trait that gets passed along. The missing heir and his wife are criminals. The medium, who is murdered for her effort, unwittingly identifies and locates them. Their ruthless challenge to UK security – the traceless kidnapping of prominent subjects in the public eye – can now be matched by their elimination, which the agents of the state cover up with arson. The portrait or pattern of psychopathy is subtle: the wife is the second wife deemed by father and son as an upgrade. Indeed father and son are more like peers; there are no secrets between them. The ransomed diamonds will buy a small world of their own, a hunting preserve free of impurity or inhibition. The authorities overlook the issue of inheritance and spare the son who was away at boarding school. When he later kills the great aunt whose property he inherits by pushing her down the stairs, we look into her mind and realise that he is repeating her own act of violence against her brother, who decades earlier took the fall of their descent. Hitchcock skips the pattern of inheritance and assigns the problem of psychopathic violence to the emptiness of a family grave.

1

One adoption of a phrase inside the American language seems to be mistaken. We give ironic expression to a feeling of being (momentarily) at a loss in the environment when we quip that we need to leave behind a trail of breadcrumbs, like Hänsel and Gretel in the more grim original. Is it just phatic filler in the dialogue when recited, for example in the sixth installment of *Friday the 13th* (1986)? While the phrase, which always elicits amused recognition, tells a joke (but also a hope or *Verhoffen*) that some sort of survivalist improvisation might be necessary in the current setting to secure a roundtrip, in the fairytale their trail of breadcrumbs was eaten up and, thus cut off from the outside world, the children were left at the witch's disposal. Of course the couple in *Friday the 13th Part VI: Jason Lives* is dispatched soon after the man utters the phrase. But first the woman counsels that they get out of there when she sees Jason: 'I've seen enough horror films to know that someone wearing a mask isn't friendly.'

After I had corrected it countless times, even treating it each time as symptomatic, I realised that the phrase (with its significantly twisted meaning) 'to have a death wish' was already inside the American language (which doesn't make it less symptomatic but does depersonalise the fault). To have a death wish means you want to die. This bruises the logic basic to the lexicon of psychoanalysis, according to which self always passes 'first' through the other's death. You always wish the other gone. Just the same, fulfilling a death wish as suicide emphasises the suicide-bombing structure of what the Germans call free death: innocent bystanders have to go with a death that is their free gift for standing by. Intrapsychically and interpersonally the suicide takes along internal objects and wounds the survivors. In a late arrival to the horror of the mask, *Bruiser* (2000), Romero allows the mask, which is either a cult object or art, to release the death wish. The mask appears on the protagonist's face (or mirror image) one fine morning – something white that cannot be removed. This horror in your face looks like a mime face that, whether on a street in Paris or on some porcelain doll, is fully immersed in the death wish. At the start of the protagonist's transformed existence his wish is granted when he kills the maid who lies about her stealing. What objects, she asks. Then he whacks her with her sack filled with the silver.

The masking (or unmasking) series, which throughout the films we are considering carries forward one of the fundamental tropes of *Schauer*, is attached to another literary property in the doubling genre Freud claimed for his reading of the uncanny: Edgar Allan Poe's 'William Wilson'. It joins Stevenson's *The Strange Case of Dr. Jekyll and Mr. Hyde*, another original inspiration for some of the earliest encounters between the doubling phantasm or literary figure and film. *The Student of Prague* was in 1913 already a first sum total of the influences crossing over into the new medium from the literature of doubling. In his 'Uncanny' essay Freud makes mediated reference to the film, namely to the screenplay by Ewers, which remains the only reference to film he ever made, even while everyone else in the immediate circle of his following or reception kept finding cinematic analogues for psychic mechanisms. From the medium he skips he reclaims doubling for his science, which, continuous with the literacy that carried it forward, is the true medium of its presentation and understanding. In *The Student of Prague* the only act that at once consummates and stops the doubling is suicide, albeit unwittingly committed by proxy. William Wilson and his double also occupy and together stagger the simul-space of vision in which they maintain a relationship of out-of-timing. The double always appears suddenly at the wrong time (in contrast to the same time) to interrupt or disrupt another two-year season of the protagonist's dysfunctioning. Doubling thus blows the high-functioning cover of the psychopath.

The story opens with William Wilson (WW) contemplating the 'origin' of his miserable years of stealing and lying. He hopes to open up a 'little oasis of *fatality*' (1992: 626). Between the heavens and hope a stormy cloud blocks understanding: but he would rather not be left a failure of interpretation. Like Aleister Crowley according to his own *Autohagiography*, William Wilson, already remarkable by his descent, became what he is by growing 'self-willed' and thus 'a prey to the most ungovernable passions' (1992: 626–7). Because he is constitutionally infirm by birthright (in which his parents must recognise their own legacy) he grows up unchecked (or neglected). When we are assured that the young child was master of his own actions, we understand that he was sent away to boarding school already in childhood.

His mastery continues among his peers, even among all classmates not greatly older than himself. There's one exception. The only fellow student who will not bend to his will bears, though there is no family relationship, the same name (they also enrolled in the school on the same day and, upon registration, the same birthday was recorded for both of them [1992: 630]).

But their doubling remains in the eyes of the beholder, the delegate of the reader of Poe's story: his 'associates, by some unaccountable blindness, seemed not even to suspect' the equality or doubling or struggle for mastery between them. The protagonist/narrator is sure that his double is in the know. 'That he observed it [their match] in all its bearings, and as fixedly as I, was apparent' (1992: 632). The certainty that the double sees what the other double sees is 'a parent', the placeholder, therefore, of a failure in – rather than absence of – parenting. Through his parents he benefited from the uplifting momentum of his descent, which refers at once to his early experience of being sponsored and held and to his fall and deprivation.

That the double is also a mask, a mirror image held so close that it's the echo chamber of the sounds of breathing and speaking, also becomes apparent when we learn of the double's sole distinguishing trait: that the volume of his voice never rises above a low whisper. And yet this whispering voice was identical to WW's own full-bodied voice in its 'key:' 'his singular whisper grew the very echo of my own' (ibid.). We have been given the key to their relationship, which will be fully embodied once the double pronounces the verdict out loud over the dead body they shared.

WW decides to play a prank on his sleeping double and make him feel 'the whole extent' of his 'malice' (1992: 633). But he finds himself walking the prank over an abyss. WW now recognises reflected back in the double's sleeping face, which is not the double's waking face, the prospect that their sameness is but the mere accretion of 'sarcastic imitation' (1992: 634). This is the best containment he can summon from his 'incoherent thoughts' (ibid.) to follow up on his first response: 'my whole spirit became possessed with an objectless yet intolerable horror' (1992: 633–4). When he doesn't wear the double-mask in which his every sound is echoed in a whisper he encounters the cutting blank of objectless disconnection.

At Eton, the next station stopover of his search for containment, WW seems in a trance state of debauchery, which he is shocked out of only by his double's arrival. He only whispers their name, which now administers with its echo 'the pregnancy of solemn admonition' (1992: 635): 'it was the character, the tone, the key, of those few, simple, and familiar, yet whispered syllables, which struck upon my soul with the shock of a galvanic battery.' Splitting on the spot, WW is already gone. But it's in their long-distance relationship that the double continues to signal changes that WW is undergoing. As his depravity grows, he is also growing older developmentally.

At Oxford WW takes his antisocial tendencies to the next level. He likes to cheat at cards by targeting a 'dupe' (1992: 637) and making off with the proceeds. He reaches back to an early spot of deprivation via gambling, a compulsion Freud assigned in the case of Dostoevsky to repression of infantile masturbation. Regression brings WW closer to the starting block from which he developed reactively and protectively antisocial tendencies. This time the double arrives to whisper the verdict and unmask WW to his fellows as cheat (1992: 638). The relationship to the double can now address loss of face or shame. When in their final encounter the double interrupts WW's attempted seduction of a married woman, we're developmentally older than that card scam now.

Although suicide is the conclusion, it is the relationship between doubles that kept its consummation deferred, staggered, and increasingly legible as hope betrayed. Speaking no longer in a whisper but in their own voice, the double pronounces the verdict: '"In me didst thou exist – and, in my death, see by this image, which is thine own, how utterly thou hast murdered thyself"' (1992: 641). In the duel the original stabs the double. Then he looks away. When he looks back all he sees is a mirror and his own bleeding form in its reflection. Before going, then, WW's double-take allows him to recognise the loss in his face-to-face. The doubling relationship is unmasked: WW hears the verdict in his own voice.

The final destination that doubling earmarks as suicidal is skewed by the span of time the protagonist/narrator has already taken and filled with reflection on his history of deprivation, the doubling momentum of his testing of the environment. Because our introduction into the impasse is out of proportion with its closure we are returned to the beginning in the mode of recovery. The other double is then the narrative of development that takes one antisocial child to the limit where he starts over (and out). At the moment the dead double declares that it was only in him that the narrator/protagonist lived, and that with him he thus dies 'to Hope' (1992: 641), we also discern that the developments we followed and now return to forestall this double loss and succeed instead (instead of descent) in preserving the lost-and-found object relation.

2

That mummy horror has no history (even the exploitation of King Tut's curse was a long time coming) is owed to the truth its name cannot conceal: look at *Abbott and Costello Meet the Mummy* (1955) to appreciate what cannot be hidden, only denied or laughed off. We must go back to the very beginning of Hollywood horror to discover the story for which Karl Freund's *The Mummy* (1932) was the sequel adaptation.

Gaston Leroux's *Le Fantôme de l'Opéra* explored the ghostly limits of the sensorium by following a phantom 'Voice' and placing the work or 'opera' of mourning in the foreground of its tale of haunting. The first film adaptation, Rupert Julian's *The Phantom of the Opera* (1925), can be watched, after the fact, as the premiere articulation of psycho horror. Toward the close of the *Psycho* Effect two or three remakes of the story fit this range of recoil. In addition to *The Phantom of the Opera* by the slasher genre's European correspondent Dario Argento in 1998, there was, eight years earlier, *Phantom of the Opera: The Motion Picture*, starring Robert Englund aka Freddy Krueger.

The Faust story, which plays in Gounod's version on stage in the background of the phantom's intrigues, enters the slasher phantom's history in 1990. This phantom sold his soul to the Devil in exchange for the ability to break through to masterpiece music and take home the love of his audiences. He asks for renewal of life. But what he forgets to ask for is what he gets (superego-style): the life he wanted to control now hangs from his person as degenerative loss of face. He can save face, the face-to-face, only for the brief duration that lies between each death mask's perfection and putrefaction.

The pieces of skin he peels off his victims and sews onto his putrid face as heterograft patchwork never last too long. To incapacitate Carlotta so that understudy Christine can rise up in her place, the phantom plants in her closet one of the stagehands, now his skinned victim, still living and bleeding. At a time when *The Phantom of the Opera*, never an opera, was condemned to be a musical, this slasher film restored the after-the-fact connection between the *Psycho* Effect and the prehistory passing through it. Throughout the *Psycho* Effect the medical-prosthetic mask, like that worn by the phantom in Julian's film, alternates with the metamorphic mangled face which, no longer underneath the firm mask, gets stitched together or doubled by a skin mask. In 1990 a pitch could be made on behalf of the gore face of Freddy Krueger as reclamation of the 'leather face', a new mask standard. As I tried to establish as 'typical' fantasy in *The Devil Notebooks*: switching bodies or assuming a victim's face as flesh mask is not in the main an external ripping off. In keeping with its infernal significance as creative act it implies entering the victim from behind.

My next example of projection of psycho horror inside Leroux's story is literary. In *Le Fantôme de l'Opéra* the phantom's control of the inside/out, above/below space of the opera, augmented by the special effects he added during the completion of the Garnier edifice, allows him to remain invisible, unless or until he wishes to leave an impression. The vaster layout of the phantom's styling with antisocial designs can be reduced to fit the olfactory canal in Patrick Süskind's 1985 *Das Parfum* (*Perfume*). The protagonist lacks any scent at all which allows him, since not personalised, to pass under the radar. In German you can express your dislike for someone by saying you can't smell him, which could mean you can't abide his stink or, literally, that the scent is missing. Erik's mask, which he puts on to be a contact person suitable for humankind, corresponds to the perfume Grenouille dabs on, the aura of an identifiable persona (though not his own). His lack of scent or a smell of his own, which is his guise of anonymity, is also his wound – like the loss of face the phantom conceals under his mask. Grenouille's sense of smell, however, is so highly developed that he can whiff out the ingredients for the best perfumes. When he catches the scent of prepubescent girls on the cusp of ripening he is inspired to capture its essence in perfume. But as in early photography (or a certain understanding of photography as vestige) Grenouille requires indexical matter, a nightshirt and the girl's hair as well as a cast of the bodily aura made with fat and sheets. All this takes time – and his subjects won't sit still. That's why he starts serial-killing choice maidens to garner their essence for his most excellent perfume. After he's been caught, convicted, and sentenced to death, Grenouille pours on the distillation of his killing spree: the aura-mask compels everyone's adoration. He gets away with it for the sake of a survival he could never enjoy. Grenouille approaches a lumpen group in the local cemetery and douses himself with the entirety of the essence of murder/merger. Thus he accepts the early object love that his hate can now abide, albeit in reverse or in masque: the bums eat him alive. The novel closes with the reflection that they had for the first time done something out of love.

In Julian's film the phantom role as a whole is the mask that the psychopath Erik assumes when he acts out and begins to hope. Under the actual mask his deprivation, the wound of accident, is in his face. The film reception of Leroux's novel transfigured the phantom's birth defect into the look of a trauma victim, whether disfigured in an accident, a trainwreck for example, or at the factory or down in the mine. Trains crossed over from the industrial era – even up out of the underworld of mining – to offer passengers transport. Every passage through a tunnel was a flashback to prehistory. But then when the electric-mediatic phase followed the industrial one, electric illumination opened the very mines to tours of proximity to danger, which afforded consumable and fortifying thrill, and provided the model for the world's fairs and amusement parks that followed. In Leroux's novel the phantom's underworld threatens or entertains Christine with its countless special effects culminating in the torture chamber, which reminds Christine of her visit to the Grevin wax museum. The metallic chamber puts the heat on its victim, thereby inflicting physical torment; but it also scores traumatisation in the psychological, internal, or mediatic sense when, like the torture camera in *Peeping Tom*, its relay of mirror reflections shows the victim the prospect of being endlessly alone with his fear.

Medical advances allowed casualties of techno crash just like soldiers to cut their losses and survive the field of destruction – testimony for all to see in the streets. The prosthesis thesis was gaining currency while both physical and psychic victims of accident began filing for projection. The psychic casualties were just as recognisable, given the high incidence in traumatic neurosis of hysterical symptoms like shaking, paralysis and grimacing. We were being mass-psychologically reorganised to accept a new horizon of technological contact in the prosthetic application to trauma survival. This was the staging area for Lon Chaney's art of a thousand faces; news of his latest transformation shared the back page with ads for what was new in medical prosthetics.

Chaney's death date was due with the advent of sound pictures. In a letter to Benjamin dated December 17, 1934, Adorno underscored that the end of Kafka's life coincided with the end of silent movies. The writerly gesture of the creature in Kafka, bereft of words, gestures across the silent screen toward music. The Meister mimic of creature features received the gesture with love. Chaney was the child of deaf parents. Something like a substitution going around his senses, spinning the dial of an extra sense, inspired Chaney's transformations. He was the only one of the deaf couple's children who could bear to face the dramatic gestures of reproach that accompanied a scolding (Blake 1995: 157). When his mother was afflicted with inflammatory rheumatism he became her caretaker for the next three years. At first drawing sketches for his mother's amusement he soon extended his bedside entertainment to acting out world or local events and mimicking the neighbours. Within a growing frame of reference, therefore, Chaney developed elaborate skits for his mother's eyes only to follow and enjoy (1995: 161).

Since Chaney refused to take direction from Julian, we watch in the series of scenes and exchanges culminating in the phantom's unmasking Chaney's direction of his film within the film. *The Phantom of the Opera* was the one film he identified with to the point of bringing it home to Colorado Springs (Blake 1995: 165). He arranged with a local theatre to offer a special screening for the students of the Colorado School for the Deaf, which his maternal grandparents founded in 1874. In the genealogy of media the deaf-mute subject models semiotic and mediatic theories of language and their prosthetic application to a bodily sensorium suspended between withdrawal and reanimation. The first robotic machine rehearsals of artificial intelligence were based on this reception of language folding out of the deaf-mute subject of study, in every sense a medium. Among the props of trauma Chaney pursued an art of identification and transformation that was akin to the modern magic of Spiritualism.

Before he was the author of *Le Fantôme de l'Opéra*, Leroux was known as 'the eternal reporter' for his skill at making copy out of the most incredible or unlikely materials. His career in journalism first took off when he turned to crime reporting.

Moving right along, the foreign correspondent started reporting on revolutions and wars. Somewhere between military formation and the newspaper layout of information he introduced the expression 'the fifth column'. While a journalist he tried his hand at fiction writing. His novels first appeared, and fared best, as serial material staggered across the columns of newspapers. In 1907 he scored a success with *Le mystère de la chamber jaune* (*The Mystery of the Yellow Room*), a locked-room whodunit. The protagonist who solves the case locked inside the yellow room is a journalist with a new perspective on crime that outdates official police work. He tests the impossible scenario – evidence of a crime perpetrated against the victim behind locked doors – the way one might investigate a Spiritualist séance. The frame of the reporter's rational investigation runs up repeatedly against the possibility that any explanation of the locked-up crime must include some other world than the rational one. Hypnotism and magic come up repeatedly within his speculations. Then the Professor's research into 'dissociation of matter' seems to propose yet another dimension. But the reporter finds just the same a logical solution behind the séance of this crime. 'Then with the right end of my reason I drew a circle around the problem. Around this circle, I mentally wrote these bright words: 'Since the attacker cannot be outside the circle, he must be within it!'... In other words, I had within the circle one person who was really two, that is to say, a being who, in addition to being himself was also the attacker' (1997: 204). The lead detective turns out to be the Oedipal twofer, the cut-rate two for one offer: he is both the investigator and the criminal, a professional acrobat and swindler (like so many defrocked mediums).

There is nothing incidental about the author of the Sherlock Holmes mysteries being a prominent Spiritualist. Modern Spiritualism, which amounted to a first theorisation of the new live mediatic outlets, at the same time required investigative journalism and detective work to secure the pro-and-con span of its claims. Testing draws us inside the site or séance we entered either to prove or disprove. According to Freud, the work of mourning deploys testing in all the station stops of memory to reality-check the absence of the remembered object. At the same time the search engine of testing keeps the missing hanging on and around, a still current address.

Telegraphy and the tapping that the Fox sisters picked up and transmitted belong to one primal scene of the modern science of communication with the long distant. The connection between these parallel worlds was the press, the first institutionalisation of new mediatic prospects. Via telegraphy the news media soon became national, soon-to-be global. What hit the headlines with the regularity of a driving force were, alongside coverage of train wrecks, for example, reports on Spiritualism, often investigative reports aimed at debunking the claims of mediums. Just the same journalism thus promoted the pressing influence of ghosts.

Spiritualism spread across the same telegraphic grid as the press – first throughout the United States, then, around the time of the Civil War, on the other side of the Atlantic. Spiritualist sessions offered themselves up as testable. Whatever is testable was already proved in some fundamental way to be acceptable, admissible in the form of hypothesis. The absence of proof is the other reality that draws testing onward. *Le Fantôme de l'Opéra* advanced its tale of haunting as both simulated and believed in, the two alternating poles of the reception of modern Spiritualism.

In *Le Fantôme de l'Opéra* Leroux, signing in as investigative reporter, gives the backstory in his prologue: he set out to explore a tragic murder that commanded the headlines thirty years ago, but which remained an unsolved mystery. Going into the recent past of the Paris Opera, the scene of the crime, what witnesses he finds are dead or are going to die (the very range of photographic subjecthood, according to Barthes). All the while he keeps stumbling across the legend of the Opera's phantom and begins to draw a connection. One of his witnesses writes to him: 'If it be possible to explain the tragedy through the ghost, then I beg you sir, to talk to us about the ghost again' (1987: 4). Not until the writing or reading of this sentence, had anyone even 'thought that there was any reason for connecting the more or less legendary figure of the Opera ghost with that terrible story'. To make the connection is to acquire what the prologue advertises in its subtitle: 'the Certainty That the Opera Ghost Really Existed.'

The ghost proves to be not real – or rather real indeed and therefore no ghost. The recordings of an opera singer's voice are to be buried beneath the Paris Opera. It is thus that we stumble upon the crypt: 'It will be remembered that later, when digging in the substructure of the Opera, before burying the phonographic records of the artist's voice, the workmen laid bare a corpse. Well, I was at once able to prove that this corpse was that of the Opera ghost' (ibid.). The prologue lifts a crypt frame that only by the end of the novel can be shut: 'Ah, yes, we must needs pity the Opera ghost. I have prayed over his mortal remains. ... Yes, I am sure ... that I prayed beside his body, the other day, when they took it from the spot where they were burying the phonographic records. It was his skeleton. I did ... recognize it ... by the plain gold ring ... which Christine Daaé had certainly slipped on his finger, when she came to bury him in accordance with her promise' (1987: 264).

Christine's work of mourning – which comprises the intervening 200-plus pages of the novel – is framed by the double movement of interment of phonographic records and disinterment of the ghost's remains. Following the death of Christine's mother, father and daughter formed a death cult that ran on music's occult medium range. The 'Angel of Music', father promised her, would pick up where the father would leave off. He will never go. Her singing goes down inert following her father's death. The opera ghost now can fill the one position he can fulfill unseen. Christine: Is he the Angel of Music, the Voice? Yes he is.

The Angel's hold over Christine appears Oedipal, since chiefly imposing limitations on her ability to marry (if she bestows her heart on anyone else the Angel must return to Heaven). But the voice has pre-Oedipal qualities: maternal but also phallic, in other words, all difference rolled up into one. Christine joins the Angel of Music through the mirror relation; she walks into her image, merges and crosses over.

The Voice isn't the father but is sent to her upon his passing. This medium or mediation between father and daughter is the mother, whose monstrous representative is the phantom. 'He fills me with horror and I do not hate him.... He has imprisoned me with him, underground, for love!' (1987: 124).

The Voice plays 'The Resurrection of Lazarus' over her father's tomb: by this point she has become the Voice's 'thing' (1987: 118). What went down just before was the chandelier accident: for the first time she worried about the Voice's safety, as though 'it' were embodied and mortal: 'I was really afraid for it, just as if it had been an ordinary person who was capable of dying' (ibid.). Following the accident, then, the Voice resurrected itself via the performance of the Lazarus piece. But now he was ready for his close-up. The Voice encounters her in the flesh beyond the mirrors on mirrors through which he draws her. But once on the other side, she feels the touch of 'a hand that smelt of death' and faints dead away (1987: 120). Her identification with the dead person she cannot see gets a rise out of the crypt inside her. First she thinks the Opera ghost has abducted her. She calls on the Voice to save her. But then she realises that ghost and Voice are one. He offers her his ghostly protection, still in the rehearsed terms of the father's legacy: 'the rest of the time would be devoted to music' (1987: 125).

As long as he's just the Voice there's no problem for Christine. But Christine has yet to bury the dad and the mummy, which is why the Voice and the phantom must come together as the one loss that the phantom alone can recognise and put to rest. For even after he has let the couple go, Christine and her Raoul, Erik still must put to rest what Christine will ultimately bury.

After Erik shows her where he sleeps, inside a coffin, Christine transgresses against his one injunction and completes the withdrawal of idealisation: she tears away his mask. Now she must face the music: 'know that I am built up of death ... and that it is a corpse that loves you ... and will never, never leave you!' (1987: 129). Christine draws back from the 'words of love in his dead mouth' (1987: 130). But now Erik wants 'to live like everybody else:' 'I have invented a mask that makes me look like everybody else...I want to have a wife like everybody else' (1987: 216). When Christine broke the phantom's rule and violated his personal space, the mask that fell was the same one his mother had put up with the shame.

Christine steps out of the line of the parents: the father never saw him; his mother invented the mask so she wouldn't see him. 'My mother...my poor unhappy mother would never...let me kiss her' (1987: 253). When he threatens Christine, 'If your answer is no, everybody will be dead and buried!' (1987: 218), the 'buried' part of the threat also marks the spot of mourning's onset. If she just says no, then every body that is already dead will be buried.

Surrounded by furniture that is all he has left of his 'poor unhappy mother', Erik announces that he's ready to die now (1987: 248). He has kissed Christine alive and farewell. The phantom is good to go. And now, like a mother, the phantom puts herself to rest. 'I kissed her alive...and she looked as beautiful as if she had been dead....It was the first time I saw my living wife....Until then...I had always seen my dead wife' (1987: 251–2). The techno journalism at the art of this opera of haunting, which set out to record the evidence of those who will have died, makes its mourning deadline.

3

Brian De Palma's *Phantom of the Paradise* from 1974 is the best motivation for going back to the reception of Leroux's novel to find a staging area of the *Psycho* Effect. De Palma even ensconced the shower scene within his update of the film adaptations of *Le Fantôme de l'Opéra*. Beginning in 1943, films titled *Phantom of the Opera* remade the composer, before he retired to his underworld, a victim of plagiarism. His life was transformed when he sought redress from the plagiarist who, to add injury to insult, threw acid in his face. Now the phantom face reflects the plagiarism of his composition or corpus or rather the violence that his attempt to reclaim his composition releases. In *Phantom of the Paradise*, the composition to be plagiarised (that is, improperly commemorated or buried) is a Faust rock musical that never leaves the setting of recording, the studios of Death Records, the corporation and label of the highly successful Swan. His ultimate plan is to build the Paradise, his own Disneyland of pop music. To open it he is looking for a new sound.

When Swan first overhears the original music of Winslow Leach we hear this time but never again, although there are many partial performances of the rock cantata in the film, a direct hit with the psychopathic destructiveness and envy attending Swan's decision to use this music. 'Like a child always poor reaching out for more, I could feel the hunger grow.' It's the immediate preamble to the Faust figure's decision, in the cantata, to sell his soul. Before Swan binds him through the terms of his own infernal contract he simply robs Leach and frames him for drug dealing. But when Leach the loser learns that Swan is opening the Paradise with his composition and that it will be performed by the despicable Juicy Fruits he breaks out of Sing Sing and commences his career as phantom. After getting his face mangled on one of his forays into Swan Records in a record-pressing apparatus he looks the part. After the accident he again tracks the precincts of the corporation for his stolen corpus but now as POV. We also hear his heavy breathing, or mangled muttering, since he also lost his voice in the accident. All this leads to his self-conscious assumption of the phantom's role upon grabbing a highly styled mask from wardrobe.

The aural markers of the subjective camera, the breathing, muttering sounds, show that POV is already a mask-like construction which the moviegoer also puts on to see what he sees and hear his own breathing at close quarters. When Swan encounters Leach the phantom in his headquarters he decides to rip him off some more. He devises a device for synthesising the fragments of Leach's damaged voice. Plugged into the machine he can sing and compose and thus conclude his Faust. But as soon as Leach is finished Swan grabs the score and orders workers to erect a brick wall at the door to the studio, which seals him inside.

Already at age fourteen, Swan decided to commit suicide to preserve his own perfection. But his mirror image proposed instead that Swan sign up with the infernal program and stay forever young. The mirror relation holds interchangeable places with the video-taping: the recording on tape – like Dorian Gray's portrait but on both video and audio tracks – will absorb and ward off his aging.

Like an alchemical solution, the tape medium is a mix of elements and energies. It is not the shadow and imprint of that which is to be depicted. The displaced aging is largely aurally marked: on tape we might recognise a senior hand briefly in front of the POV but there's no mistaking that Swan's voice is old and sinister. Rather than act as mirror, the taped record upon contact and compact with the Devil is a POV document, and the heavy breathing under the mirror mask is the living aging split off from Swan's physical appearance into the tape recording. This compact on tape, like the surveillance at the heart of the Swan corporation/incorporation, supersedes all subsequent contract signings that are also on tape: including Leach sealing his deal and Phoenix, the Christine figure, making her compact. After witnessing through the bedroom's glass ceiling that Swan has stolen Phoenix, his love object, Leach attempts suicide and, failing that, stabs Swan. But he discovers that whoever is under the original infernal contract can't die. Only destruction of the original on tape would restore all parties to finitude. For Leach that would mean the opening of the fatal wound of his attempted suicide, which was kept sealed by the deal. Tape recording holds the powerful industry of Swan's corporation/incorporation together; but it's also its defective cornerstone. Nothing easier than to destroy a tape, already and in any event a non-archival medium beset by entropy.

The other phantom figure, or his psychopathic aspect, in contrast to the traumatic psychosis that gets Leach behind the mask and then on contract, Swan takes centre (sound) stage within an 'opera' as extensive as live recording or surveillance. The film shows us the continuity between a bank of surveillance monitors and the split screen technique it applies. The surveillance on monitors and on tape serves Swan's pleasure at watching not only the pleasure of those trying out on his casting couch but even or especially Leach excluded from the pleasure only Swan enjoys, but with whom he identifies in the split whereby he watches Leach watch his pleasure on interminable standby.

Swan's psycho profile is made manifest in the tendency to spoil and destroy what he can't have or doesn't already have as his own. He steals Leach's Faust opera in order to spoil it. When Leach concludes the work Swan doesn't cast Phoenix in the leading role because he can't stand 'perfection' in anyone else. Swan revises the lead role to fit a *Rocky Horror Show*-style Frankenstein monster to be played and sung by the glam rocker known as Beef. In their shower scene, Leach warns Beef not to go on with the show. But when Beef is browbeaten into staying, a fatal jolt by the neon prop Leach hurls at him takes him out on stage. The impact of Beef's death on stage viewed from coast to coast sets a new standard for the Paradise. Now, apparently, only snuff's enough. When Phoenix replaces Stir Fry in the performance, a star is borne by Swan who now can't ignore her (since his antisocial spats do find their limit in the success stats of the mass market). Still he at the same time vows to bind her to him in order to market her destruction as forever young star. When Leach breaks into the video archive and reviews the relay of infernal contracts on tape he also discovers (the video record is also Swan's Dear Diary) that Swan's ultimate plan for Phoenix is to stage their wedding party live at the Paradise according to the fine print of their marriage contract: until death does the parting and partying.

The Turning

In *Maniac* (1980), the war-paint of scalping applies another parting shot to the slasher POV. Even before there is evidence that she is being stalked by the killer in the headlines, a nurse undergoes the kind of panic that dooms small critters. The psycho in turn picks up on her fear, the scent the hunting animal follows out to the end. The psycho, who scalps his victims and takes the souvenirs home with him, alternates between hunting instinct and self-torment, which we hear out loud, either in the voiceover of his thoughts, or in his moaning and heavy breathing when he is POV, and thus wears the POV like Michael Myers his mask.

The serial killer keeps a collection of mannequins in his home. Onto the empty heads he nails the scalps of his victims dripping blood down the blank dummy faces. These are trophies from hunting expeditions in which both he and his victim, in one sequence, become animal. We are passing through the environs of *The Texas Chainsaw Massacre*.

Psycho's tormented relationship to his mother, which comes in two distinct parts, idealism and murderous hatred, catches up with the one woman, a photographer, with whom he has entered a relationship beyond the one-night stand of murder. That she is the exception results from his respectful interest in her photography, in which psycho discerns a fulfilled wish to preserve her subjects or their beauty. But then on the way to another dinner date they stop to pay their respects at his mother's grave and suddenly he tries to kill her, too.

But she becomes the one survivor it takes to undo a serial career: she whacks him and gets away (which releases the hallucination of his mother rising up from the grave to punish him again with her stranglehold). He retreats to his lair and the mannequins, who come alive as the undead victims who now destroy him. We see him through their POV. The overturning of the masked POV in *Halloween* is given another twist: while blood drips down the lens we see through the dead eyes of the victims.

John Carpenter's *Halloween* (1978) 'introduced' Jamie Lee Curtis, daughter of Janet Leigh. Whether first introductions are accidental or not, Carpenter followed *Halloween* with its after-the-fact motivation or momentum: in *The Fog* (1980) Carpenter teamed up Jamie Lee Curtis with her mother in one screen text and scream memory.

The psychiatrist in charge of psycho killer Michael Myers in *Halloween* is named Dr. Loomis, in earshot of *Psycho*'s Sam Loomis (what's more, the actress playing Annie is in fact named Loomis). The year I pointed this out as strong sign of the uncontrollability of the slippage Carpenter introduced in name, one of my honours students was named Loomis. The student didn't think it was a particularly common surname. Loomis was the name Marion was doomed never to take in matrimony.

A rumour that once was current – up there with the improbable but 'known' gerbil story – claimed that Jamie Lee Curtis was born a hermaphrodite and a decision for the one gender over the other was quickly cut into her body. The name she bears in the middle or genital position is the streamlined (or slashed) version of her mother's maiden name between a first name often given boys and the mother's marryin' (Marion) name. Signing in right from the start with this ensemble meant that in its incorporation there would be no room for a name in marriage. According to the primal medium of rumour, then, she was born to meet more than halfway Benjamin's proactive understanding of the cut and thus overturn the psychotic application of the trans- in *Psycho* (later heightened and literalised in the case of the psycho double Bobbi in De Palma's *Dressed to Kill* [1980]).

Laurie (Jamie Lee Curtis) was psycho Michael Myers' sister only since the sequel, *Halloween 2* (1981), which was to be a conclusion, deliberately not designed for further serialisation. Hence Michael Myers (MM) is destroyed by fire: only the illuminated Jack-o'-lantern image of the mask still between us and his cremation remains at the end. A file is opened that was so secret even Dr. Loomis never knew it existed. Laurie was born to MM's parents who made it to the two-year mark after their daughter's murder but then died in an accident. Her parents feigned her adoption with the proviso that her true identity be withdrawn from circulation.

After years of observing MM, his psychiatrist spends as much time plotting his lifetime incarceration. Dr. Loomis is the eternal witness to a failure of interpretation his discourse on evil allegorises. Dr. Loomis pulls up short before MM's 'evil' and 'devil's eyes' and assigns MM to the outer limit of untreatability. Thus rather than interpret the violence he speculates on its 'trigger'. 'I've been watching him for fifteen years, staring at the wall, looking at this moment, the magic moment that would set him off.' Or again: 'I've been waiting for some alarm to trigger him off.'

In *Halloween: H₂0* (1998) Jamie Lee Curtis and Janet Leigh are on the same screen during the calm before MM's return. However any calm is the effect of heavy self-medication. Laurie, now in the position of teacher and the mother of a son, is a high-functioning case of traumatic neurosis. She's actually the head mistress of the private school her son attends. A classic shocker that ultimately cuts the tension involves Laurie, at the end of the school day, literally bumping into her secretary, whom we also didn't see coming. It's Janet Leigh, who now offers her employer 'maternal' advice. As she walks to her car we hear the *Psycho* music play.

Before this run-in, we attended Laurie's English class where the teacher is instructed by her son's girlfriend. It was Victor Frankenstein's crucial mistake not to 'confront' his monster. For this reason alone he is responsible for Elizabeth's demise. Has anyone in the room read the novel? Laurie says there's no excuse for the class's lack of preparation: 'you could have watched the movie'. The novel is plain text about Victor's superimposition of his every replacement object onto the dead or undead mother he cannot bury, let alone mourn. To this extent he is related to Norman Bates. The therapeutic breakthrough of Carpenter's film has by 1998 elided the *Psycho* Effect, and placed the *Halloween* franchise by inoculation and proxy on a par with *Scream* (which is being shown on TV in this film). Likewise I'm sure, the teen group of experts in *Scream* watch *Halloween* on the VCR in order to decode its conventions and semiology of suspense or survival. The 1998 portrait of society is a composite out of parts contributed by different films. That those afflicted by identification belong to the parental generation, whose encrypted encounter with psycho violence endangers the next in line, also cites *A Nightmare on Elm Street*. Confrontation addresses a growing sense of anyone's pre-case-history of abuse, neglect, deprivation or privation. The shift that *Halloween* introduced, and which continues, for example, in *A Nightmare on Elm Street*, coincided with the era of the child abuse charge that sparked in a milieu, brought home by their photos on every milk carton, of missing children.

What Laurie learns from her student's deluded point that Victor is responsible for the loss of his loved ones because he didn't face his fear leads her to cut off the head of MM. But in the next sequel she's locked up in an asylum deranged out of remorse over her unwitting murder of the innocent bystander who was dressed up by MM as his double and placed on mute. In the meantime she stopped taking the medication because she is vigilant in the face of MM's inevitable approach. In their showdown on the asylum roof Laurie once again fails to kill Michael; but she gladly skips the serialising ambiguity of apparent attainment of her goal and takes the leap herself to wait for him in hell.

Before any tragic conclusion between siblings, which the serialisation already overflowed, the therapeutic revalorisation of Laurie's survival was in place as the legacy of *Halloween*. The film picked up with its 1963 date mark more or less where *Psycho* left off (more or less after a period of mourning). The first victim of the five-year-old MM is his teen sister. In stabbing her MM strikes out against her neglect of him in her role as babysitter. Then he shuts down and waits for opportunities to resume his repetition compulsion to kill all teen mother substitutes. Fifteen years later it's Halloween in Michael's hometown. Laurie's dad is trying to sell the Myers place: but it's a spook house, as her babysitting charge for that night warns her. From inside looking out Michael steps in front of us (we hear his muffled heavy breathing) to remind us that it's his POV (and that we're still inside it).

Halloween developed the mask logo of end-of-70s horror – the wave of the 1980s – out of a POV that puts on a mask held in place by two eyeholes in front of the camera. The mask is not on from the start. Instead we are inside the masking while the POV is thus embodied.

Otherwise POV easily reaches consciousness as only a camera convention and not the way we in fact see. The hand-held camera as stalking device, for example in *Eyes of Laura Mars* (1978), can't really get you when you realise it's a jiggling camera. Something I recall that Carpenter emphasised in an interview: because camera vision is without context or peripheral vision, the conventional merger of perspectives cannot but call attention to the camera behind the seeing-I killing machine. In *Psycho* and *Peeping Tom* we are captive audience to our own murderous participation; in *Psycho* through the overlap or contamination of three performed, but not seen levels of the cut, in *Peeping Tom* through the relay of mirroring that loops us through the suicidal camera of horror stuck on horror, the trauma machine of the movie we are inside watching. *Halloween* accomplishes all of the above by masking the camera's POV.

Star Wars (1977), which appeared the year before *Halloween*, foregrounded the heavy-breathing mask of Darth Vader. It is the addition of the sound mask to the gallery of masks in horror cinema beginning with the phantom of the opera that motivates the group identification with the killer. (In 'William Wilson', remember, the double is this echoing mask.) The pop-cultural status of Mickey Mouse, the sadistic rodent turned cute critter or child, seems reclaimed (and reversed) by MM, Jason, and Freddy (whose mask is his malleable scar or scare face). Darth Vader is indeed the primal father who is only restored to the identifiable body of the aging Oedipal father in time for his death and his son's mourning. But while he remains within the pre-Oedipal zone he is the techno-embodied death-father of total control over mother and children alike. For Jeffrey Dahmer, for instance, Darth Vader, with libidinal focus fixed on the heavy breathing mask, became the ultimate trigger for masturbatory p-unitive fantasies of control, which he syndicated with victims. With an unconscious purpose matched only by that of certain Disney films, George Lucas's fantasy picture (which as such is ultimately happy end and Christian) cited and summoned a specialisation of S&M fantasy. Like Ed Gein's stitching together new bodily relations under the influence of his Ilse Koch book, there is in Dahmer's case of zombie enslavement of one-night stands a residual WWII reception in all that the Death Star represents.

In both *Halloween 2* and the 1979 novelization by Curtis Richards, metaphysical placeholders prop up a frame in which the evil nature of MM can be seen to pass through him from the prehistory of Halloween, which lies in the Celtic festival of Samhain. I've been advised the term is pronounced 'sow-in' (isn't it just like a dead language not to take any lip). Samhain occupied the borderline between harvest and winter, life and death. Crops and animals and, on special occasions, humans were sacrificed to the Celtic deities in great bonfires. *The Wicker Man* (1973) shows a local restaging of the Celtic ritual-burning of sacrificial victims. Richards' novel also places the beginning of the psycho violence in Celtic times: Enda is a tortured misfit (or adolescent) in love with Deirdre. When he tries to get close she screams 'Rape!' and calls him 'monster'. 'Enda's body had been deformed at birth, but not until that moment had his soul been deformed' (1979: 4). At Deirdre's wedding Enda slashes Barbie and Ken. Now it's the tribe's turn to exact vengeance. Enda's remains are trashed, not buried, and an extra curse is pronounced upon his spirit: till the end of time he must relive his crime and his punishment.

In *Halloween 2* Dr. Loomis balances accounts when he admits: 'Samhain isn't goblins or witches: it's the unconscious mind.' But at the same time, on balance: 'He was my patient for fifteen years. I was obsessed with him until I realised there was nothing in him, no conscience, nothing that was human.' According to Denis Duclos, we make the connection between Celtic prehistory and the family packaging of schizophrenia by dint of mass culture, which replaces a more direct or pure hit of Nordic cultural influence with the sale of Halloween paraphernalia, including 'plastic pumpkins shaped like scooped-out heads', each visited by 'a ghost whose mind continues to illuminate an empty skull' (1998: 150).

In *Halloween* Annie can't see her jerko boyfriend that night because he was grounded for his mischief the night before. While the celebration of Halloween was still reserved in the 1970s for costumed children who collected candy at every door in the neighbourhood upon crying out 'Trick or Treat', on the evening before, 'Mischief Night', older children and teens were unofficially free to soap windows and wrap the scenery in toilet paper. But the police were on the alert for the regular excesses in mischief that amounted to delinquent or antisocial behaviour. By some point in the 1980s, the Californian introduction of party night for teens on Halloween was beginning to go global, while the circulation of trick-or-treating children came under restrictions owing to incidents of psychopathic violence. Broken glass or razor blades in apples and poisoned candy had been handed out to the children under the mask of anonymity. The children were henceforth led by chaperones to visit only addresses of relatives or family friends (an itinerary that could be reconstructed in the event of crime).

The working title of *Scary Movie* (2000) set up two couples at either end of its span of horror, the first in recovery, recovery of momentum in reflection, the other for ignition, the intervention that led us to therapy: 'Last Summer I Screamed Because Halloween Fell on Friday the Thirteenth.' Between the date marks of their prehistories, 1963 (which is also the date in film history of the first film reference to the shower scene) and 1958 or 1957, *Halloween* and *Friday the 13th* have the origin of the *Psycho* Effect covered.

Friday the 13th, the slasher franchise that was the parallel universal of *Halloween*'s re-opening of the *Psycho* Effect under therapeutic conditions, also had to begin again before it could go serial. Parts 2, 3 and 4 are the first films in this genre to be designed for serial continuation of a story that, as in the *Halloween* franchise, lies between the first two films. Each sequel opens with extended montages from the earlier films. Do these openers remind the viewer of the story up to that point now to be continued or does the flashback to the earlier shocker get the audience into the mood for the next fix?

Jason is the undead killer only by *Friday the 13th 2* (1981). The first time around Jason's mother was killing the summer camp counsellors whose predecessors had once left her son unsupervised to drown. We hear Jason's commands and voice passing through his mother who also in her own voice speaks for him. 'What monster could have done this? A young boy drowned. The counsellors weren't paying attention. Jason should have been watched. Today is Jason's birthday. You never paid attention.' That the teenage girl counsellor gets to destroy the mother who slaps her around is another kind of payoff. It is typical for this series that whatever problem is addressed it is supplemented by a specifically teen issue, like this agon between mother and daughter. Though we don't look through the eyes of the dyadic dead end, this reversal of the encryptment in *Psycho* binding mother and son can only support one projection. A mother deranged by the loss of her son is a tragic figure whose pageant doesn't bear repeating. The norm or Norman for the serialisation of undeath requires that a son sacrifice substitutes to the preserved loss of mother. Jason materialises out of his watery grave between films, coming back in time to have witnessed his mother's beheading, the scene he has eternalised for the sequels.

In *Friday the 13th 2* one of the camp counsellors is studying to be a child psychologist. When she finds herself cornered in Jason's very lair, she recognises the significance of the mangy head on the altar – and knows how to use it to contain the violence. She puts on an oversize sweater and stands lined up with the mother's severed head, which she, now the talking head of 'no' and 'good', replaces. When Jason enters she presents herself as the animated version of his dead mother. Like an animal or like MM, he tilts his head to follow what otherwise takes him by surprise. He does obey until the mother's head comes back into view and he sees through the counsellor's transference interpretation.

Friday the 13th brought back the splatter films that *Halloween* largely elided. The new structure of serialisation supported the polymorphous eclecticism of its effects through which all aspects of psycho horror could be represented as available at once. As in Lewis's films, we pass from one special-effects staging of murder to the next one. The difference is that in the meantime a psycho horror genre had emerged with its own recent past, a concise history of repression and representation. There are also explicit references to the *Schauer* scene, in and around the shower stall, with a pronounced predilection for showing victims-to-be on the outhouse toilet. But it doesn't stop there. Every citational prop from psycho horror cinema is another station in which a therapeutic dynamic tests the allegiances to the couple and to the group which the adolescent must integrate. Thus the shower scene in *Friday the 13th 3* (1982) runs (with the giveaway music playing in the background) on empty: how the violence is administered around and outside the citational frame underscores the displacement of the mother-and-child *Schauer* by the foregrounding of an adolescent dynamic.

That the psycho killer attained mascot status in the *Halloween* and the *Friday the 13th* series owes something to the qualitative change in the status of survival in each franchise. That MM proves unstoppable also guarantees that Laurie's survival remains uncompromised by killing and rests on its own merits rather than in doubling relationship to the agent of psycho killing. The 'supernatural' status of MM, Jason Voorhees, and Freddy Krueger underscores each figure's intrapsychic significance both in tandem with the psychic revaluation of the survivor and as group mascot.

In his 1963 essay 'Struggling through the Doldrums' Winnicott gives the postwar purview. With the atom bomb, total war was suddenly totally out of the question and equation. The discipline imposed upon teens in preparation for the ventilation of violence in warfare was therefore no longer a motivated functional part of society. Taken together with contraception postwar adolescence contained itself as the site or medium of sex and violence in our society. 'Adolescence now has to contain itself, to contain itself in a way it has never had to do before, and we have to reckon that adolescence has pretty violent potential' (2000: 151). 'So adolescence has come to stay, and along with it the violence and sex that is inherent in it' (ibid.).

Group or adolescent psychology is binding only for the time being. Because the teen struggles to feel, be, and keep it real he can't compromise (for example via acceptance of the parental inheritance and the traditions passing through it). Instead he starts 'from scratch, ignoring all that has been worked out in the past history of our culture. Adolescents can be seen struggling to start again as if they had nothing they could take over from anyone. They can be seen to be forming groups on the basis of minor uniformities, and on the basis of some sort of group appearance which belongs to locality and to age' (2000: 152).

Sex gets him into this corner, the only safe place between the parental and the futural couples. Certainly the group dynamic is, in terms of recognition values, cursory, consumerist and volatile. Attack from without alone gives coherency to adolescent group psychology. What I prefer to refer to as 'groups-of-one' Winnicott terms 'isolates' who 'form an aggregate through the adoption of mutual ideas, ideals, and ways of dressing and living' (2000: 147). But: the group 'has no dynamic from within.' Instead, 'it is as if they can become grouped' (ibid.). As if!

In the absence of external stimulation, Winnicott emphasises that what keeps the group going is the ability of the members to economise with symptoms on a sliding scale of psychopathology. Teen traits range from psychotic symptoms to normal deceptiveness and self-deception. 'From this it follows that in a group of adolescents the various extreme tendencies tend to be represented by the more ill members of the group' (2000: 153). The teen group members rely on the identified patient or scapegoat, whose acting out, which exceeds what individual group members may be willing or able to do, receives the support of those who, thus, feel real and coherent. Over time – in its passage lies the cure for normal adolescence – the teen admits that compromise is allowable and thus begins to discover ways in which 'the relentlessness of essential truth can be softened' (2000: 151). When it becomes possible again, identification with the parents is Winnicott's chief example of a compromise or truth softener that helps the teen grow out of the doldrums of feeling futile.

Friday the 13th sets up the tension span between group and couple in a completely age appropriate manner. The teens working at the summer camp give themselves group licence. In syndication with the group psychology internal/external to the movie-going 'group' in the theatre a kind of group therapy was set in motion. The laughing recognition that 'in a slasher movie' the decision to play strip monopoly or to screw upstairs is to ask for elimination pays lip service to the superego which the teen doesn't in fact heed. At the same time the laugh track through the slaughter lubes the ultimate release of two more group members for coupling. *Halloween*, which alternated with *Friday the 13th* in the production of therapeutic effects, showed coupling at the more advanced stage of dating. Laurie is the girl who is maid to marry; she is the guarantor that the couple bond will fold out of the in-group of best friends.

Like *Halloween*, *Friday the 13th* is associated with a date of ill or good luck (trick or treat) at the busy intersection between pagan and Christian belief systems. The film or series of films began with speculation that 'Friday the 13th' was the next title and frame for another psycho horror projection along the lines of *Halloween*. That's all director Cunningham had, but placed in an ad it was enough to obtain funding. By the time the film was completed it was the first psycho horror film to be distributed by a major Hollywood studio. One option for the series of films (which was implemented for the TV series) was to present different horror scenarios connected by the uncanny date mark alone. The ill-fated *Halloween III: Season of the Witch* (1982) responded to a similarly open-ended plan of completely new horror variations based on Halloween-related material. The *Friday the 13th* franchise pursued a greater narrative throughout, with each sequel re-starting the story from scratch. Since *Halloween* it was possible for the dead killer to come back without forfeiting the psycho horror focus on survival. As in the game of 'exquisite corpse' each new director took the story at the fold of Jason's death and added a continuation unto the next fold.

The openness to all aspects of psycho horror in the recent past, a commitment to the conventions of horror that made room for the new group therapeutic momentum, also brought to each film in the series its exhibition value as demo for yet another technical innovation. The first film demonstrated a new portable camera which, for the duration that POV was being projected, could convincingly track scenes or shots from a running start and as ongoing, even for long periods, without all the machinery of major motion-picture cameras on train tracks. The mystery POV masks but without asking for unmasking. When the mother steps into view we didn't know that she was behind the POV. Although the killings proceed swiftly enough, through the mystery POV more and more time is won for suspense.

In *Friday the 13th 3*, which was the first psycho horror film shot in 3D, the literally eye-popping effects, which keep the new camera technique in the foreground, punctuate and promote the suspense without the more lasting psychic effect of the focus on eyes in Hitchcock, Powell or Hooper. This was also the first in the series to take up the side issue of integration of the loser within the teen dynamic between group and couple.

Shelley does not share the look of adolescence, the image in 'assimilation' that TV was still getting across. He opts for being the group clown or 'jerk' rather than the 'nothing' he claims he sees in the eyes of his date. When he walks off against the date's protestation that he's overreacting – or that he is retraumatising himself by the jerk defence he has adopted to exercise control over his outsider status – she looks inside the wallet he left behind and we see the photo portrait inside of his parents. She nods with recognition. Every teenager carries an internalised image of the couple that gets in the way. But what Shelley also leaves behind is the ice hockey mask he put on to give her a scare. After he murders the date, Jason picks up the mask that, after the fact, was his iconic accessory.

Into the niche market of the outsider a child enters the serial narrative by the fourth film. Tommy, around ten years old, is young enough to pursue a fright hobby, in particular the fabrication of horror masks, without being a jerk. He is an outsider, but only because he is the only child in the teen group portrait. Although he is not enrolled in camp he is the age of the kids the teens supervise for a summer, the age of Jason, for example, at the time of his death by neglect. (That he couldn't swim also refers to his mother's neglect.) At the end of the film, Tommy rises to the occasion of survival via his identification with Jason for which his hobbyist preoccupation with monsters prepared him. Like the child counsellor in training in the second film, he takes a psychodramatic approach. Based on the composite sketch of young Jason from the papers he models his transformation into Jason's double from trauma past. He stuns the psycho killer and then goes in for an overkill that is the overdose of his identificatory doubling. But out of this proximity a new outlet for group identification was projected. When he decided to check on audience response in a large New York theatre, the director (as recorded in the extra documentary material on the DVD) witnessed the entire audience at the instant the screen fades to white, the signal that Tommy's destruction of Jason is complete, jump up, yell, celebrate, even embrace the ones they were with. In one moment the identification with Jason (via Tommy) is the same as the identification with survival. We contemplate the mask from both sides now.

2

Roland Kuhn, who led us into the material underworld of the psychopath in the environs of *Martin*, wrote a book on interpretations of Rorschach test blots as masks. Kuhn's starting point is the atmosphere of metamorphosis that attends occasions for masking, like during Carnival. In consideration of the mask as interpersonal relationship – as 'taking someone at one's mask' (1954: 138) – Kuhn tracks to the word not taken a masked mode of interaction that in another lexicon might be considered psychopathic. In the mask relationship the outside or surface becomes the 'weak point' that one covers up. To take one at one's mask, therefore, is to take one at one's weak point. If you take the other at his mask you must expect the same treatment. Thus you oscillate between the desire to hide from the other and the need to get past the other's mask. The mode of this interpersonal relationship is that of mutual influence while the underlying experience is experimental, skilled, calculating. Ideally, taking one at one's mask belongs to a one-time encounter somewhere and some time.

With the mask you are in the momentary 'situation of the task', in which action alone counts, without consideration of past, future, or of any relationality at all. The norm stops where one is unable to modify how one takes the other to fit the given interpersonal situation. This can be observed in the 'morally defective' (1954: 139). The treating clinician takes the patient at his word while the patient can't stop taking the doctor at his weak point. The clinician who proved inflexible with regard to his form of address will be surprised to find the same patient, whose affective rapport seemed nil, displaying excellent affective relations with his 'brothers in deception' back in the ward. It is the clash between the two modes of relation that produces the sense that the one who responds by taking the other at his weak point is deceptive. If the brothers in deception didn't have the ward community as their support, only prison and the military would be suitable habitats in which their take would be a welcome attitude that fits right in (1954: 140).

If identity and unity seem suspended through or leading up to assumption of the mask, then there is a temporal suspension as well, whether withdrawal of the relationship between past and present or affliction besetting the structure of the present itself. What has been interrupted around the assumption of the mask is the continuity of the inner experience of time. The moment of disunity and discontinuity includes, therefore, a past content, which no longer counts, and a new content, which is not yet significant. The mask bans and binds this moment, granting it duration. Masked existence can ride the break in continuity like the break of a wave; it is existence on the edge, like in the wake of 'shipwreck' (1954: 142).

While the assumption of the mask blurs the responsibility and the historical sense of the individual, the mask itself threatens and punishes. The interface between assumption of the mask and its contemplation from without seems to invoke opposites: on the inside optimistic, though tending towards a manic flight of ideas; from the outside bizarre, grotesque and gruesome. At the same time both sides are brought together in close proximity. Can a lack of inhibition without a care in the world be the verso of the horror instilled by the threat of loss of existence? Both sides exhibit a similar relationship to historical development in time. The easy assumption of masks, like hysterical switching of identities or roles, suggests acceptance of death. At the same time death is just another role. If the idea of death seems overvalued, since ever present, then it also need not be taken more seriously than any other function of life. Death is but the continuity of immobility in the inner experience of time. I can't die. I am already dead (1954: 135–6). One can even take on the role of Death in life and establish, 'experimentally', the extent to which Death has being just like life (1954: 136). But it is to this end that one needs to transform oneself by assuming the mask.

The mask is key to Elias Canetti's understanding of transformation across species, 'becoming animal' avant la lettre. Transformation skewers survival upon killing. Canetti assigns the structuring of survival to the packs of prehistory. All the packs are on a dis-continuum of transformation from one into the other. In the primeval hunting pack primal man no doubt 'incorporated into himself, *by transformations*, all the animals he knew' (1988: 108). Without transformation into animals man would never have learned how to feed himself. The presentiments whereby 'primitive peoples' can recognise the approach of an animal are initial signs or residues of transformations (1988: 340). Imitation 'is nothing but a first step in the direction of transformation, a movement which immediately stops short' (1988: 370). The mask (like the death mask Leatherface rips off what's for dinner) is one of the stations in the process of transformation. Masking fixes transformation in place or face: 'it is a *conclusion*; into it flows all the ferment of the as yet unclear and uncompleted metamorphoses which the natural human face so miraculously expresses, and there it ends' (1988: 375).

The survivor is 'mankind's worst evil, its curse and perhaps its doom' (1988: 468). Everyone survives the ones who didn't survive. The survivor survives (by) killing. From the survivor's perspective, everyone else is as if dead while the survivor himself remains in a position to kill anyone at all. Like Macbeth, the survivor longs for 'the forest of his fears' to be thinned.

Survival is by command. Commands are older than speech, which is why dogs, for example, obey them and are ready for them. The addition of food as reward to the communication of the command domesticates the command, but doesn't alter its original significance. The original command results in flight, which is the final and only appeal against a death sentence (1988: 303–4). The collective fear of a herd of animals in flight is the oldest example of a crowd state, in which the origin of sacrifice lies (1988: 309). When the lion downs one gazelle, the rest of the herd can relax. Only the pack of lamenting or mourning offers a stay to murderous survival – but only until the next transformation jettisons it into another formation entirely. First there is the rush toward the dying man around whom the mourning pack gathers 'midway between life and death' (1988: 107). But then, once he's dead, there is the flight away from the man and everything associated with him (anything he touched).

Canetti's *Crowds and Power* was published the *Psycho* year of 1960. Without the translation of structuralism, the clearing within which we are given to think, the book is almost impossible to 'use'. The book concludes with a portrait of the paranoid-schizophrenic Schreber, in the setting of his delusional system, as of the same kind or kin as Hitler. Sometimes a political reading of paranoia is a paranoid reading of politics. My point doesn't take away from the importance of this document, which relentlessly pursues the themes of the *Psycho* Effect. I like that it's not user friendly. However, to make room for a transition in the therapy folding out of the Effect, allow me to make a few adjustments. Canetti's conclusion that unmasking undoes transformation, in fact counts as its 'opposite' (1988: 378), seems lost when he applies it to the paranoid tyrant, who must control all spontaneous transformation in others. The perpetrator of unmasking 'always knows exactly what he will find. He goes for it with a terrible assurance, despising all the metamorphoses he penetrates as irrelevancies' (ibid.).

Canetti's exploration of the condemned site of survival implies that transformation, in its ensemble of stations, stopovers and fixities, is the primal source of our adaptation to violence. Unmasking, as Canetti applies it, is just another kind of mask, a rigid conclusion drawn from transformation, one that touches transformation's historical line: the survivor's enforced adaptation to violence. Instead I would loop Kuhn through Canetti and allow that the mask in your face confronts you with a survival that is yours for the unmasking.

3

Before MM began his slasher career at the start of *Halloween* we joined him in flashing on and taking in the empty rooms of the house. But it was the survey of the hunter preparing to strike down his prey. Is Laurie (like Sally in *The Texas Chainsaw Massacre*) chained to what she saw, confined by MM's POV? No. There is a qualitative difference between the psycho's scanning of the vacant rooms and Laurie's revisiting the empty stations of her concluded struggle at the movie's close.

When Laurie tore off MM's mask she established another POV inside the film that is external to and remains outside the murderously superimposed POV. She delivered herself and us from that destinal camera that in 1960 swooped down from the heavens over Phoenix to fix a focus on Marion Crane and which was already always slashing, from the opening titles to the hotel's Venetian blinds. While the violence was underway, Laurie crouched helpless in the corner of the closet: the light coming through the louvre doors carried forward those same slashing lines of the *Psycho* Effect to which MM next applied his knife.

Early on in this study we consulted Winnicott on the precarious lodging of the psyche in the body as preliminary to the integration of the vampire. In the case study central to 'Mind and Its Relation to the Psyche-Soma' Winnicott addresses the mind in the proto-cryptological setting of his distinction between true and false selves as a pathogenic mask that must give way, in a span of not knowing, to transformation, indeed to the transvaluation of survival.

At some point, only the false self knows best or for sure. The patient in this case example is a head-banging psycho. '"Knowing" became transformed into "the analyst knows". The patient's whole life had been built up around mental functioning which had become falsely the place (in the head) from which she lived, and her life which had rightly seemed to her false had been developed out of this mental functioning' (1992: 250).

The mental functioning Winnicott is analysing begins, according to his theoretical construct, at birth in the bifurcation of memory with which we're familiar via Freud via Benjamin. There is given already at birth the capacity for 'memorizing or cataloguing' (1992: 248) whereby impingements that demand excessive reactions can be recorded exactly and in the correct order. This protective self-storage unit could not but commence collecting stimuli; yet its type of mental functioning is an encumbrance on the individual's continuity of being, which is constitutive of the self: 'this cataloguing type of mental functioning acts like a foreign body if it is associated with environmental adaptive failure that is beyond understanding or prediction' (ibid.). In analysis this record, say of the birth experience, can play in that linear fashion also characteristic of the client 'filling in' the analyst on his or her week. In the psychopathic as distinct from the neurotic session, less resistance and aggression against or desire to be with and inhabit the analyst means more testing for failure and objective hatred. But now the foreign-body recording, which, like acting out, informed the patient 'of the bit of psychic reality which was difficult to get at at the moment, but of which the patient so acutely needed to become aware' (1992: 249), can be turned into remembering-to-forget.

In 'Birth Memories, Birth Trauma, and Anxiety', Winnicott emphasizes that the very linearity of the record insures that the patient can deal with one impingement, experience, or reaction at a time (since two or more factors spell confusion). 'The ego effort which I have described is an attempt to hold the impingements at bay by mental activity, so that the reactions to them can be allowed one at a time and without disruption of the psyche' (1992: 192). Winnicott already underscored (indeed italicised) the down side, at least in the long run, namely that the intellect can, in relation to '*the border-line of intolerable reaction phases*', begin to work '*as something distinct from the psyche*' (1992: 191).

> It is as if the intellect collects together the impingements to which there had to be reaction, and holds them in exact detail and sequence, in this way protecting the psyche until there is a return of the continuing-to-exist state. In a rather more traumatic situation the intellect develops excessively and can even seem to become more important than the psyche, and subsequent to birth the intellect can continue to expect and even to go out to meet persecutions so as to collect them and hold them, still with the aim of preserving the psyche. The value of this defence is shown when the individual ultimately comes to analysis, for in the analytic setting we find that carefully collected primary persecutions can be remembered. Then, at long last, the patient can afford to forget them. (1992: 191–2)

We return to the patient who came to analysis to lose her mind. In this case, which Winnicott presents at length in 'Mind and Its Relation to the Psyche-Soma', the turning point of not-knowing arrived with the memory of a bird that was still except for the movements of breathing. 'In other words, the patient had reached, at 47 years, the state in which physiological functioning in general constitutes living. The psychical elaboration of this could follow. This psychical elaboration of physiological functioning is quite different from the intellectual work which so easily becomes artificially a thing in itself and falsely a place where the psyche can lodge' (1992: 251). The bird in the 'and' refers to that early foundational experience of merger with the mother that gave way too soon to the relationship to the other who doesn't answer. The totemic relationship in this emplacement is to the early mother.

In the film *The Cell* (2000), the intrapsychic scanner that allows the therapist to jumpstart coma patients can be aimed at the comatose serial killer in order to obtain the whereabouts of his latest captured victim, whose impending death is on a timer. She's back in primal time with the psycho killer as a little boy, who was a victim of nonstop paternal abuse. But when she witnesses him putting a wounded bird out of its misery she faces the untreatability of the psycho. In the end she does for the psycho's good part what the boy did for the bird.

The absence of the early mother (or the bird) is symptomatised in the household of *The Texas Chainsaw Massacre* as cannibalism. Through relations with the totemic animals we keep as pets we give ourselves booster shots of mirroring, waiting, immediate answering, the whole primal maternal deal that makes life real. In Hitchcock's *Psycho* the only place left for absence is crowded with mummified animals that stare like the camera ready to swoop down with the 'crane'. A camera POV in Hitchcock's 'sequel' *The Birds* (1963), which is perched on high, looks down upon the playground but then surrenders all comfort and respite when birds crossing the peripheral vision indicate the multitude that has in the meantime gathered in hovering flight for the next attack. Critics have made the association between *The Birds* and *Night of the Living Dead*. Indeed both start out from the unsupportable loss of the father, which discounts the mother, whose messages are throwaway, lost in transmission.

In *Halloween* MM (like Leatherface in *The Texas Chainsaw Massacre* and like the masked killers who imitate them in *Scream*) exhibits pet traits within the disarray of his compulsion to cut and kill. He shows the startle response that allows the animal to test and increase intelligence in the course of restarting from scratch to re-secure the environment as tested.

He's curious about his quarry, unprepared to follow the evidence of the lapse into lifelessness he's brought about. That a corpse is left behind is the consequence he is only preparing to face. In the end we discover that he has improvised a burial for one victim by laying her out in front of a gravestone he stole from the cemetery (though the other two are stashed to clear away his tracks in the field of hunting). MM stops short of eating the dead though he still inhabits the register of hunting at the border between animal and human where the line is drawn that he is only beginning to cross toward mourning (or unmourning). Unavailability in this regard refers to the break or 'error' in continuity installed prior to metabolisation of the mother's absence to vouchsafe her internal – eternal – availability.

Laurie is not trapped inside the psycho's hunting and haunting preserve because she is constructed in proximity to the good object. The cinematic profiling of the psycho killer includes as much evidence of destroyed but preserved relations with animals as of absent mothers whose disconnection would be preserved in the cuts of murder. A good babysitter, like a pet, and Laurie is a teacher's pet, is not a substitute. Laurie performs an answering service (in the neighbourhood of missing mothers). What was in the beginning the experience of being answered, doesn't last long except via internalisation which the experiences we have with pet animals, for instance, protect and deepen. Except for the opening season of merger, without which we would have perished, we find that our fellow humans (unlike our pets) tend not to wait or answer. But this too can be borne thanks to the good object inside.

As Winnicott argues in 'The Depressive Position in Normal Emotional Development', only once the infant has his fill of internalisation of the mother is there room for her absence. Otherwise a false self or mask emerges to protect the core spontaneous self that still lends its momentum to the psychopath searching in the break for good provisions down the endless path of his continuity error.

MM is the primal figure of the original meaning of 'hope'. Another sense or service of hope is embodied by Laurie, who carries on the answering service of early relations. She excels at babysitting, the return of the setting of baby, in the trail of the mother's Oedipal absence or failure to answer. To be on call, to answer, is to make room for regression and give hope.

Not-knowing corresponds to a 'gap in consciousness', which Winnicott's head-banging patient at first viewed as the 'bottom of a pit, for instance, in which in the dark were all sorts of dead and dying bodies' ('Mind and Its Relation to the Psyche-Soma', 1992: 251). But the gap of not knowing appeared most clearly in the course of 'reliving processes belonging to the transference situation. The gap in continuity, which throughout the patient's life had been actively denied, now became something urgently sought' (ibid.). While the portrait of the psycho killer makes this cut, the analysis Winnicott describes must transform the desire for the long-denied gap in continuity into acceptance of the not-knowing state.

> The results of this bit of work led to a temporary phase in which there was no mind and no mental functioning. There had to be a temporary phase in which the breathing of her body was all. In this way the patient became able to accept the not-knowing condition because I was holding her and keeping a continuity by my own breathing, while she let go, gave in, knew nothing; it could not be any good, however, if I held her and maintained my own continuity of life if she were dead. What made my part operative was that I could see and hear her belly moving as she breathed (like the bird) and therefore I knew that she was alive. (1992: 252)

Is it possible to transpose onto the turf and terms of Winnicott's analysis the slasher movie or movement that beginning with *Halloween* allows for the figure of affirmed and answered survival alongside and beyond the figure of the cut? Yes. *Halloween* as a whole could be seen, then, as gesturing toward a therapeutic outcome that is ultimately imparted to and through Laurie: 'Now for the first time she was able to have a psyche, an entity of her own, a body that breathes and in addition the beginning of fantasy belonging to the breathing and other physiological functions' (ibid.). We help make this possible by witnessing that she's alive.

The Crowd and the Couple

In the 1982 remake of *Cat People*, Irena's alternative to metamorphosis lies in incest (as her brother Paul selfishly reveals to her). Otherwise sex turns her into a cat and, only once the cat has been satisfied, can she turn back into human form. That she can't run away from the two-part metabolism is the message and maternal legacy she receives from her brother in a dream (following her brother's death in cat form). Their parents were brother and sister, too. Paul's initial revelation and proposal, from which she flees, does clear up her inexplicable sympathy for the panther behind bars at the zoo. After mauling a prostitute the animal was captured by the police, who were aided by a team of zoologists, and interred at the zoo. Irena is compelled to be near the panther and so gets a job at the zoo's gift shop. She gets to know a couple of the zoologists who were involved in the panther's capture, Alice and Oliver. To know them is to wreck Alice's wedding plans.

A zookeeper gets too close to the panther's cage and his arm is torn out by the roots. Oliver decides to put the dangerous animal down but the panther escapes. Was the animal her brother? The splatter scene brought Irena's compulsive sympathies to a crisis point. Now she learns that it's not a compulsion but that she is in fact a werecat. Irena enters a sexually frustrating relationship with Oliver as alternative to her brother's proposed sexual containment, which is then withdrawn when he dies. Oliver recognises the truth in her sexual predicament when he performs the autopsy on the cat-brother: a human arm pops up out of the cut and the hybrid dissolves into ash. Irena has learned in the meantime that she can complete the sex act in human form. It's in the afterglow that she undergoes metamorphosis and takes her hunger to the next level. She decides to become what she is. She didn't have to ask Oliver twice to tie her down for sex. She is unable to satisfy the cat's desire to consume the object after consummation. She thus remains in cat form. Oliver, now attached to Alice, visits her in the zoo.

One candidate for precursor of the *Schauer* scene can be glimpsed in *The Seventh Victim* (1943), a clip from producer Val Lewton's workshop of horror cinema, in which special effects were improvised in the absence of the borrowed thunder of occult literacy. However, the film produced by Lewton that was noted most likely to succeed in suggesting horror and suspense with next to nothing but the film medium itself (potentiated through self-reflexivity) was Jacques Tourneur's 1942 *Cat People*.

In the 1940s when RKO Pictures opened up its own horror series (in competition with Universal) under producer/writer Lewton's direction, *King Kong* (1933) alone had been their horror film. A Big One, indeed. But RKO didn't have the rights to any of the well-known occult figures (Dracula, Frankenstein, and company). During the WWII years and in the absence of spotlights on occult mastery, Lewton became the 'Chillmaster' in deploying 'horror spots', spots based on nothing. 'If you make the screen dark enough, the mind's eye will read anything into it you want! We're great ones for dark patches' (in Bansak 1995: 140). In *Cat People* director Tourneur's fist supplied the panther's shadow bouncing around the famous indoor pool sequence. They say people were horrified but didn't know if they had seen the panther or what. The so-called bus technique was also introduced in *Cat People*. Alice's solitary walk through dark city streets gives rise to her sense of being stalked – by someone or something. The tension is on the rise with each alternating shot of darkness or light until an attacker seems to be closing in – and then with a screech and hiss the city bus pulls up short. We need a moment to recover but the driver, getting impatient, asks if she wants to get on. The editor remembers: 'The "bus" [was] an editing device I had invented by accident, or possibly by design. I put a big, solid sound of brakes on it, cutting it in at the decisive moment so that it knocked viewers out of their seats. This became the "bus", and we used the same principle in every film' (in Bansak 1995: 137).

But these devices could only mean that filmic processes had entered or reentered the viewer's psyche. No longer is our own deep-seated alternation between identification and projection reflected back to us (as in *Dracula* or *Frankenstein*) but we are now part of the program of projection as though we were inside the film – as though the film were inside us. The 'sharpness of the cutting' gives editing the murderous edge or sharpness of our own death wishes. The film medium admits by the shadow-play relay of self-reflection its intimate bond with horror. The vacancy of the pool scene, punctuated only by shadows and indistinct sounds, is the screen itself.

The internalisation of the cut of violence and derangement was a recurring feature in Lewton's productions. In *Bedlam* (1946) one of the inmates was hospitalised because he made drawings in sequence and bound them together into a kind of flip-book. With a light behind them, the flipped-out inventor imagines, the drawings could be projected onto a screen. In *The Seventh Victim*, one woman's search for her now idealised, now demonised sister passes through a satanic hush of suspicion or conspiracy. These dimmed and muffled conditions mediate the protagonist's shower scene: she is on the inside looking (with the camera) through the curtain at the outside figure who quietly and anonymously issues the warning not to proceed with the search.

Then there's *Isle of the Dead* (1945 – say it quickly and you'll hear it too: 'I love the dead'). Its cinematic self-reflection fits a scene of live burial. We know that the victim always feared that her cataleptic seizures would lead to this misplacement. She confided her fear to the doctor who, however, also succumbs to the epidemic, which, in the rapid turnover required to keep just ahead of its spread, promotes the conditions for her premature interment. When she's taken for dead, we stay behind with the camera waiting outside while the coffin is deposited inside the mausoleum. After cross-cutting to pass the time we rejoin the casket: now we hear her screaming, scratching, banging. Water drips onto the casket. In time she can shred the softened wood. But in the meantime she has turned into a raving psycho whose unseen murder spree concludes the film.

In *The Leopard Man* (1943) ex-college professor Galbraith is a part-time museum curator, part-time psycho killer, who seizes the opportunity of an actual panther's recent escape from a traveling circus to cover the tracks of his murders under the tread of the 'Leopard Man'. Kiki, who suspects Galbraith, pays him a visit to spring his entrapment. She says she wants to watch from his museum office the procession of ritual mourners (commemorating the massacre of Indians by the Spanish invaders). To see better she asks that he turn off the lights. The serial-murder suspect hesitates. Part of him knows what will be released in the darkness in close proximity to another defenceless bystander. The death wish would instantly be projected if they were to start watching the movie – of mourning.

When you peel away the occult figures of horror, the residual supernatural that's left is transformation, becoming animal. The totemic aspect is not always spelled out, but the mask/masque of metamorphosis attends acts of violence that go unsolved or serial in the crowd. In the Universal occult horror films, what the occult covered over was the psychology of the crowd or group, which defines itself in contrast to the couple. These occult horror films guided a beset couple toward a Happy End by reclaiming the interrupted wedding night. To this end the couple spent most of the screen time working through the horror symptom, the seduction by the leader (and the pack), always attended by an expert in the occult, at the same time an analyst figure.

In *Monster on the Campus* (1959) the terrifying touch of the unknown is first absorbed by the touching of students out on a date – and then amplified once the couple recognises that it is the touch of a phantom limb. In *Crowds and Power* Canetti opens with man's great fear of the touch of the unknown against a backdrop of man's desire to see and thus recognise or identify what is reaching towards him. But then he introduces the crowd: 'It is only in a crowd that man can become free of this fear of being touched. That is the only situation in which the fear changes into its opposite' (1988: 15). In the crowd all are equal and interchangeable: 'no distinctions count, not even that of sex. The man pressed against him is the same as himself. He feels him as he feels himself. Suddenly it is as though everything were happily in one and the same body' (1988: 15–16).

The *Psycho* Effect begins in the uncontainable environs of the touch of disconnection from the mother. As a treatment protocol it sought the safer haven of the closed crowd, which Canetti addresses as the place where 'the seemingly indispensable principle of growth has been replaced by something quite different: by repetition' (1988: 25). In a Church setting, which is his example but what follows should also apply to the theatre of film therapy, 'the faithful are gathered together at appointed places and times and are transported into a mild state of crowd feeling sufficient to impress itself on them without becoming dangerous, and to which they grow accustomed. Their feeling of unity is dispensed to them in doses and the continuance of the church depends on the rightness of the dosage' (ibid.).

2

As the sequel to *Cat People*, *The Curse of the Cat People* (1944) demonstrates, even to be a child in America means to be an immigrant haunted by the past and faced with the prospect of assimilation to a new team standard of athletic happiness. In *Cat People* it's the Americans versus recently arrived immigrants from the ideological battlefield of Europe where ghost was pitted against ghost. It's true: the European hallucinates and submits to phantoms. But the American fades away into the California of unchanging spontaneity. The American lives in a perpetual present of 'no problem'. Thus our leading man is named Oliver but goes by Ollie for short (the nickname is the protectively measured cutting into the name that initiates every American team player). Ollie sees himself simply as 'quite a nice fellow'.

The European has an unshakeable primal past but no personal past. The American past is personalised; in other words it can be proclaimed loudly. Ollie was never unhappy, not in childhood, school, at work. He's known neither unhappiness nor, he realises, love until his discovery of the European Irena.

The movie begins with Oliver's first meeting Irena at the zoo. She compulsively sketches the panther and tosses each attempt just short of the trashcan. Above the can the sign reads: No littering. That she can ignore the litter of the law attracts Ollie even as he picks up after her. 'Litter' also names the doubling cluster of animal babies attached to the maternal body. Ollie approaches her as a mother (ambiguity intended). He cares for her while she gives him warmth or life. The smell of her perfume is 'like something warm and living'. She says he is her first friend in America. Otherwise she loves the sounds of the zoo next door – and the dark ('it's friendly').

A month into the marriage they're still at an impasse with the touch that can go no further. Oliver: 'I've been trying to kid you out of it. It's not the stories; it's that you believe them. You need help.' Thus she goes to her first session with the psychiatrist, Dr. Judd, who puts her into a hypnotic state with a light shining on her face. It looks like she's being filmed. In *I Was a Teenage Werewolf* (1957) the scene of cinematic self-reflexivity on the couch illuminates the force of 'adaptation' that is upon the creaturely juvenile delinquent.

The pet kitten Ollie tried giving Irena didn't take to her, 'but the cat got along with Alice, the girl I work with'. Too much information. But then Alice really lets the cat out of the bag: she lets Irena know that she made the referral to the psychiatrist. Ollie told her all about the marital problems. 'Oliver, how can you discuss such intimate things?' 'Alice is such a good egg, you can tell her anything.' 'There are some things a woman doesn't want other women to know about.'

Though groupie Alice extols love to Ollie as the group plan of mutual 'understanding', she's not telling Ollie anything he didn't already know. Alice: 'I know what love is – understanding – no self-torture or self-doubt.' Like, have a nice day. 'Nothing can change us Ollie; that's what I think love is.' But how Oliver feels about Irena is different: 'I'm drawn to her – a warmth that pulls me – I have to watch her when she's in the room – I have to touch her when she's near.'

If we bracket out the hysteria and the projection of the cat, we see that Irena is the defender of the couple against the group bond of likeability, which Alice maintains. Alice, Ollie's 'just friend' and co-worker, responds to Ollie's praise of her as 'swell'. 'That's why I'm so dangerous – I'm the new type of other woman.'

Irena sadly recognises that she is the outsider among wives: 'they're happy; they make their husbands happy; they lead normal, happy lives.' But at the same time she's the only figure with a home address in the film. Alice lives at the YWCA, Dr. Judd in a hotel, Ollie's home or homelessness is a mystery. Yet Ollie, Alice, the zookeeper, Millie the waitress – they're all part of the common place, they fit in, they're average, happy and they're willing to reproduce or reduce themselves, as good eggs, to the oneness of the group.

Irena's problem, which Dr. Judd reports back to the group, is that she fears if she 'were to fall in love and if a lover were to kiss her, take her into his embrace, she would be driven by her own evil to kill him'. Irena decides against seeing the shrink after their first meeting: when he talks about the soul he means the mind, but there's nothing wrong with her mind.

Her 'psychic need to unleash violence on the world', as Dr. Judd puts it, responds to Alice's invasion of the couple. Alice is the paternal killjoy grafted onto an inimical group bond: three's a crowd. When the threesome visits an exhibition of model boats (Ollie and Alice are co-workers in ship design and construction) Oliver suggests that Irena go to another part of the museum after Alice points out that Irena seems bored.

'I like the little boats. Don't send me away.' But she's peer-pressured out of there. That friend-ship sailed without her. The pool scene follows.

Alice tells Dr. Judd that Irena is telling the truth. Twice now (the bus and pool scenes) Irena has stalked her in cat form. When she admits she's in love with Irena's husband, Dr. Judd remarks that Irena's fear is based on the past, Alice's on the present. Irena suffers from imagination, Alice from conscience. But Alice has her robe in shreds to show. Now she gives the doctor advice: 'I shouldn't advise you to see her alone.'

But after Dr. Judd 'reaches' Irena – he assures her that her 'hallucinations approach insanity', a dangerous state for which he could have her put away, and that therefore she must forget her past and 'lead a normal life' – Irena's declaration to Oliver that she's 'ready' is greeted with 'it's too late'. Now he's changed (back): he, like, loves Alice.

Irena's deep secret? Is it that her father succumbed to a mysterious death in the forest before her birth, for which her mother was held responsible and taunted by the village children as cat woman? Not only did the mother mate with her husband once, thus conceiving Irena, but she apparently ate him too. The missingness of the father that coincides with Irena's engenderment brought shame upon her mother, a shame in which she shared, bonding herself to her mother, her greatest love. When the exotic-looking Eastern European woman – the American men say she looks like a cat – passes Irena, who is just married, and tries to establish contact by recognising her as 'her sister', a certain maternal bond that does not admit men is being evoked. She keeps alive her bond of humiliation with her mother by not allowing herself to join in the normalcy of the couple while at the same time always keeping it in view as ultimately desirable. That it can't be realised is just another form of realisation of the exclusive bond with mother. Her cat fight is addressed to every effort that would triangulate her primal maternal relation. That she is in thrall to the pre-Oedipal mother is what originally attracted Ollie.

Dr. Judd thinks Irena's sexuality is held in check by the father's murder, and that the dagger of King John Irena keeps drawing is the strong sign of this repression. He goes for the quickie cure and starts turning her on. 'You see, I never believed your story. I'm not afraid of you.' But 'wild analysis' turns her into the cat. He stabs her before she finishes him off. Though wounded, Irena is still able to go to the zoo to release the panther – only to watch the animal get run over in the street (another murderous representation of intercourse). When the group finds her dead in front of the cage it gives its stamp of approval in lieu of commemoration: 'She never lied to us.'

In the open crowd, reproduction is the outside chance, but it's always already subsumed by the happening event of replication, doubling or identification. The closed crowd or group, by entrusting itself to a schedule whereby it can reassemble, leaves open the possibility of going out of itself on a date it must keep with couplification (if only in the form of the union in psychoanalytic therapy).

There are open and closed couples, too. Every coupling takes two for the time being outside the group. But the open couple is more closely aligned with the group bond that passes its torch to the low-maintenance flame of likeability between two pals. The closed couple, the substitution to end all substitution, reaches back to the original bond with mother.

Alice, the new-and-improved 'other woman', is the cheerleader of group happiness, uncomplicated mutual identification: that's what love is. What's in a nickname attracts Alice. Their couple remains open to group bonding. Irena always called him Oliver. Their closed couple encrypted the maternal touch that the group bond spreads thin. The open couple, which antedated Irena's arrival, was broken up by the outsider's touch (and perfume). The 1943 declaration of improvement in the other woman cannot but undergo further renovation. In 1987's *Fatal Attraction* she bore the nickname but in the meantime it was unisex: Alex.

3

Freud's understanding of the group bond is summarised in an appendix at the close of *Group Psychology and the Analysis of the Ego*. Freud compares how love and identification organise two groups, the military and the church. In the military formation a relationship of love is sustained outside the ranks of mutual admiration or identification. The commanding officer holds the place of ego ideal. The soldiers under his command, who identify with each other, love him but do not identify with him. Identification with one's superior in this setting is the stuff of farce (or indication of a developing psychosis). In the organization of the church, by contrast, the relationship to the ego ideal, the thing called love, is mixed up with identification.

> Every Christian loves Christ as his ideal and feels himself united with all other Christians by the tie of identification. But the Church requires more of him. He has also to identify himself with Christ and love all other Christians as Christ loved them. At both points, therefore, the church requires that the position of the libido which is given by group formation should be supplemented. Identification has to be added where object-choice has taken place, and object-love where there is identification. (1959: 134)

That's why the army (the 'army of one') is the healthier model because it still admits a distinction between love and identification. By pulling Ollie out of love and the closed couple and back into the group and the open couple, Alice would receive the church stampede of approval. Freud identified 'this further development in the distribution of libido in the group' as the factor underlying Christianity's 'claim to have reached a higher ethical level' (1959: 135). But the Christian Mass of mutual identification led to modern mass psychology, in which he also discerned the 'psychological poverty' besetting in his day, so he claimed, America.

Freud's crowd analysis is based on a conflict often misrepresented as lying between the individual and the group. For Freud there is no individual (except perhaps the primal father himself). Most often the so-called individual is a group-of-one. The tension that crosses the heart of the socius sparks between the couple and the group. When in adolescence a viable group bond develops, the teen can come into his own. Now he accepts his sexual license from the group, not from the parents who are too off-limits or out-of-it. But then coupling begins to rise up against the peer pressure to remain in-group. Since it has no reproducing plan of its own, the group cannot but entrust its future, however ambivalently, to the couples breaking away from group membership.

The teenager rebounds back and forth between extremes and short attention spans because the two segregated sides of parental identification – the mother, the father – must be mixed into the assimilated identity of the ego or group member. But according to Otto Kernberg in 'Love, the Couple, and the Group', the couple must 'overcome the Oedipal prohibitions separating sex from tenderness' (1980: 97). The perpetual adolescence of the group unceasingly infiltrates and erodes the couple's bond. Even so-called 'stable triangular relationships' (Kernberg 1980: 82) – which include excessive telephoning and the keeping of journals and scrapbooks – not only re-enact aspects of unresolved Oedipal conflict but, more to the point, represent, again, invasion of the couple by the group. Monogamy is not just the boring artefact and aftereffect of convention. Boredom is never the transparent sign of a repression doubled by social constraints. The boredom that weighs down the couple is a symptom of the repression of a pleasure which the social group finds suspicious. Since on its own it ever verges on its potential for destructiveness, the group requires the sexual love and futurity of the couple; but the group also regards the couple with the Oedipal and pre-Oedipal envy reserved for the secret prerogative of parents.

Kernberg allows that the group does provide protection via a controlled release of mutual aggression within the couple (in other words, before witnesses). If over-isolation of the couple leads to unwitnessed releases of hostility, the internal bonds guaranteeing the pleasure of couplification grow malignant – and the couple dissolves, again, within the group. Predominance of aggression and 'deterioration of internalized object relations and sexual enjoyment' (ibid.) follow from this absorption and reversal of the couple.

Enter Alex, who, as the 'other woman' in *Fatal Attraction*, is always also the mother, but in group-syndication as groupie. She acts out or denies the dread of being cut off within a terroristic rapport with the telephone. The suicide hotline was the first support group. According to R. J. Almansi's 'On Telephoning, Compulsive Telephoning, and Perverse Telephoning', when aggression, which 'plays a central role in neurotic and perverse telephoning', has gone down, it can go out again via the call since, at least with psychotic or borderline patients, 'the telephone can maintain some object ties at a bearable distance, providing separation without loss and contact without fusion' (1985: 222). Alongside this distance, American psychoanalysis stressed the more public phone appeal of projected (that is, edited) proximity: 'Finally, the telephone often makes it easier to counterfeit genuine object ties: Since the speaker is invisible, hypocritical words will not be betrayed by the expression on his face' (1985: 226). This is the call or connection Alex would receive and put through.

A fatal or 'instant' attraction is conveyed by a name that cuts both ways along a line of sexual difference which has already dotted the screen with confusion. We are given the line about sex or difference when the unisex aspect of the child Ellen is reflected in its counterpart, a pet's underside: father Dan, who has, on the diachronic or generational side, remained unsure of his daughter's exact age, must (on the synchronic or sexual side) first hold bunny up for inspection before pronouncing the corrected pronoun 'she'.

When the pet finally falls victim to Alex's vengefulness, it has already been absorbed within the series of attacks upon the couple which swells with Alex's pregnancy. After her parents return from their first run-in with Alex, Ellen joins them in bed and lies down between them on the night which was clearly 'the night'. The enigmatic force of Alex thus conveys a confusion or blockage inside the standard exchange of sexual identities vouchsafed by the couple. In the place of uncertainty and blockage – the place reserved for Alex – it is up to little Ellen to play the role of 'founding father'. (As in the school skit: 'Miles asked me to ask you to marry him.') The spectre of this child's abuse will ultimately hold the family ('that preys') together: it empowers the wife as delegate of father to kill off the monster that fascinates and paralyses Dan. If Dan assumes, like Victor Frankenstein or like the vampire hunters in Stoker's *Dracula*, that the wife is in some safety zone, and that the phantom aims to hit or miss only him (as when, after he hears that Alex cannot be located, he drives to the police station alone, leaving the wife unprotected) it is because only in this paranoid way can Dan re-enter relations with the father's delegate. He can only rescue or re-cathect the wife who has been abused – and libidinised. Thus the wife is able to shoot (and remain in) the picture: Dan's haunting by Alex is replaced by the family photo that shuts down the projection titled *Fatal Attraction*.

Alex is a perpetual adolescent at heart, a make-believer who invades and disrupts the couple as both groupie and leader of the matricentric pack. Alex enters Dan's primal scene at a defective point of hook-up between the paternal culture of transference and its maternal outlets. Dan's scene is that of a separation and divorce which the mother asks the son to witness and co-constitute: mother asks him, her lawyer-son, to represent her case against father in the divorce proceedings: 'You can't exactly turn your mother down.' But on his first date with Alex, Dan confides his perverse imitation of a paternal position: he told his mother that he didn't practice family law. Like an analyst (or rather like an impostor-patient who can imitate all the positions of his own analysis which he has divested of transference or turned into something like a TV set before which he 'acts out'), Alex asks, 'Are you discreet?' And the seduction or rather invasion begins – of the couple by the group.

But Dan had already attended divorce court, the primal performance of *Madame Butterfly*, featuring his bond with father. And on that one occasion (which, at this point in Dan's recall, begins to exceed recollection, returning no longer via culture, fiction or family law but hallucinatorily from the real) Dan's father was nice to him. Nice? The father thus maternalised through identification is a friend and Oedi-pal. But even this brand of identification results from joining the one you can't lick in the contest over the materiality or mortality of mother, which everyone must enter and lose. There is no first meeting for Dan and Alex. Too many others had already met.

> My father took me to the old Met. I was five years old. There was this U.S. sailor setting up house with this Japanese lady. That was all fine. But in the final act after he left her my father told me: she's going to kill herself. And I was terrified – I climbed under the chair. ... That's funny. That was the only time I remember my father being nice to me when I was a kid – comforting me at *Madame Butterfly*.

The missingness of the mother has been turned into a suicide known about in advance and thus remote-controlled by father, who binds up the trauma of his preview within nice or friendly relations.

Alex reenacts the scene, but this time permits Dan to reverse the mortal consequence of the father's inevitable knowledge. By reversing the suicide, Dan gives Alex life again. At this point one attempt to split the scene reanimates the other's scene, which will never be open to negotiation. After the one-night stand, Alex begins calling in demands that Dan will be unable to fulfill, just as he cannot fulfill the long-standing maternal demand to enter divorce court and remove the father inside him or alongside him ('the wife'). But this impasse follows and confirms rules of haunting dictated by the other scene. When on their second date Dan plays dead, Alex calls him dad.

But Alex, who's sensitive, doesn't like being made fun of. 'You bastard! My father died in front of my eyes. I was seven.' But then the death of the father (which Dan has in a sense caused) can be withdrawn; the cute impostor flips through all the channels: 'He's alive and well and living in Phoenix.' Loud as denial, Phoenix names the place of resurrection and slashing. From the kitchen and meat markets to the scrapbook with newspaper obituary clippings, Alex's orbit is crowded with refuse – refusal – of relations with the dead father.

Via two tickets to a performance of *Madame Butterfly*, Alex makes or plays the attempt to integrate their acting out within a commemorative and therapeutic repetition. But Dan has already retreated from culture, Europe, the father and the mother to his support group of friends. Dan goes native, becomes hyper-American, or undergoes 'culture shock', which Howard F. Stein argues is a variant of the inability to mourn.

> 'Culture shock' refers to the rekindling of unresolved attachments, separations, and losses, and leads to nativistic attempts to deny (if not reverse) painful losses by setting up symbolic objects which will repair the broken symbiosis by halting (or reversing) developmental and intergenerational time. (1985: 171).

In the era of TV, American psychoanalysis had already taken Dan's side. Samuel Atkin, for example, in 'Notes on Motivations for War', identified what was already underway, the replacement of love and war by friendship and suicide:

> Freud states that every individual is an enemy of culture, which is a heavy burden. For Freud, culture has an *otherness*, rather than an I-ness, or a Me-ness. May this not be the feeling of unreality, the remoteness from reality, that one encounters in many sensitive and often neurotic people? (1971: 572)

In the setting of the session 'patients who talk much about external environment and on social and cultural themes in their analytic hours' are on a borderline defence budget:

> They are narcissistic patients whose development has been arrested at the pregenital level and who suffer from narcissistic neurotic problems. Their relative failure to internalize their environment, and to synthesize their socially determined drives with their more discretely personal ones, leads to a blurring of the boundaries between what is perceived as the inner life and external reality. (1971: 578–9)

Dan declines Alex's offer to return to the *Madame Butterfly* scene they split between them. Alex remains alone at home listening to the record. Catatonic and cornered in an internal representation of the film, Alex flicks the lamp on and off. In between blinks we watch Dan's nativistic auto-therapy: he, his wife, and a couple of friends go bowling and exchange racist and sexist jokes. But the group leader, Alex, switches to the audio portion of her exclusion and issues the call: the phone rings, the wife gets it, no answer. When Dan runs for the cover of an unlisted number, Alex penetrates the home and meets the wife: 'I'll keep in touch.' Henceforth the camera registers the phone in the home as the site of the uncanny. Barring the transferential outlet of *Madame*

Butterfly, which Dan unplugged and Alex only acted out, one of them gets pregnant (*Fatal Attraction* rivals *Aliens* [1986] in the supermaternal combat that soon revs up) and the other gets the phone – at once umbilicus and stun gun (as advertised on TV).

In the era of TV, gadget goes to psychoanalysis. American patients who despised gadget love missed a paternal support system – against which they only wished to take better aim. Analyst Giovacchini, for example, discovered that his patients' dread of gadgets 'came to be a means of disguising, displacing, or controlling their death wishes toward their fathers' (1959: 335). Gadget love is the norm on which the family scene opening *Fatal Attraction* is modelled or set: television, headphones, telephone. The turn at the end of the film to pre-TV media technology (photography and, by extension, film) reinstalls a transferential household in the place of liveness, oneness and openness to which Alex owes admission. Cut off from the phone, Alex has been reduced ('This is what you've reduced me to') to a taped message. But as though even gadget love has to be circuited first through sublimation of homosexuality and incest, the message playing in the car alternates between news of 'part of' Dan 'growing' inside Alex and another special report: 'You're a cocksucking son of a bitch – fucking faggot.' This is where Dan stops the tape. But when he resumes playback at home, the faggot part is somehow replayed – but 'faggot' is missing. The media-technological (or the homosexual or the incestuous) enters as re-recording and erasure of the work of (endless, unacknowledged) mourning until only the identifications of group psychology can be discerned or followed.

The film rewinds around the group's (or Alex's) stranglehold on the couple until it winds free – and ends up wound-free. The photo-commemoration at the end rescues the couple within the work of mourning. The dead and separated parents have been put to rest. Ellen, the future to which the couple reduces itself, has replaced, in a space of narcissistic reflection, Alex, the double, the leader and the pack.

Getting into B-Pictures

The psychiatric settlement of the psycho's enigma in 1960 was reversed and preserved by the transference transgressions within the therapeutic response to horror in 1980. *Schizoid* (1980) reverses the progression of the psychiatrist's culpability within the span of what the film world refers to as a 'spoiler'. We are led to suspect that Dr. Fales is the psycho killer of the women in the therapy group he leads. The shrink is Kinsky, I mean he's kinky, against a background of really poor boundaries with his daughter. There's that incestuous strain in the composition of the mother's loss. 'You dressed like that when you were eight years old.' 'You haven't kissed me good night for a long time.' When she's not running around in her mother's clothes she listens in on sessions. Confidentiality is also breached by the group therapy member who's in it only for the research; she has a newspaper column to fill. The POV stalker kills three or four with scissors before we fill a blank that's buoyed up by numerous false leads. Dr. Fales is receiving cut-and-paste letters. We see his daughter making that kind of anonymous missive with scissors of her own. 'Whoever wrote this is obviously capable of murder!' Yes, she hates his clients because he was 'listening to them the night Mommy died'. When father confronts her with the epistolary evidence she makes his supposition the sign that he doesn't even know her. Besides: 'You don't need a gun to kill me. You're killing me anyway.' Columnist Julie maintains a hot line that soon doubles as supplement not only to the group dynamic but even to the work of detection. After everyone who's not dead yet has come under suspicion, it turns out that Julie's ex, who blames the group therapy for his loss of wife, is the faceless killer.

The hot lines passing through a psychologist's phone-in radio show organise another 1980 transference transgression: *Don't Answer the Phone!* It turns out a psycho bodybuilder in Los Angeles is obsessed with the local talk show hostess

Dr. Lindsay Gale. The film opens with the bodybuilder lifting weights in front of the mirror as preamble to a 'skit' in the style of Grand Guignol.

We're with a nurse who just got home and can't wait to get undressed. The phone rings and she's talking to her mother. The killer walks in unnoticed with a stocking over his head and just stands there waiting for her to turn around and notice. After he strangles her he rips apart the uniform she was already opening up and fondles her breasts.

This is as close as we get to the police-reported molestations we keep hearing about but really never see beyond this mother connection. For one thing we saw him kill her first. According to the police account of what we saw, the perp or perv 'kept her squirming for some time'. Then 'he bit off her breast and used every orifice'. Even the psychic consulted by the police 'sees' the killer strangle the victim as he enters her.

We're given different information for assembling his profile. When he's not laughing or crying while strangling another victim, psycho bodybuilder talks to his dad, asking if he's proud of his son now, asking if he measures up. (A tour of duty in Vietnam is also in his backpack.) The psycho bodybuilder takes pictures of the fresh cadavers in countless poses. Because he sells his art photography to the local porn store the policemen tracking him get their first clue.

In the time it takes for the police to search the store and identify him and his address, psycho bodybuilder skips the usual stalking and killing of Dr. Gale's patients and goes directly to her abode. When psycho ties her up she tries some other forms of binding on him: 'Why are you trying to make me afraid of you? What does it do to you? How does it make you feel?' Now he strikes out against doctors and parents and reaches the most regressed place when he recalls a little puppy. But just as he hits bottom, the restart position of his auto psycho analysis, the police arrive from their alternate recording of sex crimes to take control of all shooting in the film.

1

De Palma's 1973 film *Sisters* opened his season of interrogation of the *Psycho* Effect (also by double featuring *Peeping Tom*). This work of twinning also metabolized Ben as Marion, splatter as slasher. *The Phantom of the Paradise* and *Carrie* would follow as stations of the Effect's crossing. His mastery at close reading Hitchcock was first projected in *Sisters*, for which Bernard Herrmann, Hitchcock's composer for *Vertigo*, *Psycho* and *Marnie* (1964), scored the music.

When twins are Siamese often only one has the outside chance of survival under conditions of room enough only for one of us. The expendable twin is dead – but not inside the surviving twin. When there's no room for the absence of the double, the single survivor splits and takes over the duo dynamic where it left off – at the point of malignancy.

The opening sequence in *Sisters* that culminates in murder keeps in almost bawdy touch with *Peeping Tom*, *Night of the Living Dead* and, ultimately, *Psycho*. Now the killer is a woman under the protection of her psychiatrist, who loves her, or at least one of the two inhabiting her. If not medicated or otherwise restrained, Danielle will turn into Dominique, the evil or vengefully dead twin, who, at the end of the introductory remix of 1960s horror, slashes Phil, the fellow contestant Danielle took home with her from 'Peeping Toms', a TV game show.

But before psycho Dominique carves him up, Danielle's robe drops to one side and we witness a large patch of textured scarring on the side of her body. But what is it? Formally, musically it has been aligned with, announced as the cut. But this cut and stitch in time marks the physical separation of the twins and their psychic union on the side, on the inside. They are reunited in the slashing that follows over Phil's substitute body.

The film opens on television. In the show 'Peeping Toms', the studio audience must predict how the uninitiated contestant will respond to the scene of exhibitionism put on for his benefit. Recalling in the mode of farce the political coincidences surrounding Ben's sole survival or singular death in *Night of the Living Dead*, the contestant Phil happens to be African-American, which throws an uncomfortable fit with the show's title beyond the laugh track of voyeurism. Danielle, wearing Fellini sunglasses while playing the part of a blind woman, enters the locker room, in which Phil is changing, and starts to undress. What's Phil going to do? For being on the show Danielle receives a set of kitchen knives; Phil's prize is a night's pass for dinner and drinks at the club 'African Room'.

The trouble with Phil is that his corpse remains lodged in the convertible couch, the hideaway solution that the psychiatrist improvised for his patient's protection. Her neighbour, an investigative reporter, alerted the cops that from her rear window she witnessed a 'race murder'. Abandoned or awaiting another leg of its journey, the convertible crypt rests on the platform of an outpost train stop. On the telephone pole across the way the detective, who was hired by the reporter to follow this lead, keeps his binoculars trained on it. That's 'The End'.

But first the reporter was discovered at the asylum on the trail of the murder the police abandoned for lack of evidence. When she entered under cover she tried to place a phone call and triggered the fit of an asylum patient whose life's mission is to keep the telephone sanitised. The telephone wires transmit diseases and, indeed, made her sick, too. Then the psychiatrist arrives and advises the orderly to take the new patient to her room.

In an art cinema setting, *Sisters* journeys internally, in black and white, through the recent history both of the twins and of film, including a stopover in *The Cabinet of*

Dr. Caligari (1920). The psychiatrist, the mad scientist of this asylum and film, wants to deliver Danielle from a whole phantasmagoria of influence. Through hypnosis he sends her on a memorial tour asking her each time to remember. After she has been given the post-hypnotic suggestion that her original charge as eyewitness was bogus, the reporter is placed alongside Danielle and becomes in the internal film's scenes the Dominque to be remembered and let go. The psychiatrist hopes that remembering will stop the split Danielle undergoes each time she is turned on sexually and Dominique takes over vengefully. While professing his love for her, caressing and fondling her, he asks her to remember that she, not Dominique, killed Phil. But she has already turned into Dominique who again jabs the knife, this time into the psychiatrist's groin. Now that the psychiatrist is dead and the asylum cover cannot be sustained Danielle is taken away and the reporter rescued. But when the police, with her own mother in attendance, reassure her that they now believe and support her, she cannot give them the testimony. All she can pronounce is the hypno-withdrawal of her complaint.

2

Dressed to Kill was a remake of *Psycho* that set out to reverse the legacy-transmission of victims and perpetrators 'addressed to kill'. What followed from this act of redress was a trilogy of films in which, in the subsequent entries, De Palma gave a B-picture treatment plan that drew on the therapeutic opening that *Halloween* had made possible.

In *Dressed to Kill* De Palma divides the Norman position between the psychiatrist, who is the figure of all splitting in this film, beginning with the cohabitant of his professional persona, Bobbi, the inner girl who makes and takes him over, and Peter, the son of the first victim, who is placed alongside the female witness inside a new niche market of survival. Kate as Marion starts out by taking back the knife of pleasure. *Dressed to Kill* opens with a shower scene that Kate enjoys as rough trade of the boring routine she gets from her husband for sexual fantasy. He's included in the fantasy scene as attractive standby while the wife masturbates in the shower. Then, still inside the stall, a stranger suddenly emerges and takes her from behind. When the fantasy is dropped we watch a scene from her everyday life: to start the day the husband pounds her and leaves her unsatisfied. Kate, like Marion Crane, is on her way out, but first she visits her psychiatrist, Dr. Elliott.

In *Sisters*, the psychiatrist used hypnosis to restore memory by implanting it, like film within film. But the hypno-therapy he applied ended up only re-triggering the split. Indeed, the one presentable malpractice charge that Schreber makes against his treating physician, Dr. Flechsig, was that he put his patient under hypnosis with disastrous results. It is at least the screen memory, Freud allows, for the origin of the sudden irruption of illicit thoughts uncontained by the transferential relationship, the transgression Freud considered the onset of the mega repression bringing on Schreber's break. In Richard Matheson's *A Stir of Echoes*, a party-favour demo of hypnosis, which a psychology grad student performs on her resistant brother-in-law Tom, opens him up to communication with the ghost of a woman murdered in the recent past and secretly buried in his building's crawl space. 'I even tried to tell myself I'd had a nightmare, that it really hadn't happened at all. Unfortunately, I knew better. I knew that something had happened to me that I'd never believed could happen to anyone. So simple to put the word itself down; all it takes is a few elementary turns of the pencil. Yet it can change your entire life. The word is ghost' (2004: 26).

But while this ghost's demand for justice is most pressing, the opening of Tom's psyche to the extrasensory is not limited release. He picks up the unconscious thoughts and wishes of everyone in the neighbourhood. He is thus thrown into the secret but all-pervasive mix of sex and violence. 'When Elsie was gone I sank down at the table and closed my eyes. I felt as if I'd just climbed out of a well. I tried to tell myself it was only imagination but that didn't work. Mind ran second again, poor competition for my emotions. I felt dazed and weakened. On the surface that was senseless. Elsie was quite ordinary, not very attractive. She'd never bothered me before. I'd always felt slightly amused by her antics. ... I almost felt afraid of her. And, no matter how I went about it, there was only one explanation. I'd seen behind her words, behind her actions. Somehow I'd been inside her mind' (2004: 37–8).

The film adaptation foregoes the inside viewing of sex and violence in the minds of innocent standbys and focuses exclusively on the ghost clue to a murder mystery. The byproduct of the posthypnotic command to open his mind is that Kevin Bacon suddenly sees a missing teenager sitting on the couch. What is installed or opened in his mind is the double of an inborn gift in his young son. When the boy talks out loud to the ghost of the murdered girl his babysitter flips out: she's the sister of the girl who's been missing for six months.

Of the two aspects of Tom's therapy-induced clairvoyance, foreign embodiment of ghost memories and traumatic sexualisation of the environment, the former is a match with *Sisters*, the latter with *Dressed to Kill*.

In that morning's session with Dr. Elliott, after recounting, first, dread of her mother's birthday visit, then that her husband 'stinks' in bed, Kate wonders whether the bad sex, like her inability to get along with her mother, might somehow be her fault. Dr. Elliott doesn't pursue the wound in the wondering and rushes instead to assure her that she's not to blame. How would he know? When she feels thus encouraged to ask the psychiatrist if he finds her attractive, if he doesn't want to sleep with her, he answers that he indeed finds her attractive but cannot act on her desirability simply because he is happily married. Wrong answer! This is where the horror begins. Dr. Elliott transgresses in and against the transference and its sublimation content and admits sexualisation checked only by contingency or hypocrisy.

This radical desublimation reflects the loss of respite and transition going through Dr. Elliott's two halves. It is Dr. Elliott himself, and not his so-called patient Bobbi, who is split between proper maleness and projected femaleness, a strict separation between one side that rejects the consequence of transsexual merger with the female identity, namely castration, and the other side (in drag) that administers the split as p-unitive by killing off the women Dr. Elliott desires. Without sublimation, there's only traumatic overstimulation or, quick split (signaled by the doctor glancing at himself in the mirror), repression carried out by merger/murder.

In *Dressed to Kill*, Kate takes the unsafety of the session along with her on a visit to the art museum, another sublimation rest stop, where she is beset by sexualisation along every line of sight. We watch her seated in contemplation of the paintings while writing on her note pad.

That she is jotting down not her art appreciation but a kind of shopping list is less a joke on her than the presentation of what is at stake. As she seeks to select and thus sort out inner and outer stimuli on her 'to do' list of social interaction, she finds in the very place where it should be given a rest that sexual stimulation everywhere impinges upon her. Soon she gets picked up and taken to his place. After the unprotected sex, she gets dressed again in the afterglow, but notices a paper trail leading to a diagnosis of venereal disease. She is beset by unprotection.

Before the slashing, Kate's ability to bear 'unattractive feelings' or 'feeling unattractive' was knocked out of her during the session with Dr. Elliott. In the elevator when she remembers the wedding band she took off and left behind up there, she reverses her downward course to go back and retrieve the ring. Like Marion before entering the *Schauer*, Kate initiates repair of what isn't really broke yet, hoping for a second chance. Not until *Body Double* (1984), the conclusion of the trilogy that *Dressed to Kill* opened, will the theme of second chance be put through unto a therapeutically happy end.

Bobbi, the psychiatrist when he's just a drag, is waiting at the next stop to turn on the *Schauer* in the elevator. Next stop a call girl, Liz, is ready to enter with her stockbroker client when he steps back horrified. (While waiting he gave her a tip of free counsel for a quick profit in his market.) Liz moves to help Kate as she lies dying and catches a glimpse in the security mirror of the psycho killer crouched in one corner. The elevator, a room with a mirror inside, moving up and down a series of floors or frames, reinstalls the shower scene inside the camera. This 1980 *Schauer* scene, already mediated by several takes on survival, transmits to Liz her delegation of Kate and Marion via technical and occult media. While making telepathic eye contact with the expiring Kate, Liz takes hold of Bobbi's razor, another mirror in the camera that caught her eye.

Sublimation is what is irretrievably destroyed at the breaking point of psychosis, according to Freud's reading of Schreber's *Memoirs*. The psychotic psychiatrist passes the loss of sublimation on to his patient like a curse or hot potato. Before the session with Dr. Elliott we witnessed between Kate and her son Peter another session, in which sublimation (or the transitional object) was transmitted intact. Peter has built a computer, which Kate identifies at once as his creation and as her gift. When Peter announces that his machine carries and holds, Kate repeats and affirms these admirable functions, which sound like carrying to term and holding the baby. But he must name his creation, Kate urges, just like Napoleon named the pastry after himself. When Peter protests her free association, she assures him that Napoleon had his feminine side, too. What Kate hands over to Peter counters aberrant mourning's under-the-counter transactions: the inheritance that both Peter and Liz, Kate's other legatee, carry out by the Oedipal work of detection. It is the frame given in the title *Dressed to Kill*. Before De Palma applied it, the title already belonged to three films of detection and under-cover investigation, including one starring Sherlock Holmes.

Bound to find her killer by the gadget love his mother raised to the power of naming, Peter gives Kate heir time: he keeps the terminal of patients, the shrink's office, under surveillance with a makeshift camera that is an internal simulacrum of the film. Gadget love allows Peter to meet the psycho killer half way – and keep him there. Gadget love also keeps Peter from turning into another Norman Bates.

His compatriot, sex worker Liz, models the rest stop and neutral hub that sublimation represents, which she uses for switching back and forth among interests and investments. She is a techno wizard in her own right who carries and holds (and forgets) in every sense that her mobile phone allows. She uses her own mother to cover up the connection between her sex work and her financial investing – which requires that she always have at least two lines open. Her sex work is not about over stimulation. She knows the value of respite.

The contrast with Dr. Elliott is provided by split screen: separately the doctor and Liz watch a TV talk show with a transsexual guest, who responds to questions about her prehistory as father of children: 'I've always been a devout heterosexual.' Dr. Elliott gives his mirror-image smile of approval. It looks like Dr. Elliott identifies the irony as fact. And that *is* the split. (I remember that the first talk show with transsexuals I watched on TV in Vienna in the late 1970s featured, unforgettably, a former young man, who, in becoming a young woman, discovered, his or her narcissism still intact, that she desired women.)

While Peter keeps watch outside the doctor's office, Liz plays the role of Dr. Elliott's new patient. Liz starts out by telling him a dream about a man with a razor who orders her to strip. We see that he begins to dissociate. She identifies her profession and tells him that she likes to turn men on. Dr. Elliott asks whether she ever has sex that isn't paid for. She promptly identifies his question as a proposition. She asks him, Are you attracted to me? Again he answers, Yes. When he looks at his mirror image, which the camera gives in close-up, we see the split before any change in costume.

Liz repeats Kate's session but with the difference that she sees through his protest that he is married and/or a doctor. She quips that among her clients she has had many married doctors. When she takes off her coat – she says it's getting warm – we see that she was wearing only lingerie underneath. She proposes that while she's off powdering her nose in the next room, he get comfortable. 'Look doc, I think you're kind of shy.' If she's wrong, they can get back to the 'mind fuck' upon her return. While she checks out his appointment book during their timeout, Dr. Elliott is getting into his Bobbi gear. When Liz reenters the office to meet not her shy client but the psycho killer, Peter hollers to let her go. This is the moment of impotence in gadget love; for all his surveillance mastery he can't intervene in what he sees. But then Bobbi is shot through the window by the officer appointed to follow and protect Liz, whose stint with Dr. Elliott was her voluntary under-cover assignment.

Survivor Liz remains unflappable at lunch with Peter. Their topic is sex change. 'How do you do that?' Matching her cool containment Peter feeds her the line that he is of course intrigued by the prospect of a new 'science project': building a woman out of his own body. As presented by Liz, the change is neither metaphysical mad science nor a gadget-loving supplement to sublimation. At lunch, to the horror of a woman at the next table, Liz spells out what would have to happen to Peter, namely removal of the testes and cutting the penis in halves to hold the approximation of a vagina. That he cannot recognise himself in the projected construction of woman out of castration is his mourning tribute to Kate.

After the two scenes of Liz's unchained survival, we witness the *Schauer* afflict her in a final dream that hides nothing from view and keeps her screaming. She knew to ask Peter if she could spend the night in his home. In Liz's dream we enter a Gothic horror-asylum, in which Dr. Elliott is a patient. Along the railing above inmates gather to cheer on Dr. Elliott attacking the nurse. Then we join Liz taking a shower. We are back inside the main film of glinting and mirroring metallic elements and edges. Liz recognises in the relay of reflections that it must be Dr. Elliott in nurse drag crouched in a corner by the door. When the camera moves up to show us more of the figure it stops at the razor in hand. Liz steps out of the shower to grab a weapon in her defence and Dr. Elliott slits her throat. When she wakes up screaming, Peter rushes into the room to calm her and she at first pushes him away. Is it enough that she establishes that Peter is not the killer, that she is not being killed, and that she, too, is not the killer? That we didn't see Dr. Elliott's head or face in the shower-scene dream suggests identification.

The final dream or film within the film leaves open the prospect of posttraumatic serial dreaming. Two De Palma films followed in which the trauma could be more fully felt or realised, and brought closer to therapeutic closure.

In *Blow Out* (1981) and *Body Double* De Palma stages in the foreground his homage to Hitchcock as one of the auteurs of cinema (together with Antonioni) but behind the scenes the protagonists seek treatment via the new B-genre of slasher therapy. As in *Sisters*, *Phantom of the Paradise* and *Dressed to Kill*, De Palma's vantage is raised by its own homage to some point outside the B-picture *Psycho* Effect. The pastiche mediation of his tributes was his debt to Jean-Luc Godard. Kept closer to the A-list, De Palma's 'Hitchcock' films offer a sovereign commentary upon rather than immersion in the Effect, which in *Blow Out* and *Body Double* makes a ghost appearance via inserts of simulated B-pictures, which do not reach out to reflect or subsume the greater film. De Palma wraps an adult profile of mourn-ability around the teen market of the Effect.

Blow Out advances De Palma's next gadget lover, Jack, to our point of identification, but this time we begin *and* end on the down side of love, the reality of loss. Jack is Peter if, while watching over Liz during her session with the psycho doctor, there had been no officer standing by to intervene: instead he would have witnessed another person dear to him fall under the knife of psycho violence. But Jack, older than Peter now, is also more fully enrolled in the media Sensurround in which the film checks its reflection. De Palma's title scores a near miss with Antonioni's *Blow Up* (1966), in which film got in touch with itself via photography. In *Blow Out*, total surveillance is where the movies go to see themselves.

A film about assassination, endless investigation or cover-up, in a word, conspiracy theory, *Blow Out* begins with a film within the film. We're inside the *Psycho* Effect when we follow the stalking, peeping POV in a slasher movie in the style of *Friday the 13th*. The panning POV takes in students partying in the dorm. The killer is reflected in the mirror as he enters a steamy bathroom. Then he proceeds to remake the shower scene with the coed in the stall. But just when the primal scene of the cut is about to commence we cut away from a screen within the greater frame of this film. We're watching the dailies with the producer-director and Jack, his sound man. They've worked together for two years now on films like 'Bloodbath', 'Bloodbath 2', and 'Bordello of Blood'. What already broke the suspense was the pitiful whine of a scream emitted by the actress. Jack needs to find a better scream to dub in its place.

Part of his job is to collect sounds. His mike is a long prosthetic affair that is neither discrete nor, seemingly, innocent. A couple feels disturbed while he is recording in the park: is he some kind of 'peeping tom', the girl who wants to go wants to know. While he's at work making new recordings to replace the 'library' wind sounds on the track of the slasher film, it happens that he also makes an audio record of a car wreck. The governor, a possible candidate for president, died in the accident. In reversal of Chappaquidick it is the compromising woman in the car who survives while the politician goes down as dead Kennedy. Jack rescues her from the car in the river. But the tire didn't blow out, it was shot out. Just listen to the tape. Upon mediatic replay, allowing the recording to speak for itself, Jack recognises conspiracy, a media 'theory' that seems to intervene therapeutically to bring him out of his B-picture limbo.

For two years Jack has been inhabiting the B-picture underworld, the medium for conversion of his despair into low-maintenance depression. In the recent past Jack wired police officers for under-cover work in sting operations. His colleague in an investigation into police corruption back then was tripped up by Jack's careless wiring – and consequently executed by the suspect he was supposed to catch on tape. In fact he was strangled and strung up by Jack's own wire. Jack's gadget love wasn't reality tested. He neglected to consider that the man he was wiring for sound might perspire under pressure. He expired under pressure. It's a painful short in the wire that blows his cover. The long of it is Jack's depressed retirement from technical support of under-cover assignments to provide sound effects for low-budget horror films.

But what gets him out of his 'library' or crypt of canned effects is that sometimes he's out and about collecting sounds hands-on. While picking up the sound of wind, rustling branches and leaves, even a night owl (and the upset date's line about the 'peeping tom'), he winds up recording the evidence of a political crime. The crime is revealed after the fact, through its mediatic echo; in real time he witnesses a crash in which one dies while the other one, Sally, the woman who was along for the ride, can be rescued. That he saves her already scores one for a more upbeat momentum. It moves him to re-enter the film medium as De Palma's delegate, proceeding from the soundtrack through still pictures to motion pictures. Only in this way can he capture the split second of the shoot.

When he detects the assassination evidence, he joins forces with Sally, the survivor and witness. Just as he seeks to atone for the discovery and death of the officer he wired, so Sally rises to the occasion offered by the taped gun shots – up from her own low point of complicity, not with the murder but with the intended framing of the politician on moral charges. She works for Manny Karp, who routinely catches and photographs her playing the female lead in yet another compromising situation. The entrapped man must pay blackmail or alimony. Manny's secret home movie of Sally and the candidate alone together was just another job that was not supposed to end in the mark's fatality. But Manny admits that for the added twist of the car wreck he was offered more money than ever before.

In the scenarios Sally performs, with Manny photographing or filming in the wings, the sexual act never happens while the victim is always willing enough to play his role. But while her day job is breaking up marriages and careers, the line of work she wants to pursue full time, all the way into the movie industry, is that of makeup artistry. Makeup is all-important, she advises Jack, especially when you want to look like you're wearing no makeup at all. She is in the ready position to 'make up', to make restitution for some failing she can't shake – and for which the scenarios are undoubtedly reenactments.

Both Sally and Jack occupy the margin of the movie industry, a place of expertise and insider access. Jack first syncs up the sound track with photos in a magazine (stills from the film surveillance that Manny sold to the publication), initially animating the cut-out pages like a flip book, but then re-photographing them to be the frames of a film. Jack updates the self-reflexivity of *Blow Up* by constructing the presentable evidence of a sound film within a sound film.

Burke, the man hired to engineer a scandal, not a fatal accident, has gone rogue, going on psycho. Though he doesn't know it, Burke has been abandoned by his original contract persons, who are no longer willing to cover for his activities. Even his idea of a car wreck had been nixed by those in charge of the operation. But then Burke, who has everything under control, decides to maintain the deception of the accident to conceal the murder. He therefore strikes out (on his own) to neutralise both the cinematic proof and the eye-witness, Sally. The first time he thinks he has succeeded in eliminating the witness, he notices that he mistook someone else for Sally. He carves the Liberty Bell icon into the victim's belly to feign the style of serial killing: in no time the press reports on the Liberty Bell Strangler. He selects his next victim only for the purpose of the deception. To perfect his crime in the mass-media setting of conspiracy the psycho climbs up over corpses and pretends to be what he is. He aims to lose the assassination of Sally in the crowd of random victims.

Even though the Law, the police, can't use Jack's testimony, the media are interested (even the police advise him to take his 'paranoia' to meet the press). Jack and Sally are invited to appear on a TV news show to present their evidence. But Burke, posing as phone repairman, tapped the calls in which these arrangements were made. Pretending next to be the TV reporter, Burke arranges to meet Sally. Jack lets her go only after repeating with her, on her person, his wiring of an undercover identification.

'I'm going to wire you — no one's going to fuck with me — If he takes the film I'll have it on tape. He won't be able to deny it.'

Sally: 'Aren't you getting a little paranoid?'

While the city of Philadelphia celebrates 'Liberty Day' Burke murders Sally, who wears Jack's live wire, with a garrote, a kind of wire cutting off her life to spite her voice. The original working title for De Palma's film was 'Personal Effects'. Jack once again cannot save the body to and through which he wired himself. He follows her screams to the spot where he must always and again, owing to miscalculation of the relationship between alive and live, arrive too late. At the end Jack kills Burke with the knife that was going to leave the psycho signature on her strangled corpse. The press (or the powers behind Burke) will cover the crime scene as self-containing: the final serial victim, before dying, killed the Liberty Bell Strangler.

In this film gadget love doesn't guarantee safe passage out of reach of traumatisation. The psycho killer (who is gadget skilled, too) may always beat you to your scene, like a double, and realise your worst but recurring nightmare.

Sound man Jack's assignment on the set of a new slasher movie to find a more convincing scream to dub into the audio track occupies the span of time of De Palma's film story. In the end he uses Sally's screaming on the record of his failed attempt to protect her to fill in the blank with its real imitation. When he listens to the film's soundtrack, his co-production with Sally, he hears, beyond commemoration, his scream memory.

4

If Jack in *Blow Out* must face the depth charges of grief and loss that were circumvented or post-traumatically postponed in *Dressed to Kill*, then Jake, the protagonist of *Body Double*, realises within the therapeutic frame of B-pictures a happy end that is grown-up and sexual. In the trilogy each protagonist, though seriously traumatised, is delivered from the serial momentum generative of new psychos, largely through the intervention of a woman who by her sex work is immune to the psychosis of influence.

At the start of *Body Double* we're on the set of a vampire B-picture. Jake, the actor starring in the picture, gets inside the coffin in order to rise up out of it. But when it's time for 'Action' we find that he can't move. Claustrophobia, as reverse shot of fear of heights, gives De Palma entry into Hitchcock's *Vertigo*. Jake leaves the set, allegedly on leave, though it comes as no surprise that he will be replaced: he comes home early and finds that his girlfriend has also replaced him. He follows the happy sounds and catches her in the act. What stays with him is her glow of passion. He mis-remembers the scene: she was on top but Jake recalls that she was lying below all aglow. Like the child reader of the primal scene, Jake plays or identifies with all the parts. Like Schreber he wonders what it would be like to get some of what she's having.

At method-acting class it is Jake's turn to go back to his primal fear. He's playing hide-and-seek. His older brothers call the game 'Sardine'. He's so well hidden that he's stuck behind the freezer in the basement. He can't cry out because this was the first time his brothers let him play. They would taunt him; he'd be the baby. But still he is afraid. 'I'm afraid' and 'I can't cry out' together produce the symptom of immobility and muteness. All the coordinates of his misconception about where babies come from, of his symptom's conception, are pressed in place, unmoving and hiding out in repression. How often the screen memory that diverts attention from the primal scene is a sibling narrative. The cheat scene conveyed that his girlfriend wanted the other man, the third person: it's their glowing union that locks him odd man out.

Sam sat in on the tell-all method acting class and now knows that Jake, the paralysed witness to a scene or screen, is suitable for framing. He arranges for Jake to live and work as substitute house-sitter in the Hollywood Hills. But Sam in fact arranges for Jake to play the part of eyewitness. Voyeurism gets Jake into the ready position. Sam shows him the opportunity not to be missed. Every night at a certain hour Jake trains the house telescope on the window through which we, too, watch a young woman strip and dance. Sam uses Jake's phobia to rivet him to the spot and slot of long-distance viewing, like the moviegoer, like the protagonists in Hitchcock's *Rear Window* (1954) and *Vertigo*. Sam finishes assembling her when he asks Jake if he saw the face of the stripper (of course he didn't): 'she's gorgeous'. Henceforth when he sees 'her' face at other times of the day (he cannot restrict his voyeurism to the happy hour) he recognises only a continuity shot. He adores one woman whose name is Gloria.

Jake takes baby steps toward making contact with Gloria, the mystery woman who comes with his view. In other words he starts stalking her. But soon he discovers his stalker-double, the so-called Indian, who begins to fit the psycho profile. Jake and the woman he watches and stalks are kept from meeting by long tunnels and other outlets for his claustrophobia. In the unbreachable gap of tunnel vision between them he catches sight of the Indian tracking Gloria at closer range than his own stalk show. Jake, paralysed in the tunnel, watches the Indian steal her purse. But then Jake overcomes his fixity, moves against his double, who gets away. Just the same, Jake succeeds in retrieving the purse. In the tunnel of paralysis and love, there is the beginning of consummation between Jake and Gloria, who embrace and kiss passionately as the camera turns. But then Gloria breaks it off and, even after all that, he still can't follow her.

One night it's not the strip-and-dance routine he watches through the binoculars. (Sam calls right before the appointed time, presumably to be sure that Jake's in position.) Instead it's the scene of the crime. The Indian uses the card he lifted from the purse to break into Gloria's place. While watching his stalker-double rob the room upstairs Jake calls her. While he is warning her, the Indian grabs her from behind and starts strangling her with the phone cord. Does Jake miscalculate the distance, collapsing it like the telescope of his long-distance viewing? He doesn't call the police. Instead he runs, a mobilised eye beam, to Gloria's rescue. In the interim Gloria is getting to know the drill in the course of suspense scenes of second chances won from the close quarters of the intention to kill.

The Indian is knocked out during his strangling efforts. When Gloria recovers she calls 911. But the strangling did something to her ability to speak. When the Indian recovers and takes the drill to her, the extension cord isn't long enough and Gloria gets another break (she also gets her scream back). Jake actually arrives right in time. But the dog immobilises him under the ceiling right at the spot where Gloria's drilling upstairs bleeds through. The dog is the father totem. Jake still can't figure out or make his scene trapped behind the screen.

But as though his self-analysis were finally at stake, Jake sets out to solve the crime. His first lead is a scene from a new porno as advertised on TV in which the blonde does the very strip and dance number he watched night after night. It's this discovery that gets him out of his depressed place. He uses the phone to locate her. This is the first time he uses the phone to triangulate the voyeur's lair.

First he recognised one of the bit parts that went into the body-doubling construction of Gloria – and of his own construction as witness double, set up for the screen but blocked from the scene. Then he reenters the film medium from another margin, pornography. Soon he joins the production team of 'Holly Does Hollywood'. He is able to enter the woman inside Gloria's media image. Sex with Holly is no problem. He gets his glow back.

De Palma first approached Jamie Lee Curtis for the surviving part. But unconsciously on purpose he ended up with a more fitting, since less specialized, Hitchcock-only mascot: Melanie Griffith, daughter of Tippi Hedren, who starred in *The Birds* and *Marnie*. The surviving part steps out of the line of her immediate predecessors in De Palma's trilogy. Liz ends up Peter's friend in a safety zone they share as starting point for work of mourning. The consummation of the love interest between Sally and Jack is on schedule, but the planned trip together is irrevocably cancelled. At the end of the starts and stops of couplification and mourning in the previous films, it is by the union of Jake and Holly on the porn film set that the trilogy comes complete. Although he starts out the most castrated of the trilogy's leading men, Jake forgets about the money shot and blows his wad inside the actress, the double of the murdered woman and as such the vehicle for his own comeback.

At the end of Hitchcock's *Vertigo*, Scottie starts assembling one woman out of two. But motivated by his rational attempt to find a cure, his denial of the haunting that filters his every move to make contact, he is not able to penetrate to a new woman, the first who would not need first to be assembled out of doubling and reanimation. But 'it's too late'. The denial will have Nun of it – and Judy takes the fall. In *Body Double* Jake does penetrate to the new woman uncontrolled by the doubling, the psychopathic masquerade, in which she played a role.

There are two endings to the film. Before the two margins of the film industry that aim for arousal of bodily sensation are conjoined in the concluding shower scene, Jake must succeed where he failed with Gloria and rescue Holly. The psycho killer knocks Holly unconscious and digs her grave next to a cliff. We see the white dog in the Indian's van moments before Jake tries to stop the psycho and in their struggle rips off his rubbery face. Sam is unmasked. But then Jake falls into the grave. Why couldn't he be satisfied with the role of witness? He had to try out for the hero role! It looks like Jake is going to be buried alive.

But then Sam offers Jake a second chance, which Jake is able to take. Sam sounds like the director of this scene. We flash back to the opening scene on the vampire film set. This time Jake insists that they try one more time. As he emerges, not only from the prop coffin, but also from the fresh grave, the dog leaps at him but fails this time to immobilise him. Instead Jake ducks – and the dog takes Sam along off the cliff. But the father as good object was glimpsed within Sam's malignant makeup. The true father is all about second chances.

When Holly wakes up to find she is alone with Jake in a grave, she mistakes this to be his scene. She doesn't know about the double elimination of Sam and the dog, which amounts to Jake's internalisation of the father. She recognises only the deadly dyad: 'You're a corpse fucker.' But she's not dead yet, she adds. It's true that only now does he like them alive, not dead or live. He asks her to come up out of the grave, the crypt, to trust him, to take a second chance with him.

In the closing scene we see that Jake was given another chance to play the glam vampire, now ready to enter the shower scene. Right before the consummation of sex and violence, however, the scene is cut and Jake freezes so the starlet can be replaced by a body double with bigger breasts before the shooting of the scene continues. This was the alleged inspiration for the film: the body doubling that went into the opening shower scene in *Dressed to Kill*. Jake, who was entrapped by a projected scene that was pulled over him via body doubling, enters into the construction of the shower scene. Holly comments to the starlet, who stepped out of the shower while her breasts were being replaced, that she'll be getting lots of dates when the film comes out. Holly affirms the paternal gift of relationality freed-up by and open for substitution as second chance. From the grave to the shower Jake no longer needs to see double because he can tolerate the doubling – the sex – in substitution.

5

While De Palma excited the outrage of 'feminist' critics with his 'trilogy', in particular the opening slasher thriller, there was a slasher series or 'trilogy' underway that, made by women for women, offered an alternate view of psycho sex and violence through a lens that was presumably corrective. *The Slumber Party Massacre* (1982) is the story of the new girl in town who wins her stripes of in-group membership in the course of surviving the psycho, another male whose idea of sex is robotic drilling. (The girls are always slow-mo and gently caressing themselves and each other, like the vampires in a Jean Rollin movie.) The outsider, Valerie (or Val), proves to be the best basketball player in gym class. In the locker room there's a *Carrie* shower scene ('Do you know what? I think your tits are getting bigger!'), which is the prelude to conflict between those who would rather shun Val and one good girl (Trish) who would like to include her. The new girl hears it all in the next row. She 'drinks too much milk', one of her detractors offers. When Trish invites her to join the in-group for a slumber party at her house, Val finds an excuse to decline.

Back home across the way from the party, Val and her little sister Courtney exchange *Playgirl* banter. These two survive, together with Trish, the hospitable member of the in-crowd. Those who weren't nice to the new girls have to go. Apparently, the writer wanted something more explicitly feminist and the director wanted to deliver a more recognisable slasher movie.

While the girls dance and strip and then change into their nighties, the excluded boys peep and, once caught, join the party. They abuse substances and finally order a pizza. During a lull in the life or death struggle one of the girls is so hungry she can't help herself. She sits on the dead-on-delivery pizza boy and eats a slice best served cold. The killer, Russ Thorn, who was hospitalised after going on a spree of five murders in 1969, is at showdown like a date gone bad. 'It takes a lot of love for a person to do this. You love it, yes!' Before impaling him, Val to the rescue strikes off the tip of his power tool and severs his hand.

Slumber Party Massacre II (1987) lets sleeping girls dream. It was time to take *A Nightmare on Elm Street* on a corrective update. We watch a serial dream with that traumatic flashback quality: 'It was just the same old dream.' Valerie, who survived the first film, is a deranged asylum inmate. But her younger sister, Courtney, has her share of 'bad dreams', too. In her dreams she encounters a crazy rock n' roll greaser. We sense that he plays back the Thorn in her sister's side. But he is fashioned out of everything that music means to Courtney. If this bit's for you, it's driller time: the drill is now attached to his electric guitar.

Courtney demands a free day since it's her birthday. On the day she was to visit Valerie with her mother she gets the weekend off to go away with her friends, all of them members of a girl band. Either the hallucinations give way to real violence or no more attempts are made to contradict the reality of the fantasy violence. When Courtney settles down with true love Matt, just as they're about to do it, the drill comes through the wall and skewers Matt, too.

Singing in the blood, the driller killer completes the music video of one traumatised psyche. This director goes one step further than her predecessor in the franchise: she folds the entire sequel out of one young woman's traumatisation by the culture industry. The stereotypes of slasher mass culture are aspects of herself that she gets to watch for the drill of it. But even after Courtney torches the driller killer the film doesn't really conclude but withdraws within a psychotic relay of dreams, awakenings, and awakenings that were dreams, and so on. In the final scene (though theoretically and formally there is no end in sight) it's still the drill that rises up out of the floor.

Slumber Party Massacre III (1990) opens with the in-group playing volley ball on the beach. Then Ken (doll), a former insider who's been away, arrives. Now that he's back, Julie, who had a crush on him all during junior high, invites him over for the slumber party. The house is cleared of parents but the injunction to keep it clean since it's for sale and must be presentable for the 'open house' is the highest law. By the proximity of real estate and trauma we know we're in California.

On the way there the first member of the in-group falls victim to the drill. First she sees just the drill, erect, in her rear-view mirror. A hand grabs her from behind and holds her tight while the drill penetrates her through the back of the seat and then moves back and forth, in and out. The officer who takes her emergency call was talking to his colleague about a cop who killed himself because he was gay. At the party Ken has impotence problems with his old flame. When Julie decides to take a bath we can see that she likes to keep her vibrator handy. Then we see the killer's hand grab the vibrator, turn on its current, and toss it into the tub. When next we follow Ken into his van we know who did it. It's filled with hundreds of burning candles fitting the mood of the psycho crypt. The cop who committed suicide was his uncle. 'Uncle Billy, this is for you!' Another targeted woman tries to talk him down: 'I know something really bad happened to you. But it wasn't me. Talk to me about it – I'll listen. Was it your parents? A girl?' Ken starts flashing back to Uncle Billy, his abuser in childhood. The black-and-white photo Ken carried with him was taken at the moment of trauma that he forgot or rather replaced with idealisation. Finally Final Girl Jackie seizes the drill and lets him have it.

In the first film of the feminist slasher trilogy, survival belongs not to a single figure but to a new in-group. Part II, which shows Courtney lost in dreamy self-reflexivity – the trauma state –, problematizes the status of survival as the bone thrown the other sex. In the third part, which was re-adjusted mid-production by the director according to her understanding of Carol Clover's *Men, Women, and Chainsaws* (see the first note on page 232), survival is again secured by one of the women from the in-group, while the hot spot of the violence is unidentified or gay. These films count as 'cheesy' – 'cheesiness' is 'camp' adapted for straight folks. Isn't the female survivor position just another male fantasy? Yes, just as giving it all to the gay guy is a female fantasy that keeps the cheap drill proximate but condemned.

The Emperor's New Closure

In 1981 Joseph Zito directed gore meister Tom Savini (whose special-effects career, which began with his work on *Night of the Living Dead*, commemorated his tour of duty in Vietnam) to enter the cut of slasher cinema and show it all. *The Prowler* showed the full penetration of the victims' bodies by the instruments of murderer, even letting the camera linger over the cutting and stabbing through the special-effects flesh. This visibility extended to the film's shower scene in which the naked young woman gets the pitchfork at great lengths (her boyfriend already took a bayonet through the head). *The Prowler* flashes back in 1981, from the high point and turning point of the slasher projection, to WWII. The voice (over stock newsreel footage) puts through the connection between immobilised soldier 'psychos' ever marching as to war and the generic psycho of horror cinema: 'For some – the psychological victims of war – it will be a long road back. These men will need time to rebuild the lives they set aside when Uncle Sam called. For others – the G.I.s of the "Dear John" letters – it means starting over, replacing what they have lost. They faced one challenge and won! They can win this one too!'

Next we pan down one of the 'Dear John' letters in which Rosemary signs off as tired of waiting and now moving on. A 'John' also designates the client of a whore. We attend the Graduation Dance of the summer of 1945. The recipient of the letter arrives to impale Rosemary and the substitute. Thirty-five years later the locals have decided to hold the Graduation Dance again. It looks like the return of the long inert tradition of the Dance re-triggered the psycho killing. Scenes of teen girls getting ready for the dance ('Disco Blood' is playing in the background) alternate with shots of the killer suiting up in the combat outfit we recognise from thirty-five years ago. It's not the same psycho killer – a continuity shot that would have personalised the war story and thrown it away. Instead copy-cut murder possesses a new psycho. What lies within the cut is the Vietnam War.

In *A Nightmare on Elm Street* a middle-class neighbourhood confronts the return of repressed memories of the recent violent past. What the parents don't want to remember returns just the same, but first befalls their adolescent children, who were born following the traumatic incidents under repression. The violence has the momentum of catastrophe, for which the kids from greater LA are prepared in their waking state. We no longer need to pretend we're in a small town in the Midwest (*Halloween* was filmed in Pasadena). That's why earthquake weather is the first try by the teenagers to contain mounting fear around the sameness of their nightmares (which threatens to overflow the group container by way of forecast and reality-effect).

In the 2010 remake, when the teens disagree what it means that they are having the same nightmare, we know that we have switched from transgenerational trauma to the individual format of repressed memory. Now 'five' is not the age of a murdered sibling but the marker of each teen's own murdered childhood. First the teens think that they are suffering the repressed memory of their own crime of fabulation whereby the gardener at preschool was falsely charged and executed. But then this flexing of responsibility is but the first layer of internalisation and reversal whereby the crime of abuse was in fact forgotten. Molester Freddy sought his current afterlife in their dreams by manipulating not only their little bodies but also their memories, which continued to play hide and seek.

In 1984 the parents on Elm Street want to sleep or pass out – want to forget – while the kids try to stay awake: the parental repressed is so dangerous. To avoid further dreaming Nancy takes 'stay awake' pills and watches horror movies. Stay awake drug administration is first introduced, at least in Nancy's class, in the context of cramming for school exams. Like the sound of Freddy's nails, just like the screech of chalk on the blackboard, this abuse of all-nighter medication underscores the transferential setting of Freddy Krueger's transgressions.

President Reagan was known for sleeping well; it was the often-touted testimony to his good conscience. Nancy Reagan, however, kept on tossing and turning, even with the gun in her night stand. During the 1980s, anxiety gave way to or accelerated into the specialised disorder of panic: we turned down the Valium and enjoyed chiasms of calming Xanax. To summarise the panic attack: to sleep is to die.

By the influence of this franchise, the figures from the neighbouring series, like the counsellors in *Friday the 13th*, became so wealthy and so accessorised that the initial sense of responsibility and history (reaching back into the anti-Vietnam-War movement), which their occupation once entailed, became tenuous. On Elm Street the kids were ensconced within a Sensurround of gadget-loving connection – and ignored or neglected. The parents were too busy self-medicating for high anxiety and repressed depression. The pressure was on to conform – to family values.

In *A Nightmare on Elm Street* we proceed down two alternating tracks: the transferential and the psychotic. The metamorphic equality of Freddy Krueger's ghost appearances relies on the close discursive association between all-out hatred and self-hatred. At around the same time as Freddy Krueger hit the screen standup comedy switched from the aggressive neurotic style of the Lenny Bruce era, in which projective hostilities were brought to consciousness through the forced participation of live audiences. TV-style comics began in the 1980s to switch their own channels in disconnection from the live audience. Henceforth the audience would be as-live and the comic a psycho.

The sound that signals Krueger's approach, the shriek of chalk coming at the blackboard from the wrong angle, which makes skin crawl across the student body, was already on the verge of becoming collectible in 1984. It belongs more properly to the public fears of the parental generation.

Her parents assume that Nancy won't be going to school the day after her friend Tina was murdered (she was Freddy's first victim). But when your high school girlfriend dies you go back to school to mourn (or not). In class the teacher talks about *Hamlet* and chancre (close enough to 'cancer' in the panic Sensurround). The teacher addresses Hamlet's awareness of the rottenness in mother. Hamlet digs into her with his questions like a gravedigger into her mound. *Julius Caesar* is next. (Surfer dude reading Shakespeare out loud in class is a scream memory of the best years of my life teaching Californians.) When we hear 'the sheeted dead', Nancy hallucinates a visitation by Tina in her body bag. Nancy runs with the vision or dream, running down corridors between sleeping and waking states. When Nancy in her dream ignores the admonition of the proctor in the school hallway, the tormenter with the steel nails emerges from the figure of delegated authority.

In no other slasher story is the school so central. Although the same basement subtends both institutions, the high school is the alternative to the family. Even though the teacher automatically reminds Nancy that she will need a pass for the hallway on her way home, a reminder at once protective and rote authoritarian, her interpretation of *Hamlet* demonstrates that she not only represents or substitutes for parental guidance but also, just like a therapist, calls the parental authority into question.

Nancy goes to school to drop off in class and share her dead friend's nightmare. In dreams we witness the return of the dead. The belief in ghosts arose from these dream visitations. Arthur Schopenhauer argued that if Spiritist contact with the departed were in fact possible it would be via transposition of the 'dream organ' to the waking state. In *A Nightmare on Elm Street* we see for all the metamorphoses always ultimately the same basement and the same threatening figure. Ernest Jones argued that nightmares were originally considered the visitation of a demon who sat upon the sleeper's body, fixing it in place, applying pressure, sucking out breath and bodily fluids, even copulating with the sleeping form. This demon, 'mara' and 'Alp', is inside 'nightmare' and the German 'Alptraum', respectively. The Romans added to the primal incubus a succubus, a female version, thereby keeping the sexual difference straight. Jones further aligns the double sense of incubation with the incubus of nightmares. Incubation, the slow time of disease growth, was first applied to the ritual of sleeping in temples or on graves, which proved a means of sexual congress with divinities, spirits, and the deceased. The historical counterpart of incubation in both senses is the process of inoculation, a more current sense of which can be historicised as the *Psycho* Effect.

A Nightmare on Elm Street stages the occult understanding of the nightmare as the visitation rights of a demonic foreign body. But there is also a recent past of traumatisation underlying the serial dreaming, which fits inside the basement boiler room, the lair of Freddy when he was a figure in waking reality and history.

When Nancy empties with the tub below bath level in a dream-scream fit of bottomlessness, her mother, who comes knocking at the door, interrupts the drain of thought. Over-anxious about Nancy's continued existence, mother says that as many people drown falling asleep in the tub as die slipping and falling getting out of it again. Before drifting off Nancy was hum-singing one of those jump rope songs but with 'Freddy' in it ('nine, ten, never sleep again'). But does she remember the ditties from childhood? They seem rather to be the background music for her mother's apprehensions.

Nancy's mother reveals to her daughter that Fred Krueger's dead because 'Mommy killed him.' She 'even took his knives', which she can show her daughter after Nancy brings his hat back from her nightmare. Twenty years ago (one year after Michael Myers' first murder) Fred Krueger, psycho killer of children, targeted their neighbourhood. The mother says she knew the children. She also says that she was among the parents who stepped outside the law as vigilantes and burned up the psycho killer acquitted on a technicality. Nancy is fifteen years old. She was born five years after this incendiary event. The children killed would seem to belong to a first generation of older siblings whose comings and goings have been withheld from Nancy's generation. As the stress starts to show and tell, Nancy declares that, Oh My God, she looks like she's twenty years old. The lost generation was deposited inside the replacement generation.

The unstoppability of Freddy's return, which is admitted right from the start and does not need to rise up with the momentum of sequels, does not compromise Nancy's status as new survivor on Marion's behalf. Nancy, who even says that she is into survival, builds booby traps and related diversions. Going into the making of his film, Craven was interested in the reports of unexplained deaths associated with nightmares in deferred relation to the traumatic events of the Vietnam War. Three Cambodian refugees were beset by nightmares after one year in the United States; soon they refused to sleep for as long as possible, but then when sleep came they woke up screaming – and died. There was no identifiable cause of death, like heart failure. Nancy survives as a survivalist, in other words within the symptom picture of someone suffering post-traumatic stress disorder.

Boyfriend Glen told Nancy about the Balinese understanding of dreams, that they manifest the dreamer's energy, which the dreamer gives but can also take away again. After Glen goes, and her survivalist traps only slow Freddy down, Nancy accepts this view, her dead boyfriend's delegated New Age rescue and cure. Self-help is the new subject position that allows for survival in the midst of threats and dangers that can't be tuned out but can be kept at one remove in a mediatic environment of station switching or channeling. By the remote control of will power one channels the fluidum of energy that can be turned on and off.

2

McLuhan's reading of TV, which determined his genealogy of media, dates *Understanding Media* as another exhibit in wonder rooms dedicated to projections of a future that never happened – alongside LA's layout of endless automobility, as in the found footage that recycles through early science fiction films as the setting prior to the end of the world. The centrality of TV in McLuhan's reading reflected the synthesis he claimed for the latest mass mediation unto globalisation between Anglo-American literacy and Continental European tribalism or between democracy and totalitarianism. Because of the denial of TV-Führer psychology, which belied the alternating opposition of McLuhan's argument, *Understanding Media* can't simply be reclaimed and realigned for consideration of what was new in digital media.

The concomitant pressures of mass mediatisation occupied the foreground of horror films as fragmentation, disfigurement, masking, unmasking and doubling. In 1984 the rebound from the projected digital acme of mass or global dominance of live media as interactive surrealism became the premise of *A Nightmare on Elm Street*. We entered the borderland of dream and psychosis in our encounter with violence under all-pervasive conditions of live surveillance, which the horror film was already well equipped to stage and reformat in terms of the self-reflexivity of its own medium nature between film proper and its hybrid predicament with TV. In the course of the reception of Hitchcock's *Psycho*, to which *A Nightmare on Elm Street* still belonged, albeit at the tail end of trying to wag the already sleeping dog, film was becoming more and more like television – just as film reception was becoming continuous with TV reception. Acting out or group therapy in front of the set or screen was in the 1980s as important as watching the visuals.

What was fundamentally different about the frame of reference of *A Nightmare on Elm Street*, however, was that it violated a new space of privacy, no longer the bathroom like in *Psycho*, but now the sleeping, dreaming mind. Skipping the private space where the victim faced the look of trauma at close quarters, *A Nightmare on Elm Street* slashed the boundaries between dreaming and waking to open up, ultimately, hallucinatory states or cyberspaces of loss and torment.

Freddy Krueger's knife hand tore tracks through cloth, which was continuous with the movie screen itself. The glove, which also bore the date mark of its own history as cyber glove, was the key in the legend to the surreal special effects that kept the audience coming back for more. But this phantasmagoria was also what soon dated the franchise. The analogical mapping in anticipation of the prospect of digital mediation and its special effects, conducted in the *Nightmare* franchise as spectacular boundary blending between dream and reality, under the aegis, however, of surveillance, is another exhibit for the wonder room of projected futures.

In the 1960s McLuhan saw through the phantasmagoria of the new but his futural reading was premature. What was 'new' about the digital medium was the total synthetic access it afforded both synchronically as sensorium and diachronically as medium of return of every name, era and category in history. The novelty item in the genealogy of media since the early nineteenth century is and remains live transmission, both the phantasm and its ever growing approximation. The digital relation is the closest fulfillment of our fantastic preoccupation with supplemented simultaneity. What it redelivered as immediately accessible in a space of extended simultaneity was not so much a flow of information but the total archive complete with its demarcations for renewed access, its internal returns.

In the pre-digital era of opposition between projected and live media, the stretch marks of conflict and assimilation, even incorporation, could be observed in film's relationship to TV's traumatic influence. All that meets and crosses over in the digital hub of everyone's workspace – in virtual reality, in other words – largely stays there, at least when it comes to film.

At the border to the digital media the reality shock of the new was staged as virtual reality with the navigation device of Freddy Krueger's glove leading into so-called cyber space. In conversation with Paul Virilio, Friedrich Kittler pointed out that virtual reality would only then commence when one monitor was portal to all mediatic transmissions in a household. In the early 1980s TV was still in the way, overstaying its welcome on the mat of the new, overdetermining the imagining of the digital change as narcissism of chaos at a border that could still be projected at the cutting edge but inside the frame of self-reflexivity.

After the franchise was over – so over that in *Scream* Craven directed the line written by Williamson that only the first *Nightmare* was acceptable slasher fare – *Freddy vs. Jason* (2003) constructed the relationship of *A Nightmare on Elm Street* to the *Psycho* Effect in terms of strategies for restarting the old serial horror. In Ronny Yu's film, one defence against Freddy is a new drug that eliminates dreaming from sleep while risking the side effect of permanent coma.

Freddy wants to return but his 'children' no longer remember him, no longer are afraid of him. Freddy can return, it turns out, only if the prehistory dominated by Jason (and Michael Myers) first returns. Freddy places an order with Jason and his mother. 'The children have been bad on Elm Street. Hear my voice and live again. Make them remember me Jason!'

But then the point (of administration) comes when Freddy wants Jason to stop so that he can take over where Jason leaves off. Freddy needs Jason (and his more immediate proximity to the *Schauer*) self-contained before he can come back – surprise attack – at the intrapsychic border to psychosis. *Freddy vs. Jason* thus stipulates in terms of inoculation administration the paradigmatic differences between the first generation of slasher mascots and Freddy.

A Nightmare on Elm Street was the summit or summation of the *Psycho* Effect, which already was in the decline of its containment, but which was forced to return for one last hurrah in the ultimate nightmare. Derrida pointed out on several occasions, but in the mode of a sustained reading in *Rogues*, that the problems of auto-immunity apply to any system that relies on immunity or immunisation to protect itself against external dangers, such as violence, spectacularly represented in scenes of psycho killing. The AIDS crisis was up and running during the span of time *A Nightmare on Elm Street* and its sequels occupied. In the first sequel the connection is made explicit in terms of a new homosexual panic. A system built on immunity runs the risk of turning against itself, containing the shock, in Benajmin's view, as immunising shot to the point of neutralising the vitality to be protected. Even the survivor body can turn into its own anti-body. That is the significance of the destabilisation of the boundaries of reality, sanity or health in *A Nightmare on Elm Street*. At the conclusion of the *Psycho* Effect Freddy Krueger offered last call for the *Schauer*. It took its last stand and understanding within the props department of the contained Effect but now in your dreams, and drew on it to dismantle psychic reality as safely grounded in the certain boundary between dreaming and the waking state.

Freddy was the sole survivor of the immunisation practices applied to the *Psycho* Effect, which was grounded and ground up in reference to actual cases of psycho murder. The by now contained fears – the containment of which must be maintained – spark a kind of battery power that ends up running Freddy, who returns from his containment as, theoretically at least, uncontainable. He operates at the remove of nightmare but with the reality-shaking force of the psychotic break. And yet there is a limit to his inoculation-run charge – as *Freddy vs. Jason* illustrated. First Jason's violence must be contained between the monstrous son or mother and all the substitutes. Within the half-life of the contained violence Freddy emerges out of the impossibility of low-maintenance rest in peace.

With *Psycho* we entered the close quarters of direct or first contact with trauma, with the look of trauma. We occupied for the duration of the *Psycho* Effect – the two to three decade long phase of our working through it – the staging area of our immunisation against the annihilating shock of disconnection. With *A Nightmare on Elm Street* we entered the inoculation itself right where it is lodged at the border to psychosis.

3

Once Craven had succeeded in springing a horror series from the closing season of the *Psycho* Effect, he couldn't help wondering, like Napoleon's mother, how long it could last. In 1989 Craven attempted to introduce a new psycho killer at the front of the line of a newly projected series. In *Shocker* the shock of electricity, of violence control and the media, brings an executed serial killer back to avenge himself against the witness who turned him in. The psycho, Pinker, was a TV repairman and the young man who facilitated his arrest was the adoptive son of the investigating detective and sole survivor of the family that Pinker tracked down and murdered. But the survivor is telepathic and in his dreams he followed Pinker and led the police to his capture. Pinker sold his soul to the Devil to harness all the shocks for his returns via various bodies he doubles or enters on contact. But postmortem he can travel only via the electric flow of TV shows. The telepathic adversary devises a plan to bring Pinker into the real world (and out of his deathless mediatic transport). But first the showdown traverses in the style of *Zelig* (1983) or *Forrest Gump* (1994) TV shows in which we watch Pinker and his adversary on one set with the regulars or inserted into newsreels.

Wes Craven's New Nightmare (1994) supplies an alternative mode of legibility that turns up the contrast with *Shocker*'s short circuit of speculative serial expansion. In the 1994 film, the roles and the actors (and the audience) were all interchangeable (because in our media culture they already were). The film nominates the story alone as the containing force of violence and identification. It's a story that's fixed, which allows for only so much variation on dream versus reality or self-reflexivity.

It's Heather, the actress who played Nancy in the 1984 film, who wakes up from the nightmare about the making of the *Nightmare* series we watch at the start of *Wes Craven's New Nightmare*. It's an earthquake that brings the nuclear family back together again and allows reality-tested everyday life to start over. Heather, who now plays herself no longer knowing if she isn't Nancy after all, has been receiving harassing phone calls. Like: 'Freddy's coming for you.' Although the film is also the seventh installment of the *Nightmare* series, Freddy is treated this time around as the fictional character of the movies while the actor Englund joins the other actors in a new setting for which the Northridge Earthquake supplies the reality effect.

The Northridge Earthquake, which hit during production of *Wes Craven's New Nightmare*, provided ready-made sets free of charge. The aftershocks punctuate; they mark the transition or boundary-blending between dreaming and waking. Like all the other characters, the earthquake is both what it is in the *Nightmare* film narrative and what it is in reality (both inside and outside the film).

Mother, Heather, or Nancy, reads the Hänsel and Gretel story, which was her son's special request. She balks when the plot sickens. But her boy, Dylan, wants it all.

Dylan's stuffed dinosaur, Rex, gives under the covers protection for or against lower extremities. Mom decides to air the sheet: 'There's nothing there, see.' Dylan: 'It's different when you're gone. Daddy can follow the breadcrumbs, right?' 'Right.' 'If the birds don't eat them first.' We cut to daddy falling asleep at the wheel: Freddy's fingers grab dad's crotch and the car careens off the road.

With father gone, and the nightmares recurring, Dylan gets to join his mother in bed. But this is the Oedipal setting for Freddy's comeback, the vengeful return of the dad, castrated by the mechanical hand of prohibited masturbation. In one dream within a dream, Freddy takes possession of the psychiatrist, the transferential stand-in for the father. But Freddy also possesses the boy on occasion. It couldn't be made more explicit: Dylan must come to terms with his identification with a father he also wished, on occasion, gone, a goner.

Otherwise a good mother when it comes to her bond with Dylan, Heather fails in the face-to-face containment of turbulence. She tries to separate her son from the bad influence of her *Elm Street* films or from that of the Grimm fairy tale he wants her to read to him over and over again. In this sense Heather fits the psycho's family history (as first assembled in 'The Sandman').

Dylan has started sleepwalking. He's singing in her pain: '1, 2, Freddy's coming for you.' 'Dylan, where did you hear that song?' 'On the phone.' 'On TV?' 'In my bed. That man's trying to get up into our world.' 'That only happens in the movies. But I'll be here when you wake up. And I'll be sure that nobody gets your toes.' Is there epilepsy in the family, the psychiatrist asks. 'I'm convinced those horror movies can drive an unstable child over the edge.' In the Dr.'s stage whispering to a colleague we overhear 'all the signs pointing to schizophrenia'. But Heather, who has an implanted sensible memory from her other life as Nancy, insists that sleep deprivation alone can produce those symptoms.

Heather decides to visit Wes Craven, who lets her in on the reality of the Mara or Alp of his new nightmares. The entity is very old and lives for the murder of innocence. It can be captured by storytellers like the genie in the bottle. But when the story waters down for a long spell or sell, when the story dies, the entity's let go. But it can't just go anywhere. In the guise of Freddy, the entity has grown accustomed to this time and place. The series of films is over – and now Freddy can't contain himself. He's decided to cross over, come out of our films and into reality. There is one gatekeeper Freddy has to get by before he can make it into this world: 'it's you. Because you were the first after all to humiliate him as Nancy.' 'But that was Nancy, not me.' 'But you gave Nancy your strength.' There's method acting in this madness. The only way to stop him is to make another movie. 'You have to decide whether you're willing to play Nancy one last time.' (We read along these very words as they appear on Wes Craven's word-processor screen.)

The first *Nightmare* plays on the unplugged TV set while Dylan drops sleeping pills like breadcrumbs. Heather takes a pill to join him, then takes another one. The third one gets her there. It's the opening dream set. She finds the script and reads: 'The more she read, the more she realised what she had in her hands was nothing more or less than her life itself. That everything she had experienced and thought was bound within these pages. There was no movie. There was only … her … life ….' Heather fast forwards to the last pages while Dylan is speaking for his part pre-scribed. She goes ahead and joins in. She tells the story of the claw that came back to life.

This is as good a place as any to say that I part company with Carol Clover's *Men, Women, and Chain Saws*, which also came out of the UC assembly line of instruction during the same period of my own first contact with the slasher phenomenon. Clover's folklore frame, down to its component parts, claims to be timeless. That Americans have a long memory of ad images and their jingles is the format for recalling Freddy Krueger. While the Hänsel und Gretel story can be remembered and retold in *Wes Craven's New Nightmare*, the Freddy Krueger story isn't memorable that way. The pre-interactive-media surveillance fantasy can only simulate archetype with another oldie: teletype.

4

The curator of the documentary exhibition 'Freud: Conflict and Culture', which opened in LA in the summer of 2000, claimed as inspiration for the show Freud's own interest in the past, and how Freud's interest was in the meantime part and portrait of the past. Indeed, the mass culture props in the show (from Hitchcock to *The Simpsons*) functioned not as current signs of ongoing influence, but as dated relics of an influence that was history. So what was the controversy about? The protesters, who sought to stop the show in its planning stage, all specialised in making a killing out of putting the era of Freud's science in historical perspective – in other words, behind us.

Freud's allegation of the psychological poverty of the groups comprising America was based on the para-psychotic boundary blending he discovered (even in his own American Psychoanalytical Society) between political and intellectual standards of correctness. Since when has thinking been about everyone getting a turn?

Among flashcard keywords like 'Repression' and sitcom clips that featured phrases purloined from psychoanalytic theory there were blown-out-of-proportion cautionary epigraphs headlining the display cases. In addition to the opportunistic interventions by authors who owed their recognition value to the science they would terminate, there was one quote from Derrida that appeared – in its hovering contextlessness – to be a rhetorical inquisition directed against Freud, when it in fact belonged to a brilliant reading of and with him. My favorite slur was made by Frank Cioffi, who asked himself whether he would buy a used car from Freud.

Freud's critics view psychoanalysis as out and about to seduce us into a following that they for one-for-all cannot distinguish from understanding. Yet it was hard to imagine another exhibition of documents from the life of a famous historical figure which would have required the same integration of the latest criticism of that figure's thought, as though it would be politically dangerous if words of caution were missing from the show's labeling. Maybe a show of Hitler artefacts would draw this kind of preemptive fire. Even pop therapy's return in the 1980s to the seduction theory (which Freud had discarded in order to inaugurate psychoanalysis proper) and which turned up full blast again in the 1990s as the cottage industry of repressed memories, could be interpreted by Crews (on another exhibition poster) not so much as resistance to psychoanalysis as, even as resistance, the project just the same of Freud's dangerous legacy.

In an *LA Times* article about the show, the curator was cited as admitting, whimsically I suppose, that he, too, probably could have signed that big protest petition (submitted by Peter Swales and signed by Gloria Steinem and the rest of the Crews) that stalled the show for two years. Indeed. What made him think the show wasn't the repetition of all those middlebrow historical receptions – pro, con or whatever – of Freud's influence? Swales took to the headlines with his soap opera plotting of Freud's bio around an affair with sister-in-law Minna. The former promoter for the Rolling Stones attacked the show for 'using a federally funded institution to stage a public relations campaign'. Crews was either cited or his barking was validated for calling Freud's dream interpretation the work of a 'pseudo-scientist'. Crews, I guess should know, having been your average English prof before he hitched his wagonload of correctives to Freud's star. Last time I took notice, Steinem was publishing the political recant of her inner child. It seemed by the 1990s Freud's detractors had all undergone a change of political and therapeutic standards from criticism to correctness.

For as long as I can remember, there has been another rebuttal of Freud's dream theories or affirmation of their scientific validity in the headlines about every two years. Each time is like the first time. By the late 1980s Freud's great-granddaughter Emma Freud was a TV star, who hosted her 'Pillow Talk' show in bed side by side with her lie-in guests. It was the same bed – of Oedipus – that the generations in *A Nightmare on Elm Street* had put to the test, somewhere between brain wave research and New Age beliefs, when Freddy, the perpetrator of dreams that cross over boundaries to become indistinguishable from waking reality, skipped the generation of his loss or murder and came back, surprise attack.

'The only time I see Freddy in my mind's eye' – as Robert Englund relates in an extra-feature interview accompanying the video release of *Wes Craven's New Nightmare* – 'I had gone to sleep in my trailer with the makeup on. So I got up to pee or something in the middle of the night, and I had the dimmer switch on my makeup mirror on very, very low, which gives off this ghostly sort of dimmer light. And there was this disgusting old crone or a man there looking back at me. Freaked me out! And of course it was me. And I still occasionally have a dream of that moment. It made a little crease in my brain matter, and it will find its way back into my dream state occasionally.' This doubles one of Freud's personal examples of an uncanny experience via the mirror in his train compartment. To see yourself without recognising yourself, but instead glimpsing the vengeful, threatening intruder or spook is just about as close as you can get to experiencing your own death.

There may be some material crease that confirms the reservations held in Englund's dream state. But how does that take away from the haunting staying power of the shock of recognition or preclude association and interpretation. What every Freud resister tries to head off at the impasse of dream interpretation is the medium of the transference. How do neurological discoveries, beginning with REM sleep, disallow Freud's interpretation of dreams, both as wish and, after WWI, also as rerun of the scene in which traumatic shock took you beyond the basic anxiety defence and which dream interpretation alone can, by eventually producing the missing anxiety, absorb and control release after the fact?

Trauma lies at the origin of identification, even the mistaken identification of oneself as spook. On Elm Street the parents who seek to guide their children past nightmares to the safety zoning of neurology are completely ineffectual. Instead, it is up to Nancy, the parentified teen, to work with the unconscious. She admits the unstoppable return of Freudy.

By Rule of Tomb

The title of Jeff Lieberman's *Just Before Dawn* (1981) identifies the time and light of the panorama pan of the mountainous sylvan landscape at the start and conclusion of the film. Upon closer inspection the human trace in the natural setting is backwoodsy and over the hill. Hunters take a drinking break inside an abandoned chapel. While one wants to take something along that he must first pry loose from the wall, the other one performs the sacrilege of impersonated preaching at the altar. When he pitches his address to the heavens we catch our first glimpse of the psycho looking down through a hole in the roof. As in the opening of *Night of the Living Dead* desecration (ultimately disrespect to the dead) is reflected back in the psycho violence that follows. The faux preacher rushes outside when the truck is brake-released and crashes into a tree. He takes the outside chance of flight when he sees that the psycho (he calls him a 'demon') took out his buddy, whose cap the killer now dons. We watched the psycho stab him in and through the groin (a groiner!).

Then a van bearing five hikers enters the environs. That they are also recognisably TV actors makes them family. The odd man out, a younger brother along for the ride, looks out and recognises a photo op: twins. After he takes the picture he wonders out loud why there are so many of them up here. A possible counterpart to the desecration scene: the van hits a buck but the responsibility for the animal stops here. The driver, Warren, walks around the van, but is too creeped out by the surroundings to continue a proper search.

The local forest ranger stops the van and warns them not to go to the mountain. Warren owns property up there. 'The mountain can't read.' After they set up camp, one of the couples – Jonathan, who doesn't know how to swim, and Megan, who's constantly refreshing or redoing her makeup – goes skinny dipping. Under conditions of backwoods camping, these bodies of water, which are basins below waterfalls, replace bathtubs and showers. He likes to scare her with his disappearance and drowning. She likes dunking him. Psycho enters the basin at the waterfall. Again Jonathan disappears after she dunks him. But now arms grab her from behind. Oh Jonathan! But then she sees that he's on the shore. Was it a demon?

The psycho drowns Jonathan for real. At the same time, in another part of the forest, Megan and the photographer, Jonathan's younger bro, discover the chapel with its surrounding cemetery. A photo op: he takes pictures of Megan lying on one of the graves. They think Jonathan is playing games so they pretend to be making out. But it's the psycho, who stabs the photographer. Megan runs into the chapel and looks out at the psycho playing with his camera trophy. But he is also inside with her. While one double kills her the other one takes the pictures.

The main couple, Warren and Connie, enters the next scene in nature's shower. But then Jonathan's dead body washes down upon them and they are out of there. But Warren has to go back to the body to find the keys and the SOS whistle still in Jonathan's pockets. When she's attacked on this schedule of ambivalence, she gains time by climbing up a tree. The forest ranger saves Connie, from, as is now explained, one of two psychos. Yes, they're twins.

Connie's theme throughout is that while she knows how to pitch tents, she can't get it up to defend herself when violence threatens. The first step in her transformation is trauma shock. She starts wearing missing Megan's makeup and even quotes her earlier line, given in response to Connie's rhetorical questioning of her desire to continue making herself up out here in the sticks: 'You never know who you might meet up here. Some demons are kind of cute.' Then the other twin, grunting like a pig, attacks. He stabs Warren but prefers crushing Connie in his arms. But then she shoves her free arm down his throat until he dies. Now she's whimpering like one of the psycho twins. A residual charge of psycho violence enters her transformation into the survivor.

1

In addition to adopting the foregrounding of the visual sense in Lacan's mirror stage theory for my presentation of Freud's reading of the uncanny over the years (closing ranks, thus, with the pedagogical imperative of coeducation), I also in turn tended to flesh out the mirror relation as object relation. But last time I reread Lacan's brief essay I noted that the insistence on the mirror (and on the media that fold out around it) is rather nonnegotiable. In 'Mirror-role of Mother and Family in Child Development', Winnicott opens with Lacan's influence on him, even though he must correct the French colleague, who placed the mirror before the mother's face. Though Winnicott characterises 'actual mirrors' as signifying 'mainly in the figurative sense', he does allow that mirrors in the house give the child opportunities 'for seeing the parents and others looking at themselves' (1996: 118). Glancing to the side, where prospects for endless support grouping open up, Winnicott identifies in this prop department opportunities to repair early damage in the face-to-face. Think in this regard of Erik contemplating Christine as Marguerite on stage in the mirror scene of Gounod's *Faust*.

Within the perspective of Winnicott's 'psychopathic analysis' (in contrast to what he himself termed 'neurotic analysis'), the crux of so-called good-enough mothering is the utter vulnerability of the makeshift arrangements constitutive of what can be taken for granted as the basis for object use.

> A baby is held, and handled satisfactorily, and with this taken for granted is presented with an object in such a way that the baby's legitimate experience of omnipotence is not violated. The result can be that the baby is able to use the object, and to feel as if this object is a subjective object, and created by the baby. (1996: 112)

When the mother looks at her baby, what she looks like is related to what she sees there. 'All this is too easily taken for granted' (ibid.). Thus little one drops out of the school of good-enough mothering when the mother 'reflects her own mood or, worse still, the rigidity of her own defences' (ibid.). When babies look and don't see or find themselves they start searching for other ways to get something of themselves back from the environment. Mother's moods in baby's face can raise a whether-or-not forecaster of the good-enough motherological conditions. Winnicott ventriloquates: 'Just now it is safe to forget the mother's mood and to be spontaneous, but any minute the mother's face will become fixed or her mood will dominate, and my own personal needs must then be withdrawn otherwise my central self may suffer insult' (1996: 113). But such patterns of predictability bring up baby 'in the direction of pathology': the baby is strained 'to the limits of his or her capacity to allow for events. This brings a threat of chaos, and the baby will organize withdrawal, or will not look except to perceive, as a defence. A baby so treated will grow up puzzled about mirrors and what the mirror has to offer' (ibid.). Little one henceforward only looks at the mirror that doesn't bear looking into. Beauty is no longer in the eyes of the beholder nor is it in the holding environment. When this one grows up, falling in love with beauty will be the fixated detritus of what lies before finding and feeling the beauty that is there in and about the one you love.

One patient 'is particularly sensitive as a judge of painting and indeed of the visual arts, and lack of beauty disintegrates her personality so that she recognizes lack of beauty by herself feeling awful (disintegrated or depersonalized)' (1996: 115). Another patient was high functioning except at the start of every day. She seriously disturbed her relationship to her husband, in other words to her mother, when she spent every morning putting on her face as the only painstaking resolution available for 'the paralysing depression' which 'came each day when at last it was time to get up' (1996: 114). She was only deferring the 'chronic depressive state which in the end became transformed into a chronic and crippling physical disorder' (ibid.). And yet what is illustrated by this case, which begins with the face and ends with the body, is that it 'only exaggerates that which is normal:' 'the task of getting the mirror to notice and approve. The woman had to be her own mother' (ibid.).

When he allows the thought to cross his mind that this patient might have been helped out if she had had a daughter, he pulls back from the horror prospect of transmission of the mask impressed upon such a daughter 'because of having too much importance in correcting her mother's uncertainty about her own mother's sight of her' (ibid.). The average daughter 'studies her face in the mirror' to reassure 'herself that the mother-image is there and that the mother can see her and that the mother is *en rapport* with her' (1996: 113). In the midst of case examples, Winnicott addresses the reader, whose thoughts he can read: 'The reader will already be thinking of Francis Bacon' (1996: 114).

Winnicott enters the painter's process: 'in looking at faces' or recreating them 'he seems to me to be painfully striving towards being seen, which is at the basis of creative looking' (ibid.). Bacon seems to remain caught in the act of 'seeing himself in his mother's face, but with some twist in him or her that maddens both him and us' (ibid.). Winnicott is able to bring home the Bacon reference to one of his patients, who expresses a desire to lend him a book about the artist in which she has already marked as of interest to him the detail that the artist prefers to see glass over his works so that when viewers look at them they might at the same time see themselves. 'After this the patient went on to speak of "Le Stade du Miroir" because she knows of Lacan's work, but she was not able to make the link that I feel I am able to make between the mirror and the mother's face' (1996: 117). But he holds back from premature interpretation. Psychotherapy (a word Winnicott at times uses to mark the divergence between his approach and 'neurotic analysis') must ultimately give the patient, that is, give back, only what the patient brings. 'It is a complex derivative of the face that reflects what is there to be seen' (ibid.). Winnicott follows his therapeutic standard of good-enough mothering in this formulation of seeing or receiving (as one's own, of one's own making) that which is at the same time given to be seen.

2

Wes Craven almost turned down the offer to direct *Scream*, which at least as screenplay, in particular the opening sequence, caused him to flash on *The Last House on the Left*, his 'deeply disturbing' first film, from which he wished in the meantime to keep his distance. Of course, even if the slice is right, *Scream* couldn't be more different as horror film. But a more pressing point of contrast lies between *Wes Craven's New Nightmare* and *Scream*, with the former, not only directed but also written by Craven, falling short at the same self-reflexive game that *Scream* would win two years later.

Directed by Craven, shot straight from what's hip in Kevin Williamson's screenplay, *Scream* is perfectly happy-faced to represent us, the audience, as a teen culture of experts in the slasher genre, experts who enjoy a testing relationship to the films. Of course the rules get broken, or, once again, the boundaries transgressed: but the gadget-loving audience takes pleasure in the film's and its own self-awareness or preparedness. It is not along the lines of selfhood or through the finite stories of tradition that the audience into *Scream* gets off. For starters, 'ghost face' makes the crowd of those who identify with his transgressive anonymity and dress up in the same store-bought Halloween costume. While in *Wes Craven's New Nightmare* the actors played themselves in the off, stepping out of the film, but of course in open denial that they were still inside the film, in *Scream* the film boundary is reclaimed and projected outwards via the claim that everything is film. The deregulated sensorium of recording backs the claim. Every psycho killer in the trilogy is 'directing' another slasher film. These internal films aim to displace Sid Prescott in her starring role as survivor. The advanced self-reflexivity of *Scream* enters the loop of the controversy kept going in the headlines around each new high school shooting spree: Did the culture industry dictate the criminal behaviour of the teens? Did the movies make them do it?

Not even one year has passed since the murder of Sid's mother. Cotton Weary, one of the mother's extra-marital affairs, was charged right away and sent to prison. But then a serial murder spree commences over the bodies of Sid's fellow high school students. After the first murder the teen group meets for therapy (we're still on Elm Street, though we're back to denying that we're in LA). Their classmate was slashed open and emptied of several organs. Stu jokes when his girlfriend seems squeamish during the in-group debriefing that they should liver alone. It's a groaner that sets the double track of the movie (and trilogy): a tragic element on one channel, a laugh track on the other one.

The mother's 'ghostliness' takes the form of the static on Sid's lines of trust, beginning with the mother who posthumously introduces trust issues. The *Scream* trilogy marks periods of passage that fall short of the mourning period Sid is hard pressed to set at the end of her mother's death sentence. The onset of mourning is reopened over and again through new revelations about the mother and her murder. In the after-the-fact expansion and differentiation of knowledge about her mother, it is the murdered mother who, just like a ghost, keeps on growing, remaking herself, acquiring greater depth in personal history and psychology. By the end of the trilogy the missing mother dominates the story.

The father keeps to the sidelines, popping up on occasion to encourage Sid to get on with her life. That in the first film he must be saved by her at the critical moment is a byproduct of Sid saving herself. He falls out of the closet, an afterthought to the scene of survival. But all that also means that he's safely inside her.

It turns out Sid was right all along in her recurring suspicions of her high school sweetheart, Billy, which alternated with her accepting blame and shame. Like in *The Texas Chainsaw Massacre* Sid survives because the killers become preoccupied with their comedy routine. Billy didn't work alone but with his pal Stu. To prepare the scene of Sid's demise, the psycho buddies start stabbing each other for reality effect (they aim to be around for the sequel). But for some reason they like stabbing each other more deeply than planned. While this farce is underway Sid gets away. In no time she's at the other end of the cell phone exchange, terrifyingly unlocatable, now giving it to them. She makes her ghost appearance in the *Scream* costume and stabs Billy with the umbrella. Now Stu wants to consummate his long longed-for thing for her. 'In your dreams,' Sid says and knocks the TV or monitor (*Halloween* is playing) onto his head. This tribute to *A Nightmare on Elm Street*, and commentary on the media essence of its interpretation of the *Psycho* Effect, is one of over fifty references to horror films in the first *Scream*, both enacted and verbatim.

While teen group members were gathered around the set, giving gadget-loving attention to *Halloween*, testing the in-group comprehension of 'the rules', they were also under surveillance via a device that newswoman Gale Weathers smuggled inside. However when she gets back to her cameraman parked outside, they discover that there is a thirty-second delay in the live transmission. Of course every live transmission is produced and is as such open to tampering and displacement. Derrida pointed out that globalisation – or globalatinisation as he called it – still spread, via the live media, the word wide web of Christianity. In other words, the live report from Baghdad must be believed in: the reporter asks us to believe in him and his broadcast, the word made flesh. That surveillance as fully functioning system is in the first place a belief system is so obvious no one can recognise it. In *Scream*, the cameraman's belief in the liveness of the surveillance coverage is such that he forgets the accidental delay and as a result miscalculates his relationship to the events inside the house as displayed on the monitor in his truck. When he remembers the delay that propels the violence on screen on fastforward it's too late. He steps out of the van to get out of there and gets his throat slashed.

There are cognitive 'continuity errors' in *Scream* formally figured by the thirty-second delay in liveness. *Scream* admits to being a world in which the main characters watch slasher films incessantly, to the point of the genre becoming transparent to them, down to the rules they recite. Why, then, does no one notice or comment on Billy's last name, Loomis? It is a blind spot that looms as large as Billy's claim that Norman Bates lacked a motive. He mentions this in tandem with the correct observation that Hannibal Lecter pursues his cannibalism without motivation. *The Silence of the Lambs* is up in the lights that blind this post-Psycho-Effect film to the personal effects that litter the opening wounding of slasher cinema. Billy's denial of the intrapsychic motivation in *Psycho* amounts to another rule: unacknowledgment of the contributions of mourning (or unmourning) to the cut of disconnection that *Psycho* introduced. Although the denial doesn't go away it becomes clear, after a brief delay, that it doesn't cover Billy, who spills his motive, the loss of his mother, who split over his father's affair with Sid's mother. But then Billy jokes that his abandonment issues make for good mass media coverage and reader's digestion of his crimes. Stu has no other motive than peer pressure. He's like the rest of us who watch psycho movies without being psycho. But to watch these movies is to want to make one yourself.

The blind spot surrounding Billy Loomis, whereby he cuts himself slack or lack of motivation, is further displaced in *Scream 2* by his mother. Her partner in the new serial spree occupies the returning theme of lack of identifiable motivation. He just wants to become a celebrity criminal by claiming before the court that the movies made him do it. Mrs. Loomis found him in an Internet chat room and now, while revealing herself to Sid in preparation for the finale, finds him dispensable. As she herself says, her motive doesn't belong in the 1990s (which her dispatched partner's lack of motive apparently embodied). Indeed her 'old-fashioned' revenge motive, since she is the mother of a dead son, brings up the first *Friday the 13th*, which had to be refigured in the sequel so the series could begin. *Scream* opens over the slashed body of the recognisable star who failed the psycho's phoned-in test question, who was the psycho killer in *Friday the 13th*. It's a trick question she gets wrong because it is the series she remembers. Knowledge of the places exchanged between mother and Jason separates, in the spirit of survival terrorism, the expendable groupies from the experts, who make the next round. However, Billy's undercover avenger lets the tragic element slide when she goes off in eye-popping slapstick as psycho mom. She's tired of the parents being always at fault. Just the same, it is a shame that the blame rests with Sid's mother. This establishes the trajectory of irresponsibility that Sid must set right.

At one point in *Scream 3* (2000), Sid talks to her father, who is visiting her in her retreat or hideout where she therapeutically occupies herself with taking calls, pseudo-anonymously, from other people in crisis. He encourages her to return to the world of the living. She says that if it weren't for his wife and her mother, for all the difficulties she introduced through her secret lives, none of this would have happened. But understanding her mother's bad influence doesn't save her from what follows. Sid sees her mother's ghost scratching on the window pane, condemning Sid to bring destruction, just like her mom, to those she loves. Sid sees her murdered mom up against the pain.

In the world Sid fled a new serial murder is underway which is following the script for the new film 'Stab 3', currently in production. This film is based on the events in *Scream* and *Scream 2*. But aren't 'Stab' and 'Stab 2' already matched with *Scream* and *Scream 2*? We never see 'Stab 2'. But the opening of 'Stab' was a close reenactment of the opening of *Scream*. Thus the self-reflexivity of the trilogy within the trilogy pulls apart and gets lost in *Scream 3*. At times 'Stab 3', like *Wes Craven's New Nightmare,* seems to follow or dictate *Scream 3* like its double in the present tense. But then we discover there are three versions of the script.

The killer in *Scream 3* has been leaving photographs at the crime scenes. Each photograph is yet another portrait of Sid's mother as a young woman taken at a time officially missing from all known 'histories' of her life. It turns out that Sid's mother, when she was more or less Sid's age, left hometown for Hollywood to act in horror films. Traumatised at some producer's 1970s swinging party as up for grabs, she went back home and stamped her Hollywood time repressed. This abandoned date mark (and rape) returned when, four years earlier, one year before *Scream*, Roman, her illegitimate son from back then, tracked her down. She wasn't interested in the reunion. That casting-couch victim was dead, which gave Roman the idea.

The abandonment issue prompted Roman's first turn to filmmaking. He shadowed his mother with his home-movie camera and ended up with a record of her extra-marital affairs. The abandoned Hollywood son, who in *Scream 3* is the director of 'Stab 3', showed Billy his document of Mr. Loomis's involvement with one bad mother. Thus he 'directed' Billy to make the 'movie' of the mother's murder. But then Billy and Stu made their own movie directed against Sid and her father. Under the cover of a slasher series, this subsequent film was out of Roman's control. It wasn't in his interest to watch the legitimate daughter rise to the status of victim and survivor-heroine. Beginning with the second film, then, the *Scream* trilogy carries the meta-theme of envy of the survivor role. (*Scream 4* adds itself to the series but doesn't go near the mother issue, which remains inside the trilogy.)

Roman does not intend to make 'Stab 3', which even while in production is still stuck in the development hell of script versions and revisions (a situation that apparently reflects the making of *Scream 3*). The production is the vehicle (or disposable costume and mask) for the murder spree whereby, under Roman's direction, the out-of-control movie will be reclaimed. He will frame Sid as killer (as unhinged by the revelations about her mother) and himself as star survivor. But when Sid rejects his sense of motivation or entitlement that he is the true victim she triumphs once again.

The self-reflexivity of the first two *Scream* movies followed out the continuity between the culture of real crime and, whether via profiling on the side of detection or via the media efforts of the psychos themselves, its projective syndication or PR campaign in the movies. Williamson's inspiration for the original screenplay was the Gainesville killer, who specialised in rearranging his victims and styling with mirror shards. It was this psycho's final cut of the view to the kill, which the crime scene's discovery and reception would transmit. In the foreground of *Scream 3* and *Scream 4* another self-reflexivity extends through deregulated movie making by consumers internal to digital mass-media culture, the endless looping between pocket cameras and website posts. In this sense, too, a serial or spectacular crime is immediately a movie.

Sid's half-brother Roman emerges, then, out of her mother's past to start the series rolling. His success story was the original killing, which he 'directed'. The only film of his we see is the home-movie surveillance tape of his abandoning mother conducting affairs. That lies in the prehistory of *Scream*. The trilogy folds out of the renewed attempts by various psychos to direct sequels, to make their own 'movies'. Each new movie marks the failure of the psycho directors, since Sid keeps on surviving and starring.

The destruction of psycho brother – whereby justice would be served on the murdered mother's behalf – opens up a clearing where before there was haunting. That in *Scream 2* psycho mother Loomis adopted the reporter role as her cover identity underscores a line of doubling of the mother passing through the ambivalently regarded role model Gale Weathers. As proxy breakthrough that reflects a related internal change in Sid, investigative reporter and detective can marry following the busting of the ghost in *Scream 3*.

The gadget-loving experts of the *Psycho* Effect, both out there in the theatre and inside the film, organise *Scream* and *Scream 2*. But the rules for trilogies are off this mark. The in-group expert leaves on tape to be played in the event of his death instructions specific to trilogies.

Out of the prehistory that is taken even further back for the ultimate surprise attack, the antagonist emerges in the third part of trilogies always with supernatural powers. While that isn't true of the psycho brother, this ruling does reflect the ghostliness of the mother, who in a sense is the other opponent. The best advice given Sid comes from the detective, who is called in whenever the homicide is industry-related, because murder in Hollywood is his specialisation. Hollywood, he says, is about death. Sid walks onto the set of 'Stab 3' and passes through her reconstructed neighbourhood, the setting of her mother's murder. Even the room in her home in which her mother died has been reconstructed. We see this room for the first time. Repression is beginning to lift. The detective says that when it comes to trilogies all bets are off. *Scream 3* has not been rehearsed, will not be repeated.

As self-conscious staging of the end of the *Psycho* Effect the *Scream* trilogy straddles the defence between tragedy and comic relief. The working title for *Scream* was originally 'Scary Movie', while another one of *Scary Movie*'s working titles was 'Scream If You Know What I Did Last Halloween'. There is a vacancy or emptiness in *Scream* that *Scary Movie* fills with laughter.

Part of the comic relief is that the motivation for serial murder seems to get lost in the crowd of possible motives. In the trilogy the motives for killing include revenge, personal trauma, desire for fame, peer pressure, psychosis, psychopathy and the influence of the movies. What we are left with in the emptiness of therapeutic closure is the inscrutable persistence of violence and the interminability of its interpretation, representation and containment. As long as violence is mediated, one place to which the perpetrator and victim alike can track back is everyone's prehistory with mother. Mother is the ultimate medium and live or life transmission. But we can also join Sid in recognising that the psycho movie mom to whom we all have easy access is not our responsibility.

In *Scream 3*, when Sid whines up her lament that she never knew who her mother really was, the detective points out that there was the mother she knew. All the prehistories and psycho versions of her mother can't take that away from her. The basic relationship cannot be displaced by the vengeful ghost business of psycho killers, with her half-brother at the front of the line. Thus she rejects Roman's victim claim, his abandonment issues, and the blame he lays on their mother. 'You kill people because you choose to,' she tells him: 'Take some fucking responsibility.' *Scream 3* suggests an alternative for the secular mind, which lies in responsibility in the sense of remembrance of one's early response and in the direction of mourning. By responding to the loss of the mother she knew, Sid takes responsibility for mourning her, the good object inside her — not to be confused with the other woman in the projections and home movies of the psycho killers.

3

Sometimes it is the mother's depression or rather its repression that lies upon the daughter. Recognition of the provenance of what afflicts her gives the daughter, like Sid at the end of *Scream 3*, a lift that takes her out of the psycho horror and gives her a new responsibility toward herself and toward her mother.

In 'Development of the Theme of the Mother's Unconscious as Discovered in Psychoanalytic Practice', Winnicott treats children who, because they must otherwise entertain depressed mothers, succeed in preventing Winnicott's 'depression or what might be boredom in the clinic' (1989: 247). But it's a near-miss since he does after all notice. Thus these children were showing him that they were 'making reparation in respect of the mother's destructive tendencies' and 'that at home the mother had to deal with the other side of this, namely the child's inability to keep up counteracting the mother's mood all of the twenty-four hours' (1989: 248). Because the patient can't take the audience of extramural contacts home with him, also because the success of lifting their depression communicates the fatality of his failure in the other place, getting to the start position is the greater effort preliminary to restarting, which never really happens: 'Always it seems that success, instead of bringing the patient to a new position, simply brings him or her to the starting point, and there is no question of further progress because the patient is exhausted by the effort of getting to the place from which a start might be made' (1989: 249).

In session the patient wants to knock up against hatred and 'arrive at being persecuted without losing the sense of being sane' (1989: 250). But there's a big difference between the mother's hate and her repressed and unconscious hate. Children can deal with being hated and make use of it as ambivalence. 'What they cannot ever satisfactorily use in their emotional development is the mother's repressed unconscious hate which they only meet in their living experiences in the form of reaction formations. At the moment that the mother hates she shows special tenderness. There is no way a child can deal with this phenomenon' (ibid.).

In 'Mother's Madness Appearing in the Clinical Material as an Ego-Alien Factor', Winnicott sorts through in the mind of his young patient Mark 'the muddle introduced into his life by certain characteristics of the mother' (1989: 375). Winnicott relied on a doodling or squiggle game to construct a child patient's history. Each takes a turn making marks on the page, developing earlier marks and commenting on them. In the opening interview with Mark, each squiggle exchange is yet another opportunity for him to bring up the theme of 'funny' (1989: 376). When on another page he leaves a mark that suggests that it is part of an 'M', he can identify it for Winnicott: '"It's a nothing." He had reached an extreme defence, for if he is a nothing then he cannot be killed or hurt by the worst trauma imaginable' (ibid.). The page before he tore while drawing vigorously. Then, upon dropping his pencil, he continued with a penknife. He goes back to this otherwise blank page after he has signed in as 'nothing' and draws the engine of a train. 'He was getting towards the traumatic express train, which evidently reminded him of Mother' (ibid.).

What he showed Winnicott was that he had to be nothing to let the traumatic thing arrive. It turns out mother goes mad in front of Mark sometimes. However, she's in treatment now. Mark needed Winnicott to know both that he is alone on occasion with his mother's madness and that his mother was otherwise good. Mark too must understand what he's after during the game. With the 'funny' squiggles 'he plays around with personal madness', thereby 'testing out' Winnicott's ability to take it. Then he shows his own extreme defence of nothingness or invulnerability. With the express or repress train that was passing through, Mark tells Winnicott 'about an immense potentiality for destruction' (1989: 381). When he next suddenly goes mad he shows 'that he is *possessed by madness*. ... The express train is rushing through the station while the local train is standing still in a siding. "Nothing" is not being destroyed by the mad "something"' (ibid.).

Transmission-impossible accomplished and the boy leaves the session happy. 'He is confident in this mother whose going mad has now been shown to me, whose going mad has become objectified and limited by its own boundaries. Mark has now become something instead of nothing, and he can play again, even play at absurdities which, being part of his own madness, are not traumatic so much as comical and laughable' (1989: 381–2).

The ghostliness of her mother is another formulation for the maternal delegation of mental states Sid works through in the *Scream* trilogy. In contrast to these films and Winnicott's case studies, two films selected from the *Psycho* Effect restate the inheritance of the mother's depression in the plain text of untreatable aberration.

Mother's Day (1980) stages on level ground the showdown between women from the city, who periodically fortify their pack bond by going out together alone into the wilderness, and the shitkicker clan of two boys and their mother. When one of the women defiantly puts her captor down as a hick, he quickly corrects her. They may not live in the city but they know all about the world as seen on TV. Didn't she notice that she was strapped to one of the latest models of exercise equipment! It would seem, then, ideologically self-important to consider the hungry of splatter cinema disadvantaged, abandoned (in *The Texas Chainsaw Massacre*, for example) by whatever economic mobility allowed their former neighbours to move to the city. Even a mass phenomenon like zombieism had to get its start cross sectioning the middle class of consumers.

Before the support group of women friends must undergo the psycho training camp of mother and sons, *Mother's Day* opened in group therapy, in which the members are all adults trying to identify with one another like teenagers. At the end of the marathon session everyone kisses the neighbour and declares, 'I love you.' The older woman, soon to be revealed to be the psycho mom, feels that the guru, Ernie, must make his mother so proud. The young woman's bandana is as much a put-on as the therapeutic lilt of her language: 'Once you know what you know you act on it.' She and her hippy boyfriend hitch a lift with the older woman, who is the perfect mark. She agrees to give them the ride since they're hardly strangers after all they've been through together. A nicety will get literalised for laughs: 'How beautiful people are underneath!' While the couple plots the next move that will off the driver and scoop out her possessions, the driving woman's psycho sons swoop down on the car and its cargo, decapitating the guy and capturing the bandana gal for gallows humor. Mother, proud of her sons, repeats 'I love you' to her victim.

In addition to working out with machines, the boys are drilled in outdoor exercises (supervised by mother wearing the uniform of a whiplash collar), which seems a Schreberesque scrambling of the military training one might pick up from TV shows. When the boys first bring the women body-bagged in their own bedding, the absolute leader greets them: 'Let's see what you brought mother.' While the other two wait their turn tied to the exercise equipment, the first one up must play with the boys in shows for the mother's viewing pleasure. The first skit in which the captive player is set up for surprise attack sitting on a park bench reading a magazine wasn't really satisfactory. But the Shirley Temple sketch on the next channel provides the transition to fatal rape on mother's watch.

We are inside the household of mother's depression which the evil clown sons manically deny. The 'daughters', who only appear to come from the outside of socio-political changes and their new in-groups, are linked to 'mother' by the same depression. After the two women have settled the score, a chthonic, deformed creature, suitably named Queenie, is the ultimate psycho-mom to emerge out of the crypt that joins the survivors to the hillbillies unto death.

In *The Baby* from 1973, to give another example of maternal adaptation to a bad place and its delegation to the next generation, a young man of diminished capacity is still being raised as the baby of the house by middle-aged mother and young adult sisters. To care for someone afflicted in this manner of bringing up baby is a good example of manic denial of repressed depression. A social worker takes an interest in the case. Baby's family doesn't trust her investment. We too wonder about her motives. Doesn't she find the situation abusive? With her mother-in-law on hand to comfort her, the social worker watches home videos of her deceased husband.

Baby also has a babysitter. She's on the phone to her boyfriend. Of course she has panties on. Will they meet later that night? OK, she won't wear any. But now we hear the cries of baby upstairs. It's OK, it takes getting used to, but she has to go now. Baby's diapers have to be changed. Baby wants to play. Baby hits his head. She comforts baby, who goes for the breast. Mother and sisters are back home. When they enter, baby is sucking the sitter's teen tit.

Whack!

The violence, however, lies in watching 'what a big baby'. Then there's violence in the mother's protectiveness of her baby. But the surprise violence lies in the court of the social worker, whose husband isn't dead but mentally impaired by a car accident. After she kidnaps baby and his clan arrives to take him back with a vengeance, she kills the young man's sisters and buries the mother alive (all of the above with her mother-in-law's help or guidance). At the happy end the social worker watches her two babies play together. It's a scenario only a mother, a very depressed mother, might enjoy.

The Renewal of Psycho Horror by Compact with the Devil

1

In the lexicon of horror film reception the notion of 'the spoiler' propitiously asserts itself as near-perfect taboo observance. Check out the countless on-line accounts of almost as many slasher films, and you will find that the revelation of the killer's identity is withheld. If you don't remember the identity of the serial killer in a particular film, it seems at times that no 'plot synopsis' is willing to help you out; you have to fast forward to the end and watch the revelation scene one more time. I discovered this group-supported ritual of withholding spoiling when I inadvertently gave away (I don't come to the B-genres from adolescence and thus never received the group instruction that comes with membership) the twist in the then brand new movie *The Sixth Sense* that Malcolm (Bruce Willis), the protagonist and child counsellor, was another ghost. The entire theatre into which 900 students were packed resonated with groans, gasps and curses. (If only because there were still several weeks to go in the course, the incident was not beyond repair.)

I taught in California for almost thirty years. After the first ten years I had a large student following: half were Rickels-heads, the other half drive-throughs who were given something to talk about at the nightly forget-togethers. No doubt we all thought I was stuffing Freud down the throats of B-genre consumerism. Part 3 saw the dismantling of my series of courses on occult and technical media by the administration, from the Department Chair and College Provost to the higher offices of university decision-making. That this arc of UCSB authority should have finally and resolutely spoiled my undergraduate reception, the pedagogical relationship that once made history at UCSB, is one of those enigmatic excesses that Melanie Klein spent her career trying to contain, at least in theory. One of the themes I addressed early on in the class on psycho horror cinema can in fact come true in one's own neighbourhood.

UCSB collapsed from progress that was once made toward distinction, beginning in the 1980s, back upon its death drive, the suburbia of adaptation to psychopathy. Klein's re-theorisation of the drive in terms of envy, the impulse to spoil not only the advances of others but one's own goodness as well, would also seem to fit a case of institutional suicide.

Klein's notion of envious spoiling, whereby she introduced an exemplary manifestation of the Death Drive as fact of life, is admitted by Winnicott into the contractual fine print of our contact high of illusion (our contractual relationship to the given as our creation). The young child must never be confronted by caretaking adults with knowledge of the transitional object's makeshift character, its random or extraneous provenance, or its real inefficacy. The injunction not to question the transitional object must succumb to the sweep of reality testing. Winnicott formulates his social contract as the open invitation to spoil early childhood at the onset, which is then the foundation for individual development. In contrast to the constitutional blows of envy in Klein's thought, which ultimately can make it impossible for a patient to benefit from analysis, what follows from the spoiling of the transitional object in Winnicott's psychopathic analysis is the relay of provisions, environments, managements that keep deprivation open to after-the-fact renegotiation at the maternal group level. Winnicott recommends spoiling the antisocial child by the family he seeks to transform into a care centre for the child's treatment, also because the spoiling by the mother will prove that the mother wasn't good enough and that the therapist is also therefore the hateful cause of the deprivation. The child learns to hate the mother in the family setting of the therapy. Psychopathic therapy does not invite the past into the session via transference but relocates by the force of regression all the parties to the setting in the past.

The willingness to spoil the child and spare the rod recommends parents for assistance in the therapy of their ill child, which Winnicott fully sketches out in the first interview and which the family must flesh out with support for the child's need to heal through regression. 'Spoiling here means giving a limited and temporary opportunity for the child to regress to dependence and to a material provision which belongs to an age that is younger than that of the child at the moment' (*Therapeutic Consultations in Child Psychiatry*, 1971: 217). The family that spoils together can be made over as site for the child's recovery. In the double meaning or application of 'spoiling' lies the second chance Winnicott gives the family system: to cancel out the earlier spoiling with the spoiling of regression therapy.

Spoiling refers to the inevitable breach in the transitional contact as well as to the inevitable therapeutic rejoinder that must make the best of a situation that's just not good enough. It is the setting in which psychopathy is grounded and unfolds. If it's too late to retrofit the family to host the dual conditions of the breach, juvenile delinquents find the institutional counterpart in a relay of holding cells.

Academics are another at-risk population treated in the institutional correlative to what's in the name alma mater. By the requirement that they practice self-management in exercises in the recognition and prevention of harassment, the institution acknowledges the ease with which academics often enough assert the performative interchangeability between discursive positions and acts of real violence. They should know. Scholarly exclusion is a typical act of delinquency, ranging from theft to extinction. The author commissioned to supply one of the essays for a 1994 edition of *Death in Venice* told me that the editor forbade that he refer to my reading in *The Case of California*, and the reference was deleted from the essay and edition. Academia or, as D. Harlan Wilson dubbed its condition, placquedemia (in a slasher novel that plays it close to the tooth), is the other walk of life in which psychopathic criminality runs rampant.

University service could spoil the life of the productive scholar; now it is spoiling therapy for losers. Once the rewards program whereby those who weren't productive in research could nevertheless upgrade their status, by the new millennium committee service was compulsory for the entire faculty, a form of occupational therapy administered to and by psychos. And whereas it was once a good thing to be a controversial rather than a likeable instructor, it certainly brought in the crowds, instruction came to be restricted to a limbo loop that transmits to the students the blanks they learn to fill in with positive evaluation, the vital circulation of a non-producing faculty.

UCSB once had an interim chancellor whose flighty comment when it was time for him to move on now resounds loud as prophecy. The UC campus, like the Santa Barbara airport, bears a Santa Barbara postal address even though the history of the institution's expansion brought about its relocation to the next town, Goleta. Unaware, perhaps, of the signifier appeal of certain place names, or aware indeed of the denial in a name, the outgoing substitute chancellor asked: why don't they change the name to UC Goleta? It's a name somewhere between deprivation and anonymity that adds plain speaking to the psycho holding cell.

2

Is *The Sixth Sense* even a horror film? Anne Rice called it a 'classic' horror film (I know this because her praise for my book *The Vampire Lectures* was part of the same fan-phone-line outgoing message, recorded and dated September 24, 1999). I take 'classic' to refer to pre-*Psycho* horror. While the *Psycho* Effect was still with us, earlier films, like Julian's *The Phantom of the Opera* and Freund's *Mad Love*, seemed re-projected in anticipation of the excess that hit the screen in 1960. By the late 1990s this monopolisation and metabolisation of horror began to fade out. The treatments had over the years secured a cure.

But when I watched *The Sixth Sense* the second time, I had the second thought that, like *The Blair Witch Project* (1999), it was engaged in a reformatting of the end of horror post-*Psycho* by the renewal of contact with the medium as sight unseen. *The Sixth Sense* packs a surprise ending that sends the viewer through a flashback loop in part given or modelled at the end of the film. Both *The Blair Witch Project* and *The Sixth Sense*, though certainly in different ways, exceeded the frame of the single screening (as contained in, as containing, a body of work) by networking with outer-corpus experiences of media manipulation and the two-timing of surprise.

Mark Z. Danielewski's 2000 novel *House of Leaves* presented a study and documentation by an internal author of a legendary film document, *The Navidson Record*. Model for this fiction of a film was *The Blair Witch Project*, which took as its outer and preliminary form (and forum) Internet rumour of a real encounter with the supernatural raised to life-or-death stakes. The outside chance that *The Blair Witch Project* was a real posthumous document of a group's violent contact with an unholy abyss, which was repeated and rehearsed on the Internet prior to the film's release, allowed it to break through the impasse at which horror was already headed off.

In *House of Leaves*, what appears to be press information about the publication's prehistory is also internal to the novel's construct. According to the cover blurb, years ago a preliminary version of the novel was first being passed around: a 'heap of paper, parts of which would occasionally surface on the Internet'. But what's being passed around is the internal fiction of a 'small but devoted following' that spread through 'older generations, who not only found themselves in those strangely arranged pages but also discovered a way back into the lives of their estranged children'. Now we hold in our hands in book form these very pages, excerpts and their first reception. The book comes to us across the gap in generation – the death in adolescence – a delegation of mournful identification.

The jacket material identifies as the content of the novel not the study of the film, which is overlooked, though it remains legible, but instead that which is never really available, namely Will Navidson's document 'of creature darkness, of an ever-growing abyss behind a closet door, and of that unholy growl which soon enough would tear through their walls and consume all of their dreams'. Navidson, a prize-winning press photographer, decides to film the happy document of his move with partner and children into a country house in Virginia where he plans to renew vows with family life. One day there is an extra room where before there was none. This room proves to be the opening of a labyrinth in which one can get lost (or find that one is at a loss) not according to a fixed design but because it is a space without borders that can undergo instant abyssal changes. *The Navidson Record* is thus the video- and audio-recorded document of a traumatically close encounter with this supernatural house.

Though the record cannot be shown, the book (or its internal relay of documents) renders itself at once visible and legible at crucial points of crisis. Thus when the passageways of the labyrinth close in on Navidson, which the video record allegedly shows, the margins start shrink wrapping the text in bits that must squeeze through these straitened circumstances on pages left largely blank, like the grey zones that presumably sustain insubstantial traces in the documentary film record of the unknown.

Upon discovering Zampanò's unfinished study and documentation of the legendary film in the apartment he takes over from the blind man upon his death, Johnny Truant decides to conclude the interrupted work. Truant's notes also record as diary entries the psychopathology of his everyday life that this editorial work either illuminates or triggers. Within the relay of his diary entries there is a story in the mode of 'The Sandman' organised around the so-called Gdansk Man, who, like the paternal Sandman figure in Hoffmann's story, cruelly enforces the high fidelity values of Oedipus at the expense of the libidinal vitality of his wayward sons. Because they messed to varying degrees with his girlfriend Kyrie, Gdansk Man, who 'is now officially on some kind of Halloween rampage' (2000: 348, n. 310), has targeted Johnny and his friend Lude for retribution. That Johnny doesn't die in consequence (as Lude does) is owed to Johnny's own potential for 'psycho' violence that he has kept in reserve since childhood and which Gdansk Man's attack releases as a kind of doubling on contact.

Zampanò's study of *The Navidson Record* completes its range of references within a (largely simulated) scholarly apparatus. In the labyrinth there is always bull: but there is one track in the footnotes that is free of the recycling language of the simulated or neurotic academe. It belongs to the troubled youth Truant. His tract is ultimately framed, like a Gothic novel, by the relationship to a missing mother.

Because he unravels (along the dotted lines of a maternal legacy of psychosis) there is another editor who must give Johnny Truant's wrap the stamp of completion. While a group of editors has turned the internal relay and withdrawal of documents into *House of Leaves*, each group member takes over where another leaves off. *House of Leaves* re-stages this staggered transmission of its document, its internal posthumous relations, in a closing series of appendices. The trace of survival is inscribed in the 'final shots' Navidson takes one Halloween night. 'Navidson does not close with the caramel covered face of a Casper the friendly ghost.' He cannot end with a recognisable representative or representation of group survival. 'Letting the parade pass from sight, he focuses on the empty road beyond, a pale curve vanishing into the woods where nothing moves and a street lamp flickers on and off until at last it flickers out and darkness sweeps in like a hand' (2000: 528).

3

While the first *Scream* appeared after *The Silence of the Lambs* (which coincides with or confirms the end of the *Psycho* Effect), the third one appeared right after *The Sixth*

Sense. The contrast between the responsibility of mourning and the therapeutic wrap that *The Sixth Sense* administered through its double take finds its point of articulation in Cole's treatment of his mother's depression.

The only dead person in *The Sixth Sense* to make contact with Cole, whom he knew in life and who thus represents a loss to him (and to his mother), is the grandmother. Otherwise his ghosts are dead strangers in transit; they're neither identified with nor necessarily internal/eternal. Instead something from this life makes them stick around, but only for the time being, until their business is finished. Before we are left with Malcolm putting himself to rest and us to the test of identification with the undead, we leave Cole putting through a communication from his grandmother to her daughter. Up to this point, Cole's relationship to the good dead was fundamentally trans-parent, dedicated to his grandmother, in doubling circumvention of the static of Oedipal relations. Once Cole took Malcolm's counselling and started listening to the ghosts that appeared to harass him, he immediately accepted a mission of rescue and justice that brought him (and us) into contact with the poisoning mother. This blinding spot in the face-to-face relationship between Cole and his mother is thus contained. In the end Cole transmits a message from grandmother to mother: Yes, her daughter had always made her proud, every day. With this proof of Cole's extra long-distance sense, the mother's blocked grief is overcome.

In 1999 one of the ghosts in *The Sixth Sense* was the *Psycho* Effect itself. The Vincent scene was a genuine shower scene: just as child psychologist and wife settle down in the bedroom, psycho Vincent pops out of the master bathroom, stripped down for full Effect. The psycho is a former child patient the psychologist treated but did not help. Vincent could not bear to be alone with his ghosts.

What can drive one as though possessed to the gunpoint of violence is the refusal to listen to your ghosts, to attend to their unfinished business. But what are ghosts animated by unfinished business? Therapy fictions. Unfinished business would correspond to the transferential relationship in session that cannot always be subsumed by the finitude of the therapeutic task at hand, which upon successful completion can be let go.

Shyamalan's precursor was Stanley Kubrick, the director famous for cinematically reinterpreting each new genre to which he contributed one film, the mantle Shyamalan hoped to assume twenty years later. Kubrick's *The Shining* set up its portrait of the haunted child at the very turning point (in 1980) of the therapeutic engagement with Hitchcock's *Schauer* scene. As Stephen King acknowledges in hindsight, ghostliness was for the author but an analogue for the effect upon the father of traumatic memories of abuse. The tendency in the novel to establish the hotel as less haunted and more infernally possessed is not an option in the film. The hotel may be possessed but not by infernal agency but rather by the murder victims and the evil dead perpetrators. That Kubrick understood the context in which he was intervening is evident in other changes he introduced into the story, which were cite specific, for example aligning the plot with the slasher/splatter thematic of survival: Hallorran, the African-American cook who shares the boy's telepathic prowess, is not admitted into the open-ended survival of the boy and his mother (in the book he even remains behind as the good father). Kubrick followed Diane Arbus into the tight spot of what Roland Barthes would address as punctum, the point of the medium where the violence in mourning is enigmatically contained and directed.

Although Shyamalan, like Kubrick, doesn't admit the Devil into the horror film, he secures the 'perfection' of his film by linking and limiting haunting to the finitude of a therapeutic outcome, the new nihilism in the wake of the contained *Psycho* Effect. If the ghost isn't clear and the psycho is contained, then a new clear text was expected. Already *The Blair Witch Project*, for all the diversion of new rumour media, gestured in this direction.

The metabolism of horror film requires surprise dosages now of hiding, now of showing it all, now of serial interminability, now of termination in time. Following the success of *The Sixth Sense* therapeutic closure itself came to be targeted as laughable or even horrifying. This is where we put *The Ring* (2002) on it. This film grabbed us just when and where we thought it was safe to see dead people (in other words in the movie theatre as therapy setting). The adults have tended to the unfinished business of the tormented girl, granted her proper burial and so on. But when the mother, all upbeat about having done the right thing, tells her son (who is the counterpart to the boy in *The Sixth Sense*) about the good deed and dead, the boy is horrified. Don't you know that she won't stop, that she doesn't sleep, that her violence cannot be buried or let go?! Now the mother knows – and now we, too, know – that the anger of this ghost is interminable and the psycho violence contained in the ghost's video and phone call as death sentence in seven days' time can be circumvented only by passing it on before the deadline is reached. You must spread the viewing of contained violence – its death threat – to ever more potential victims or survivors and collaborators.

It is the spell or curse of black magic (as prescribed in the most ancient manuals of necromancy) that can best be kept off its mark by passing it on. In Jacques Tourneur's *Curse of the Demon* (1957), the written spell wasn't simply activated when cast; first it was secretly deposited, whereupon it had to set its spell, during which time the person under its curse still had a second chance, theoretically, if he knew what happened and could find the spell, to pass the piece of writing on to yet another address in the developing chain. In *The Ring*, the ghost, in fact a demon, prefers the spreading scenario to the carrying out of the death sentence. Each viewer who dies of fright after seven days closes off a tributary of her influence. The demon rules through the violence we contain, survive and pass on. Infernal violence is attached to push-buttons of certainty, but pressed down in the service of control of the finite span of d eferral.

But what is personalised and staggered through this infernal compact with the curse of violence, whereby one intended victim must pass it on to the next consumer, is the 'divine' frame or plan of surveillance. During the era of the *Psycho* Effect, we were also, in everyday life, in the media, in politics, under the growing impression that they've got us all on tape. The medium in which sound engineer Jack in Brian De Palma's *Blow Out* keeps running up against the limits of his gadget love is also the doubling medium in which that love is realised, but as posthumous. De Palma's *Body Double* also underscored how mediatic doubling of our senses can be constructed via surveillance as *evidence* of our senses. Wes Craven's *A Nightmare on Elm Street* conveyed the sense that your dreams, your unconscious, including your repressed memories, can be known, placed under super-vision and transmitted intact from one psyche to the next. The research clinics in *A Nightmare on Elm Street* – as already in *Exorcist II: The Heretic* (1977) – suggested that science (in other words, the film medium) had caught up with demonology in regard to control of access to your dream states. In *The Serpent and the Rainbow*, Craven's 1988 zombie film set on contemporary Haitian occult beliefs and practices of Voudon, the dictator who is intent on destroying the visiting researcher assures his opponent in yet another showdown: 'I know what you dreamed last night: I was there.'

In the 1980 slasher film *Prom Night*, the killer witnessed how years ago the group of friends now in the graduating class had caused the death of a younger child, Robin. 'See you at the prom,' the anonymous caller assures one of the graduates responsible for the crime back then: 'Do you still like to play games?' This twist in the plot of psycho killing reaches the foreground seventeen years later in *I Know What You Did Last Summer* (1997). Whereas in *Prom Night* a witness remembers and avenges the murder of the victim, in *I Know What You Did Last Summer* the surprise is that the victim lives on. In *Prom Night*, Kim, sister of Robin, takes away the axe the psycho killer has to grind and knocks him out with the handle. But when the killer is unmasked, she faces her brother, who saw her date and his gang kill their sister. Eyewitness testimony courses tragically through the sibling bloodline.

The savvy that Williamson demonstrated in disclosing the structure of slasher therapy in *Scream* is also evident in his screenplay for the 1997 movie, in which he elaborates a shift in the crime scene. No longer do revenge and recognition catch up with the illicit secret crime, allowing everyone in the end to take it interpersonally. That the proof, like the murder victim, lives on is an uncanny continuity, which, lacking the suspense of motivation, must undergo diversion through an 'urban legend' of a demonic reaper, which is no less throwaway than the identity of the killer.

Between the two films (and in the case of *I Know What You Did Last Summer*, between the novel and its film adaptation) the status of evidence had come under a new aegis of certainty. It is not that of testimony, like the visual recording on tape as proof. The doubling of the evidence of the senses always admitted the constitutive possibility that it had been manipulated, even simulated (which is why its omnipotence was fantasy material). But then a new standard of certainty established itself in crime investigation, which could not but change our relationship to the spectrum of proof and its attendant fantasies. The ensuing prominence of the lab in crime shows as seen on TV found in horror cinema a parallel universal: the reemergence of the Devil. That *Hello Mary Lou: Prom Night II* in 1987 breaks with the original by turning to possession by a hell-bound spirit as the continuity shot linking the prom in the 1980s to a prehistory in murderous jealousy thirty years earlier amounts to a replacement of the traditional Oedipal setting of the whodunit. Infernal possession by 'evil beyond imagination' became the motor of return for *Prom Night* sequels III and IV.

The Devil Dad, at once the primal father of prehistory and the pre-Oedipal father in every individual history, is a figure of early monopolisation of sexual difference as penetration, for which the anal theory of birth provides the premier outlet. Before taking the leap of faith toward acceptance of the reality of reproduction, as Freud argued notably in his case study of the Wolfman, young children derive from their sense-certain relationship to their own excrement, now as loss, now as gift, a sure-fire understanding of where babies come from.

The only sexual difference or distinction wielded as penetration in this setting belongs to the Devil Dad, who sires the excremental babies. This certainty of creativity and origin in terms of excremental replication is reflected, by upward displacement, in the contractual terms of the relationship selected clients enjoy with the Devil. The Devil's best offer, finite quality time without interruption or compromise by death or trauma, extends the paradoxical comfort of a certain deadline. The Devil rejects as immortality neurosis the grief that gets in the way of the upgrade of substitution and accepts as clients under contract only candidates free of inhibition, including that of attachment to what's gone.

The Devil's clients are, then, psychopaths, whose violence finds secular elaboration as mystery in crime scenes. In the setting of psycho horror, the diagnosis of psychosis supplied a stopgap in the failure of interpretation of psychopathic violence. But psychopathy, while apparently impossible to treat and interpret, takes us by surprise in the environs of quasi normalcy. The utterly psychopathic psycho (heir to the Devil's clients) is the fitting candidate, if not the mascot, for the new possibilities of identification at the scene of the crime.

4

Leaving 'he said, she said' behind, the criminologists of *CSI* (Las Vegas) must follow the evidence – even if they don't like where it's taking them. In episode 7 of the first season, the evidence leads them to know who, how, and what. Although the CSI team is satisfied with knowing 'all the truth except Why', the leader of the team, Grissom, does care about the outstanding Why. 'I don't like holes. What are they hiding?' This leadership or readership that we follow to know the Why passes through two lines from *Macbeth*, the first and last lines of one stretch of Lady Macbeth's sleep-talking: 'Out, damned spot! Out, I say! One; two. ... Yet who would have thought the old man to have had so much blood in him?' (V. 1).

Lady Macbeth encapsulates within her breakdown address both her former resolve, which she used to motivate her hesitating husband, and her own initial hesitation. She couldn't murder Duncan because asleep he looked like her father (like her dead father). Often one recognises a parent's likeness in one's own child. To motivate her husband she swore that, if that had been her resolve, she could snatch her own baby from her breast and smash its brains out against the wall. Since she added that she knew what it means to nurse an infant, we must assume that in this badgering with courage her dead child is being carried forward. That she lets her two already-goners succumb to second death, which is murder, is what qualifies her as Freud's character type 'Wrecked by Success'. It is from the top of successful mourning that her aspirations with her husband will succeed. But the success that would secure the succession of inheritance by substitution for loss wrecks her best played plans. Getting rid of Duncan amounted for Lady Macbeth to losing the loss of her child and giving a wide berth/birth to the afterlife of successful mourning. From start to finish, Lady Macbeth proves unable to put the dead to second death. Now as she withdraws into madness and suicide, Lady Macbeth re-counts in the blood that won't wash clean her resolve to kill her dead father and child, the two successes that have wrecked her. In *CSI* episode 7, titled 'Blood Drops', we start counting one, two spots, drops or murder victims inside the compulsion's loop through the recent past. While for Lady Macbeth mourning was in the blood, another relationship to the father is recounted in the blood drops of the criminal investigation. The episode is the very allegory of a shift in the realm of verification that coincided in the 1990s with the ending of the *Psycho* Effect.

In contrast to *Columbo*, which places the titular hero in the double position of sleuth and psychoanalyst, in *CSI* a team (which embraces leader and the pack) follows the evidence to some point beyond psychological speculation. In the first episode of *Columbo*, the detective faces the enigma of a writing couple, in which one partner was murdered. And yet it proves next to impossible to separate out the two partners into the different cases required for causal sentencing. Columbo asks the murdered writer's widow to utter any and all thoughts crossing her mind associated with the two writing partners. She knows what he's after: 'It's like analysis without the couch.' We don't witness the talking session. But Columbo emerges from it with a sense of the ending of the case.

CSI foregrounds the team effort of investigation of evidence in which new and improved gadgets often take centre stage. On the sidelines there are the interpersonal relations among the team members, which come up for analytic understanding. In

'Blood Drops' the two women on the team face their relationship to children in the light of abuse or neglect charges. Childhood – or a relationship to childhood as missing – sets the stage for the final revelations both in the team context and, by proxy, out in the viewing context in front of the TV set. The question that remains to be raised is the one Grissom works to answer. It's the Why that everyone else is willing to forego.

Up to a point Grissom (or Petersen) in this CSI episode reprises his role as Will Graham, the detective in Michael Mann's *Manhunter* (1986), who must be brought out of his retirement in melancholia to crack a new case of serial murder. In this adaptation of *Red Dragon*, another Thomas Harris novel of serial-crime profiling and detection, the psychiatrist cum cannibal Hannibal Lecktor shares the psycho position with the killer at large, but as expert otherwise contained in his prison cell. Before retiring early, the detective withdrew from the scene of his successful identification and capture of Lecktor into his own mental illness occasioned by the identification work. The reason for his success in this line of work is that he can open himself to thinking the thoughts of the psycho killer. When Lecktor proclaims it inconceivable that his greater intellect could have been grasped by a lesser quotient, Graham confirms that this indeed would have been impossible, if Lecktor's mind hadn't been diminished by psychosis. To which Lecktor responds with renewed attempts to enter Graham's mind at the breaking point – and ultimately by letting the unidentified killer know where Graham lives.

In *Manhunter*, profiling is diverted by the quest to understand the psycho. Nobody knows becomes the psycho's desire to metamorphose beyond boundaries. Jonathan Demme's adaptation of Harris's *The Silence of the Lambs* runs with the big idea of metamorphosis, which is not really represented in the novel. Harris cast the maniac Buffalo Bill as Ed Gein reference complete with a mother-identified profile. But it remains unclear whether he is rebuilding his mother out of the long-distant meat vehicles for her comeback or whether he is continuing to lose and find his souvenirs of her in a nether realm of film references. The question remains, in the psychic terms which underlie the mediatic ones, does the projection of horror make room for absence – or is this projection constrained instead to fill a void with more gaps or cuts? As Diana Fuss shows, Demme's film has all its antagonists lined up as interchangeable, like the hole that's a hole, before the picture opens. What's writ large as metamorphosis is the identification required for understanding the other, which the moviegoer recognises on the double.

That there are sophisticated close readings of the film adaptations of the Harris complex attests to the confluence between academic and journalistic tendencies. At some point in the 1990s the members of the Hollywood teamwork of filmmaking had attended undergraduate classes informed by post-Freudian structuralism. As Klaus Theweleit points out, there is nothing of academic import in the receiving area of the Harris complex that needed to be imported. Overall we are left with a foreshortened range of speculation installed between Deleuze and Guattari's 'becoming multiple' and Lacan's arrival of the letter always at its destination.

The POV is wielded by Graham as the frame of his most profound application of 'profiling'. The profiling POV in the service of detection proceeds on one track while the clinching evidence pops up as a surprise out of the periphery of its oversight. The case can close once Graham knows where the killer works. Gateway is the lab where the home videos of the victims we have been watching together with the investigative team were developed. The surveillance videos themselves were the killer's link to a divine perspective beyond the good-looking and his own bad and ugly.

Graham keeps revisiting the scene while 'dictating' the identification with the psycho killer, which dictates to him: 'I see me desired by you in the silver mirrors of your eyes.' Thus he enters the psycho's super vision in order to imagine the interest the killer took in his victims, all the while observing the lives he would take. But the investigation was suspending a screen memorial of the killer's rituals in the blind spot of the address label on the video box. While the investigators did attend to the basics of the production of the videos, and already knew the place or address of their production according to the top label, they didn't know that each label of product identification covered up yet other labels in evidence of the process of subcontracting and outsourcing.

The open secret of our relationship to identification lying in the splitting image of different but superimposable addresses is what Melanie Klein called projective identification, which she fully explored in the course of analysing Julian Green's Faustian novel, *If I Were You*. The infant's fantasies about entering the mother's breast and body to scoop out the resources of her creativity alternate with the fantasies in return that the mother's body is out to devour or reabsorb the infant. 'In such phantasies, products of the body and parts of the self are felt to have been split off, projected into the mother, and to be continuing their existence within her' ('On Identification', 1984: 142).

The projective identification that fits Green's narrative of protagonist Fabian's body switching, entered upon via compact with the Devil, reflects the earliest conditions of formation of the self within intrapsychic networks externalized through outsourcing. 'Identification by projection implies a combination of splitting off parts of the self and projecting them on to (or rather into) another person' ('On Identification', 1984: 143). Splitting is only an effective primal defence 'to the extent that it brings about a dispersal of anxiety and a cutting off of emotions. But it fails in another sense because it results in a feeling akin to death' (ibid.).

Klein allows that although a patient might anxiously feel that he doesn't know where the parts went that he dispersed into the external world, this sensation belongs to the defensive function of splitting itself, which has the effect of rendering estranged parts of the self inaccessible both to the patient and to the analyst. It seems that more is retained and carried over than annihilated in the splitting – which Green demonstrates in the course of his protagonist Fabian's infernal body switching. 'We should conclude therefore (in keeping with the author's very concrete conception of the projective process), that Fabian's memories and other aspects of his personality are left behind in the discarded Fabian who must have retained a good deal of his ego when the split occurred' ('On Identification', 1984: 166). The retention of 'a good deal', like the compact with the Devil Dad, is one option for self-containment in the turbulent setting of projective identification.

Another option is reserved for the object relation, which balances the act of splitting by working through the primal scene that Klein redefined as the 'combined parents', the double backed union that in the course of development can be separated out into whole objects to be recombined in identification and love. That this development is under arrest in Fabian's case is evident, Klein underscores, inasmuch as it never crosses his mind, not even, for example, while in the throes of his fixation upon the baker woman, to enter the person of the woman's husband.

In Freud's 'A Seventeenth-Century Demonological Neurosis', the painter who signed up to be the Devil's bodily son portrayed the infernal father embodying a mix of gender traits. According to Freud, the painter was struggling to reach back through the pre-Oedipal relationship to hit bottom and begin to mourn. The early father is inside the pre-Oedipal mother's body, much as the Devil depends on the witch for all magic of embodiment. By summoning the Devil Dad's combined corpus, the grieving son circumvents the order of substitution grounded in the father's symbolic status as DOA and the mother's individuation as parent.

In *Manhunter*, the underlying Gateway label is discovered and the cover of product identification blown just as the serial killer blows his wad on his first real date. Can his murderous sense of betrayal by his blind coworker be considered inevitable within his psycho reality – or is it rather the kind of inevitability (static on the lines to the other of couplification) that under better-managed conditions he would have been able to work through, like another teenager? After the first date he cries. In becoming a unit he finds that he's depressed. This, however inadvertently, is evidence of something like clinical insight.

Graham was looking to identify the transformative POV, the mask or double, which the killer strapped on while watching and filming his future victims. In Poe's 'The Purloined Letter', Dupin lines up his seeing I by identification with the minister who stole the letter he then hid away. Dupin's inspiration was a schoolboy he once knew who was prodigious at guessing correctly even or odd by means of assuming the expression on the face of his opponent and assessing the thoughts that thus came to mind. The minister is not only a mathematician but also a poet and a diplomat who excels at intrigue. The transfer of the mathematical cast of mind to other mindsets and discourses makes mistakes of oversight, like those constraining the police inspector's investigation. But Dupin is able to see oversight from both sides. While the police investigation went so far as to divide up the thief's environs into a grid for the irreversibly exhaustive overturning of evidence, Dupin espies the letter, which is under the cover of another address label, in an interview with the minister conducted as intraview between two masks of ennui.

Before it was a convention of cinema, POV operates in Dupin's recognition that loss of sight of the periphery follows from the transfer of a mathematical perspective. It was by the logic of surveillance, applied to and illuminated by POV profiling, that Graham's assumption of a mise-en-scène of rehearsal and repetition oversaw and overlooked the product-mediation of the encounter. But the label is also key to the delusion of bodily transformation beyond gender identification. The identifying label 'Gateway' is literally stuck beneath all the others, the bottom line of a gummy tumescence. Once lifted out from under its blind spot, the dirty inverted letter dangling over the fireplace in Poe's story could be recognised by Marie Bonaparte as the anal penis. As he did with Klein's essay 'Mourning and Its Relation to Manic-Depressive States' in his reading of *Hamlet*, Lacan climbs up over the corpus of Bonaparte's study, once again unnamed, to intercept the past and make the score for Dad certainty on his turf and terms of name of the father. The itinerary of the letter as plain text of destiny is, as Derrida could show in *The Post Card*, a bum steer.

5

The first reconstruction of the crime scene in 'Blood Drops' would appear to be on the same page as *Manhunter*. While Graham retraces steps of the killer we already followed in the film's preamble, dictating his observations to a machine rather than to an assistant, the reconstruction of the killing culminates in evidence that the husband/father, even with throat slit, rushed to block the killer's movement toward the children's bedrooms. While Graham is very much on his own, a kind of method actor in detection, Grissom hovers over a team structure spanning a sensorium of evidence that provides the container for the criminal mind.

In 'Blood Drops' the team has detected in the evidence that one of the surviving teenager's boyfriends committed the crime. His confession can be confirmed by lie detector test. In the evidence gathered against Tina, the surviving teenager, from a veritable fraternal horde of suitors, a profile of the father as primal begins to emerge. But now that one couple has been identified, the rhetorical question is posed to the confessed killer: Did he do it so he and Tina could continue to be together? Was her father against their union? Not according to the results of the lie detector test. We are in the environs of the unanswered Why.

The father's blood drops on the hallway floor have to be read more closely. The father was not going toward but rather coming out of the younger daughter's bedroom.

A closer examination of the young girl's skin via a special device reveals evidence of abuse. It shouldn't be a surprise that Tina was, in her turn, a survivor of the paternal regime of abuse to which her mother and brothers adapted. But she drew a line in the blood over her younger sister whom she now, however, calls 'daughter'. Thus at age 13 she gave birth to her father's daughter, who in the meantime reached the age that turns on the father as midnight abuser.

'Blood Drops' seems exceptional in the *CSI* series for the virtual lack of new and improved detection gadgets, techniques and tests. The closest we get is when we can't help but hear in a team member's assurance – that they should find a pair of jeans under all the blood – the 'genes' for which one tests blood. Under the blood Grissom instead discovers the actual referent of the only word the traumatised child can utter at the crime scene: 'Buffalo.' It is a pendant among the father's effects, which helps identify the crime that precedes the murders.

At the very opening of the episode Tina rushes out of the house crying murder – and cites the scene in *Halloween* in which Laurie called out for help throughout the immediate neighbourhood. In 'Blood Drops' the citations of slasher films are diversions. But the Manson Family-style cult citations, the occult symbols painted on the wall with the blood of the victims, though they are indeed 'imitation, not butter', count, Grissom recognises right away, as a 'message', one that strikes home. Alone in the crime-scene bedroom with one of the team players, Grissom asks her: 'Do you feel this?' In general one senses that for Grissom the event of trauma is endlessly decodable within the ectoplasm of evidence. Outside he tells his team: 'The killer was here two hours ago. He left part of himself behind.' But in answer to his séance-style question, raised over the murdered mother's body in the bedroom, his colleague offers: 'Her soul's still in the room.' But Grissom counters: 'there's something else'. We're back inside the fundamental concern and question that Hamlet raised at the opening of secular subjectivity: is what I feel in this absence of life the identifiable ghost of the lost loved one or is there something else, a demon from hell? The first reconstruction of the crime scene saw the mother as the first victim: at the end we know it was the father, coming out of his little girl's bedroom, who was cut down first.

Tina's opening reenactment of the scene in *Halloween* is followed by a close-up of the figurines of rabbits in the front garden. Beyond their libidinal significance as bunnies, they are part of the totemic chain culminating in 'buffalo', the father who comes every night to sacrifice childhood to his desire. They are also mascots of the testing for certainty in reproduction. The 1927 pregnancy test, which observed a change in the animal ovaries following injection of the woman's urine, became as the 'rabbit test' part of the English language by 1949, like the phrase signifying a positive test result: 'the rabbit died'.

What introduced the missing piece of certainty into the test situation, which 'Blood Drops' allegorises in its close rereading of the entry and exit of the father, is, of course,

DNA. In criminology DNA testing became by the 1990s the standard for examination of evidence. But it emerged as the byproduct of its success in paternity testing, which concluded its prehistory. 'DNA fingerprinting', which is how it was dubbed in 1984, was first applied to crimes of rape and murder in the UK. In the United States the switch from DNA paternity testing to criminal trials hit the headlines with the solution of a sensational case of rape and incest. DNA testing of tissue taken from a thirteen-year-old girl's aborted fetus identified her father as her abuser. The identification of the criminal coincided with identification of the father.

DNA, discovered in 1953, developed via paternity testing over two decades unto the reversal of that symbolic range of evidence, according to which sensual certainty was ascribed to one's relationship to mother and the uncertainty of paternity was valorized for the father's role in the spiritualisation of the object relation, which was essentially one of adoption, of being chosen. The certainty of maternity was always sinister, but was put to good use to add a certain understanding of psychosis to the enigma of psychopathic violence: disavowal of paternal spiritualisation and the malingering on of maternal sense certainty. The paternity that can now be proven belongs, however, to the pre-Oedipal father, the Devil Dad, whose embodiment is secured through the subordinated pre-Oedipal mother. In 'Blood Drops' the father abuses and impregnates his daughter and then raises his daughter's daughter to be the next recipient of 'buffalo'. While reproduction and heterosexuality remain nominally intact, the father only made recourse to reproductive biology under the excremental experimental conditions of his family as lab space in order to renew his vows always only with the same interchangeable outlet.

Freddy Krueger, the first slasher killer unincorporated by the bond with mother, was also the first demonic psycho mascot, although his infernal status wasn't made explicit until the 1991 sequel *Freddy's Dead*. His original double identification – at once child murderer and repressed memory of vigilante justice – came to be replaced by Devil-dong prongs: he was the trauma spawn of his mother Amanda's gang banging by 100 maniacs and the willing signatory to a deal with the dream demons.

6

That by the new millennium another relationship to psycho violence became available via an infernal frame of reference (and evidence) does not appear new as such. But the frame in which the replacement took place was therapeutic, secular, and finite. We had arrived at the surprising turning point Benjamin identified in *Origin of the German Mourning Play*. There comes the time when the secular allegory of the Baroque stage inevitably cuts to the Devil, the hidden anchorperson of allegory itself, bringing allegory into the extinguishing light of Christianity. This turn-around, however, goes once more around the half-life that allowed secularism to emerge out of Christianity in the first place and now brings back from the props department a Christian ending to relieve the secular strain (evident even in therapeutic finitude).

While *Scream 4* still extended the frame of self-reflexivity through digital moviemaking, albeit to the imploding point, the *Saw* franchise kept resolutely outside this frame. The formal suspense in *Saw* (2004) between the locked-room or torture-chamber mystery and the flashbacks is constructed toward the resolution of the Who, What and How. (Otherwise we would be abandoned to the same sexualisation of the restroom, with a dead man in the middle, close to the border of the Schreber case.) The Why belongs to the film's resemblance to David Fincher's *Seven* (1995), in which a Christian psycho staged his murder of sinners according to the significance of the deadly sin each victim embodied, teaching not only them a lesson, but also preaching to the choir. In *Saw* the psycho killer Jigsaw presents through his traumatic staging of the shortcomings of his victims a code of conduct supported by the Christian Church and recognisable to Satanists. The flashbacks filling in the Why, which have the unambiguous quality of post-traumatic returns to original sites, reveal the staging area and era of this franchise.

By using the supplement of the new Web access, *The Blair Witch Project* in part externalised what *Saw* includes within its four screen walls. As the alleged document of a 1994 mishap, *The Blair Witch Project* was in its entirety a flashback, but suspended between investigation and black magic. It's only in the lexicon of Christian morality that the demonism of these films can express itself. Satanism is what the secular criminal mind is reduced or elevated to within the Christian frame of reference. The slasher film is revalorised, reclaimed, even redeemed as demon film. The demonic killer wields certainty in violence, but also as counter measure against neuroticising neglect. Psycho horror films with demons on board counter and contain neuroticising influence the way possession functioned in William Friedkin's *The Exorcist* (1973).

Beginning with Michael Myers in *Halloween*, the psycho killer became an object of mass identification (also through the concomitant issue of the young woman's survival, which came to have a value of its own). In becoming recognisably therapeutic (and group therapeutic) – and thus aiming toward the end in sight and the survival of treatment – slasher movies also became increasingly demonic in range of the ending of the *Psycho* Effect. In the series of *Halloween* and *Friday the 13th*, a demonic aspect eventually emerged to supply not another turn in the burial plot but the new plot twist of Dad certainty.

Spurred by the slasher momentum of the *Psycho* Effect Robert Bloch composed his own sequel, *Psycho II*, in which a psychiatrist deranged by identification with his patient Norman Bates kills off the lookalike actors performing in the first film adaptation of the Bates case. In his 1990 conclusion of the series or trilogy, *Psycho House*, Bloch updates the psychiatric frame whereby the psycho horror of mad murder can be contained. 'There was a time, up until just a few centuries ago, when it was generally accepted that the mentally ill were possessed by demons. Today we're starting to believe there may be a physiological basis for certain types of schizophrenia – evil organisms instead of evil spirits. For all we know demons may turn out to be just molecules in a DNA chain' (1990: 199).

From book to screen Friedkin streamlined the topic of possession as demonic only. In William Blatty's *The Exorcist*, possession ambiguously bordered on melancholic identification with the ghostly departed. In 2009, *Paranormal Activity* offered documentation of a haunted house. But the milieu of ghosts was blocked by the switch to the house's possession, out of which a demon emerged. While retrenchments of Christian evil in the horror film were not new – consider *The Amityville Horror* (1979) – they were exceptional, against the grain of terror.

Whether nominally secular or occult the horror plots of B-pictures have tended more recently to subscribe to a controlling interest that is demonic. Lars von Trier's *Antichrist* (2009) could still count on surprising its A-list audience with a lurching twist of the demonic, which reveals itself in the midst of mourning sickness to be the all-subsuming prehistory.

Although adumbrated by the look of trauma, the flashbacks in the *Saw* movies fill in blanks without question or narratological ambiguity. In alternation the live feed sequences reinforce the primal significance of testing and questioning through trial by torment. For the inquisitioning mind the confession that was obtained by torture was the truth without question. Torture-testing restores the live or life transmission under its true aegis, the survival instinct.

In *Saw II* (2005) we get to know John, the psycho renamed by press and police Jigsaw after the shape of a missing puzzle piece he cut out of his victim and left behind. He discovered that once his life was shattered by the diagnosis of a deadline his survival instinct had returned, too late in a sense. But in another sense: those who can't, teach. The blank in the puzzle was not his signature but the symbol of the missingness of the survival instinct in the human condition.

Through his testing he would restore the instinct in his subjects. Those subjects who cannot follow the rules and fail the test thus sentence themselves to punishment unto death. They pay, like the victims of the psycho preacher in *Seven*, for their sins of attrition, though in *Saw* it is always and again the deadly sin of sloth or apathy.

The locked room, in which two men wake up with a corpse at the start of *Saw*, is a combination bathroom/boiler room, a station to remember that the *Psycho* Effect passed here and that now it's gone. It most closely resembles the set of torture porn films that transfixes the protagonist of Cronenberg's *Videodrome* (1983). Adam, one of the two men chained to pipes at either end of this space, identifies the opening set of *Saw* in reference to 'reality TV'. He also wonders if he isn't the victim of the latest genre of psychopathic criminality: theft of spare organs for auction on ebay. (In *Saw II* the reality-effect reference is to the war zones transmitted on TV, including the

cells in which journalists are held for many years.) But as so often in digital communication and entertainment we're back inside a classroom under surveillance taking
tests.

In *Saw II* Jigsaw passes on and into Amanda, the first survivor in the prehistory
of Jigsaw's game, which we flash back on in *Saw*. It is the only game in the original
short version, also titled *Saw* (2003). As shown in the feature, Amanda, a drug addict,
followed the rules and carved the key needed to remove the 'reverse bear trap' in her
face out of the stomach of the 'dead man' lying next to her in the room of this trial.
But by drug overdose the body she cuts into lies there not already dead but rather
between life and death. That the operation itself is fatal is the one difference added
to the ordeal borrowed from *The Abominable Dr. Phibes* (1971), Anton LaVey's favorite
'Satanic' movie. In the diagnostic realm of verification of signs of life the vegetable is
not alive but can, legally, be harvested for organs. The moral of Jigsaw's teaching or
preaching, that without the survival instinct up and running one is already dead, is
illustrated by the embodied life a drug addict throws away, which, though still barely
living, no longer meets scientific criteria for being or meaning 'alive'.

I remember asking a student what the appeal of *Saw* was: she said that when she
watched the film she had to wonder if she would be able to do that, cut off her own foot
or carve up a comatose body, in order to survive. What Amanda had to do to survive
changed her life. The death-wish trajectory of the cut in *Psycho* was left behind –
at Marion's door. At the end of the sequel Amanda administered upon her first 'test
subject' the program of instruction in survival instinct she inherited from Jigsaw. The
test for survival reverses the android test for empathy (as developed by Philip K. Dick
and adapted for the screen by Ridley Scott in 1982) in order to give the highest score
to psychopathy's heirs. The one remove of inheritance is key to the main ambiguity in
the series, namely Jigsaw's claim that his teaching is not to be confused with murder.
By *Saw III* (2006) the shaky introduction of the delegation of Jigsaw's instruction is
withdrawn. Amanda's appointment as heiress was a test she failed because rather
than give the test subjects instruction in the importance of survival she gave them
short shrift and executed them instead.

According to D. W. Winnicott, the psychopath's testing of his environment for its
ability to withstand emotional turbulence leads down a relay of holding cells. The
spontaneous or true self that Winnicott saw as still alive and kicking in the psychopath
is to be redeemed in *Saw II* from its stowaway position in the hold. All the test subjects
are graduates of the psychopathic course of self-containment, all damaged goods. But
they were all caught within a span of corruption involving the arresting officer, who put
them away by manipulated evidence. This detective is summoned by Jigsaw to find
the group on the monitor, which includes his delinquent son. Only the detective's son is
'safe' in the end (literally inside a safe), while his father will be tested by Amanda unto
death: 'game over'. As is the case with the possession and exorcism in *The Exorcist*,

Jigsaw's infernal intervention, by treating the child in the parent, saves the child from succumbing to the psychological impasse of the parental generation.

To be relieved of one's death-wishing participation in the murder of Marion Crane, which was the goal of three decades of slasher and splatter filmmaking, could only be viewed from the infernal perspective to be hypocritical and dishonest. It is within this switch of perspective (beginning in Freddy's dreams) that the Devil Dad (accompanied by the survivor as witch) came to administer the horror hub of identification between the jigsaw of surgical separations and the puzzle (of evidence) it leaves behind pre-assembled. Book over.

Filmography

28 Days Later. Directed by Danny Boyle, 2002.

Abbott and Costello Meet the Mummy. Directed by Charles Lamont, 1955.

The Abominable Dr. Phibes. Directed by Robert Fuest, 1971.

Aliens. Directed by James Cameron, 1986.

The Amityville Horror. Directed by Stuart Rosenberg, 1979.

Antichrist. Directed by Lars von Trier, 2009.

The Baby. Directed by Ted Post, 1973.

The Bad Seed. Directed by Mervyn LeRoy, 1956.

Bedlam. Directed by Mark Robson, 1946.

The Birds. Directed by Alfred Hitchcock, 1963.

Blade. Directed by Stephen Norrington, 1998.

Blade II. Directed by Guillermo del Toro, 2002.

Blade: Trinity. Directed by David S. Goyer, 2004.

The Blair Witch Project. Directed by Daniel Myrick and Eduardo Sánchez, 1999.

Blood Feast. Directed by H. G. Lewis, 1963. *Blow Out*. Directed by Brian De Palma, 1981.

Blow Out. Directed by Brian De Palma, 1981.

Blow Up. Directed by Michelangelo Antonioni, 1966.

Body Double. Directed by Brian De Palma, 1984.

Bruiser. Directed by George Romero, 2000.

A Bucket of Blood. Directed by Roger Corman, 1959.

Buffy the Vampire Slayer. Created by Joss Whedon, 1997–2003.

The Cabinet of Dr. Caligari. Directed by Robert Wiene, 1920.

Candyman. Directed by Bernard Rose, 1992

Candyman 2: Farewell to the Flesh. Directed by Bill Condon, 1994

Candyman 3: Day of the Dead. Directed by Turi Meyer, 1999.

Carrie. Directed by Brian De Palma, 1976.

Cat People. Directed by Jacques Tourneur, 1942.

Cat People. Directed by Paul Schrader, 1982.

The Cell. Directed by Tarsem Singh, 2000.

Color Me Blood Red. Directed by H. G. Lewis, 1965.

Columbo. Created by Richard Levinson and William Link, 1968–2003.

The Crawling Hand. Directed by Herbert L. Strock, 1963.

The Crazies. Directed by George Romero, 1973.

CSI: Crime Scene Investigation. Created by Antony Zuiker, 2000–.

The Curse of the Cat People. Directed by Gunter von Fritsch, 1944.

Curse of the Demon. Directed by Jacques Tourneur, 1957.

Cutting Class. Directed by Rospo Pallenberg, 1989.

Dawn of the Dead. Directed by George Romero, 1978.

Day of the Dead. Directed by George Romero, 1985.

Demons. Directed by Lamberto Bava, 1985.

Dexter. Created by James Manos, Jr., 2006–2013.

Les Diaboliques. Directed by Henri-Georges Clouzot, 1955.

Don't Answer the Phone. Directed by Robert Hammer, 1980.

Dr. Jekyll and Mr. Hyde. Directed by Rouben Mamoulian, 1931.

Dracula. Directed by Tod Browning, 1931.

Dressed to Kill. Directed by Brian De Palma, 1980.

Eaten Alive. Directed by Tobe Hooper, 1977.

The Exorcist. Directed by William Friedkin, 1973.

The Exorcist II. The Heretic. Directed by John Boorman, 1977.

Eyes of Laura Mars. Directed by Irvin Kershner, 1978.

Eyes without a Face [*Les Yeux sans visage*]. Directed by Georges Franju, 1959.

Fade to Black. Directed by Vernon Zimmerman, 1980.

Family Plot. Directed by Alfred Hitchcock, 1976.

Fatal Attraction. Directed by Adrian Lyne, 1987.

Fido. Directed by Andrew Currie, 2006.

The Fog. Directed by John Carpenter, 1980.

Forrest Gump. Directed by Robert Zemeckis, 1994.

Frankenstein. Directed by James Whale, 1931.

Freaks. Directed by Tod Browning, 1932.

Freddy vs. Jason. Directed by Ronny Yu, 2003.

Freddy's Dead: The Final Nightmare. Directed by Rachel Talalay, 1991.

Frenzy. Directed by Alfred Hitchcock, 1972.

Friday the 13th. Directed by Sean Cunningham, 1980.

Friday the 13th 2. Directed by Steve Miner, 1981.

Friday the 13th Part III. Directed by Steve Miner, 1982.

Friday the 13th: The Final Chapter. Directed by Joseph Zito, 1984.

Friday the 13th Part VI: Jason Lives. Directed by Tom McLoughlin, 1986.

Ghost. Directed by Jerry Zucker, 1990.

Gone with the Wind. Directed by Victor Fleming, 1939.

Halloween. Directed by John Carpenter, 1978.

Halloween 2. Directed by Rick Rosenthal, 1981.

Halloween III: Season of the Witch. Directed by Tommy Lee Wallace, 1982.

Halloween 4: The Return of Michael Myers. Directed by Dwight H. Little, 1988.

Halloween 5: The Revenge of Michael Myers. Directed by Dominique Othenin-Girard, 1989.

Halloween 6: The Curse of Michael Myers. Directed by Joe Chappelle, 1995.

Halloween H20: Twenty Years Later. Directed by Steve Miner, 1998.

Halloween Resurrection. Directed by Rick Rosenthal, 2002.

The Hand. Directed by Oliver Stone, 1981.

The Hands of Orlac. Directed by Edmond Gréville, 1960.

The Hills Have Eyes. Directed by Wes Craven, 1977.

The Hills Have Eyes 2. Directed by Wes Craven, 1985.

House of Wax. Directed by André De Toth, 1953.

Hostel. Directed by Eli Roth, 2005.

I Know What You Did Last Summer. Directed by Jim Gillespie, 1997.

Isle of the Dead. Directed by Mark Robson, 1945.

I Spit on Your Grave. Directed by Meir Zarchi, 1978.

I Was a Teenage Werewolf. Directed by Gene Fowler Jr., 1957.

Just Before Dawn. Directed by Jeff Lieberman, 1981.

The Last House on the Left. Directed by Wes Craven, 1972.

The Legend of Hell House. Directed by John Hough, 1973.

The Leopard Man. Directed by Jacques Tourneur, 1943.

Leprechaun. Directed by Mark Jones, 1993.

M – Eine Stadt sucht einen Mörder. Directed by Fritz Lang, 1931.

Mad Love. Directed by Karl Freund, 1935.

Manhunter. Directed by Michael Mann, 1986.

Maniac. Directed by William Lustig, 1980.

Marnie. Directed by Alfred Hitchcock, 1964.

Martin. Directed by George Romero, 1976.

Monster on the Campus. Directed by Jack Arnold, 1959.

Motel Hell. Directed by Kevin Connor, 1980.

Mother's Day. Directed by Charles Kaufman, 1980.

The Mummy. Directed by Karl Freund, 1932.

Night of the Living Dead. Directed by George Romero, 1968.

Night of the Living Dead. Directed by Tom Savini, 1990.

A Nightmare on Elm Street. Directed by Wes Craven, 1984.

A Nightmare on Elm Street. Directed by Samuel Bayer, 2010.

A Nightmare on Elm Street 2: Freddy's Revenge. Directed by Jack Sholder, 1985.

A Nightmare on Elm Street 3: Dream Warriors. Directed by Chuck Russell, 1987.

A Nightmare on Elm Street 4: The Dream Master. Directed by Renny Harlin, 1988.

A Nightmare on Elm Street 5: The Dream Child. Directed by Stephen Hopkins, 1989.

Nosferatu. Directed by F. W. Murnau, 1922.

Orlacs Hände. Directed by Robert Wiene, 1924.

The Omega Man. Directed by Boris Sagal, 1971.

The Parent Trap. Directed by David Swift, 1961.

Peeping Tom. Directed by Michael Powell, 1960.

The Phantom of the Opera. Directed by Rupert Julian, 1925.

Phantom of the Opera. Directed by Arthur Lubin, 1943.

The Phantom of the Opera. Directed by Terence Fisher, 1962.

The Phantom of the Opera. Directed by Dario Argento, 1998.

Phantom of the Opera. The Motion Picture. Directed by Dwight H. Little, 1990.

Phantom of the Paradise. Directed by Brian De Palma, 1974.

Pieces. Directed by Juan Piquer Simón, 1982.

Poltergeist. Directed by Tobe Hooper, 1982.

Prom Night. Directed by Paul Lynch, 1980.

Prom Night. Directed by Nelson McCormick, 2008.

Prom Night II. Directed by Bruce Pittman, 1987.

Prom Night III: The Last Kiss. Directed by Ron Oliver, 1990.

Prom Night IV: Deliver Us from Evil. Directed by Clay Borris, 1992.

The Prowler. Directed by Joseph Zito, 1981.

Psycho. Directed by Alfred Hitchcock, 1960.

Psycho. Directed by Gus Van Sant, 1998.

Psycho II. Directed by Richard Franklin, 1983.

Psycho III. Directed by Anthony Perkins, 1986.

Psycho IV: The Beginning. Directed by Mick Garris, 1990.

Raising Cain. Directed by Brian De Palma, 1992.

Rear Window. Directed by Alfred Hitchcock, 1954.

Return of the Living Dead. Directed by Dan O'Bannon, 1985.

Return of the Living Dead Part II. Directed by Ken Wiederhorn, 1988.

Return of the Living Dead 3. Directed by Brian Yuzna, 1993.

The Ring. Directed by Gore Verbinski, 2002.

Rope. Directed by Alfred Hitchcock, 1948.

Saw. Directed by James Wan, 2003 [short].

Saw. Directed by James Wan, 2004.

Saw II. Directed by Darren Lynn Bousman, 2005.

Saw III. Directed by Darren Lynn Bousman, 2006.

Scary Movie. Directed by Keenen Ivory Wayans, 2000.

Schizoid. Directed by David Paulsen, 1980.

Scream. Directed by Wes Craven, 1996.

Scream 2. Directed by Wes Craven, 1997.

Scream 3. Directed by Wes Craven, 2000.

Scream 4. Directed by Wes Craven, 2011.

Séance on a Wet Afternoon. Directed by Brian Forbes, 1964.

The Serpent and the Rainbow. Directed by Wes Craven, 1988.

Seven. Directed by David Fincher, 1995.

The Seventh Victim. Directed by Mark Robson, 1943.

Shadow of a Doubt. Directed by Alfred Hitchcock, 1947.

The Shining. Directed by Stanley Kubrick, 1980.

Shocker. Directed by Wes Craven, 1989.

Silence of the Lambs. Directed by Jonathan Demme, 1991.

Sisters. Directed by Brian De Palma, 1973.

The Sixth Sense. Directed by M. Night Shyamalan, 1999.

The Slumber Party Massacre. Directed by Amy Holden Jones, 1982.

Slumber Party Massacre II. Directed by Deborah Brock, 1987.

Slumber Party Massacre III. Directed by Sally Mattison, 1990.

Snow White and the Seven Dwarfs. Directed by David Hand (supervising), 1937.

Star Wars. Directed by George Lucas, 1977.

Stir of Echoes. Directed by David Koepp, 1999.

Der Student von Prag. Directed by Stellan Rye, 1913.

The Tales of Hoffmann. Directed by Michael Powell, 1951.

The Texas Chainsaw Massacre. Directed by Tobe Hooper, 1974.

The Texas Chainsaw Massacre 2. Directed by Tobe Hooper, 1986.

Thirty Days of Night. Directed by David Slade, 2007.

True Blood. Created by Alan Ball, 2008-2014.

Two Thousand Maniacs! Directed by H. G. Lewis, 1964.

Underworld. Directed by Len Wiseman, 2003.

Vampires. Directed by John Carpenter, 1998.

Vertigo. Directed by Alfred Hitchcock, 1958.

Videodrome. Directed by David Cronenberg, 1983.

The Virgin Spring [*Jungfrukällan*]. Directed by Ingmar Bergman, 1960.

Wes Craven's New Nightmare. Directed by Wes Craven, 1994.

The Wicker Man. Directed by Robin Hardy, 1973.

The Wolfman. Directed by George Waggner, 1941.

Zelig. Directed by Woody Allen, 1983.

Zombieland. Directed by Ruben Fleischer, 2009.

Bibliography

Adorno, Theodor. 'Prolog zum Fernsehen.' *Gesammelte Schriften*. Ed. Rolf Tiedemann. Volume 10/2. Frankfurt a/M: Suhrkamp Verlag, 2003: 507–17.

____ 'Fernsehen als Ideologie.' *Gesammelte Schriften*. Volume 10/2: 518–32.

Almansi, Renato J. 'On Telephoning, Compulsive Telephoning, and Perverse Telephoning: Psychoanalytic and Social Aspects.' *The Psychoanalytic Study of Society*, 11 (1985): 217–35.

Atkin, Samuel. 'Notes on Motivations for War: Toward a Psychoanalytic Social Psychology.' *The Psychoanalytic Quarterly*, 40 (1971): 549–83.

Attali, Jacques. *Noise: The Political Economy of Music*. Trans. Brian Massumi. Minneapolis: University of Minnesota Press, 1985 [1977].

Bally, Gustav. *Vom Spielraum der Freiheit: Die Bedeutung des Spiels bei Tier und Mensch*. Basel/Stuttgart: Schwabe & Co, 1966.

Bansak, Edmund G. *Fearing the Dark. The Val Lewton Career*. Jefferson, North Carolina: McFarland & Company, 1995.

Barker, Clive. 'The Forbidden.' *Books of Blood*. Vol. 5. Sphere Books Limited 1985.

Barthes, Roland. *La Chambre claire. Note sur la photographie*. Paris: Gallimard, 1980.

Benjamin, Walter. 'Critique of Violence.' Trans. Edmund Jephcott. *Selected Writings*. Ed. Michael W. Jennings. Volume 1. Cambridge, Massachusetts: Harvard University Press, 2002: 236–52.

____ *The Origin of German Tragic Drama*. Trans. John Osborne. London: Verson, 1998.

____ 'On Some Motifs in Baudelaire.' Trans. Harry Zohn. *Illuminations: Essays and Reflections*. Ed. Hannah Arendt. New York: Schocken Books, 1969: 155–200.

____ 'The Work of Art in the Age of Mechanical Reproduction.' *Illuminations*: 217–51.

Blake, Michael F. *A Thousand Faces. Lon Chaney's Unique Artistry in Motion Pictures*. Lanham/ New York/Oxford: Vestal Press, 1995.

Bloch, Robert. *American Gothic*. London: W. H. Allen & Co. Ltd., 1975.

____ *Crimes and Punishments. The Lost Bloch*, Vol. 3. Burton, Michigan: Subterranean Press, 2002.

____ *Psycho*. New York: TOR, 1959.

____ *Psycho II*. New York: Warner Books, 1982.

____ *Psycho House*. New York: ibooks, 1990.

Bollas, Christopher. 'The Structure of Evil.' *The Christopher Bollas Reader*. New York: Routledge, 2011: 155–77.

Bonaparte, Marie. *Edgar Poe: étude psychanalytique*. 3 volumes. Paris: Denoël et Steele, 1933.

Bouzereau, Laurent. *The DePalma Cut. The Films of America's Most Controversial Director*. New York: Dembner Books, 1988.

Canetti, Elias. *Crowds and Power*. Trans. Carol Stewart. New York: Farrar Straus Giroux, 1988 [1960].

Canning, Victor. *The Rainbird Pattern*. London: Heinemann, 1972.

Capote, Truman. *In Cold Blood. A True Account of a Multiple Murder and Its Consequences*. New York: Random House, 2007 [1965].

Chion, Michel. *Audio-Vision: Sound on Screen*. Trans. Claudia Gorbman. New York: Columbia University Press, 1994.

Clover, Carol J. *Men, Women, and Chainsaws. Gender in the Modern Horror Film*. Princeton: Princeton University Press, 1992.

Cohen, Tom. *Hitchcock's Cryptonymies*. 2 volumes. Minneapolis: University of Minnesota Press, 2005.

Crowley, Aleister. *The Confessions of Aleister Crowley: An Autohagiography*. Ed. John Symonds and Kenneth Grant. London: Arkana, 1969.

Danielewski, Mark Z. *House of Leaves*. New York: Pantheon Books, 2000.

Deleuze, Gilles and Felix Guattari. *A Thousand Plateaus. Capitalism and Schizophrenia*. Trans. Brian Massumi. Minneapolis: University of Minnesota Press, 1987 [1980].

Derrida, Jacques. 'Above All, No Journalists.' *Religion and Media*. Ed. Hent de Vries and Samuel Weber. Stanford: Stanford University Press, 2001: 56–93.

____ *La carte postale: de Socrate à Freud et au-delà*. Paris: Flammarion, 1980.

____ *Droits de regards*. Paris: Minuit, 1985.

____ *Rogues. Two Essays on Reason*. Trans. Pascale-Anne Brault and Michael Naas. Stanford: Stanford University Press, 2005.

Doyle, Arthur Conan. *The Coming of the Fairies*. Lincoln and London: University of Nebraska Press, 2006 [1921].

Duclos, Denis. *The Werewolf Complex. America's Fascination with Violence*. Trans. Amanda Pingree. Oxford/New York: Berg, 1998.

Eisner, Lotte. *The Haunted Screen: Expressionism in the German Cinema and the Influence of Max Reinhardt*. Trans. Roger Greaves. Berkeley: University of California Press, 1969.

Freud, Sigmund. 'Delusions and Dreams in Jensen's *Gradiva*.' *The Standard Edition of the Complete Psychological Works of Sigmund Freud*. Trans. and ed. James Strachey. Volume 9. London: The Hogarth Press, 1959: 7–95.

____ 'Dostoevsky and Parricide.' Volume 21: 173–94.

____ *Three Essays on the Theory of Sexuality*. Volume 7: 130–243.

____ 'From the History of an Infantile Neurosis'. Volume 17: 1–122.

____ *Group Psychology and the Analysis of the Ego*. Volume 18.

____ *New Introductory Lectures*. Volume 22.

____ 'Notes upon a Case of Obsessional Neurosis.' Volume 10: 151–318.

____ 'Psychoanalytic Notes on an Autobiographical Account of a Case of Paranoia (Dementia Paranoides).' Volume 12: 1–84.

____ 'Some Character-Types met with in Psychoanalytic Work.' Volume 14: 309–33.

____ 'Thoughts for the Times on War and Death.' Volume 14: 275–300.

____ *Totem and Taboo*. Volume 13.

____ 'The 'Uncanny.'' Volume 17: 219–52.

Fuss, Diana. *Identification Papers*. New York/London: Routledge, 1995.

Gagne, Paul R. *The Zombies That Ate Pittsburgh: The Films of George A. Romero*. New York: Dodd, Mead & Company, 1987.

Giovacchini, Peter. 'On Gadgets.' *The Psychoanalytic Quarterly*, 28 (1959): 330–41.

Gottlieb, Sidney, ed. *Hitchcock on Hitchcock. Selected Writings and Interviews*. Berkeley: University of California Press, 1997.

Grahame-Smith, Seth. *Pride and Prejudice and Zombies*. Philadelphia: Quirk Books, 2009.

Hagen, Wolfgang. *Radio Schreber. Der 'moderne Spiritismus' und die Sprache der Medien*. Weimar: Verlag und Datenbank für Geisteswissenschaften, 2001.

Harris, Charlaine. *Dead Until Dark*. New York: Ace Books, 2001.

____ *Living Dead in Dallas*. New York: Ace Books, 2002.

Harris, Thomas. *Red Dragon*. New York: Dell, 1981.

____ *Silence of the Lambs*. New York: St. Martin's Press, 1988.

Hervey, Ben. *Night of the Living Dead*. BFI Film Classics. London: Palgrave Macmillan, 2008.

Hoffmann, E. T. A. 'The Sandman', *Tales of Hoffmann*. Trans. R. J. Hollingdale. London: Penguin Classics, 1982.

Jones, Ernest. *On the Nightmare*. New York: Liveright, 1951 (new edition).

Kapp, Ernst. *Grundlinien einer Philosophie der Technik. Zur Entstehungsgeschichte der Kultur aus neuen Gesichtspunkten*. Braunschweig: Verlag George Westermann, 1877.

Kernberg, Otto. 'Love, the Couple, and the Group.' *The Psychoanalytic Quarterly*, 49 (1980): 78–108.

Kersten, Karin and Caroline Neubaur, eds. *Grand Guignol. Das Vergnügen, tausend Tode zu sterben. Frankreichs blutiges Theater*. Berlin: Verlag Klaus Wagenbach, 1976.

King, Stephen. *The Shining*. New York: Pocket Books, 2001 [1977].

Kittler, Friedrich A. ''Das Phantom unseres Ichs' und die Literaturpsychologie: E. T. A. Hoffmann – Freud – Lacan.' *Urszenen. Literaturwissenschaft als Diskursanalyse und Diskurskritik*. Ed. Friedrich A. Kittler and Horst Turk. Frankfurt a/M: Suhrkamp, 1977: 139–66.

____ *Draculas Vermächtnis. Technische Schriften*. Leipzig: Reclam, 1993.

____ *Grammophon, Film, Typewriter*. Berlin: Brinkmann & Bose, 1986.

Kittler, Friedrich and Paul Virilio. 'Die Informationsbombe. Paul Virilio und Friedrich Kittler im Gespräch.' TV interview, Arte, November, 1995.

Klein, Melanie.. 'On Identification.' *Envy and Gratitude and Other Works 1946–1963*. New York: The Free Press, 1984 [1955]: 141–75.

____ 'Mourning and Its Relation to Manic-Depressive States.' *Love, Guilt and Reparation and Other Works 1921–1945*. New York: The Free Press, 1984 [1940]: 344–69.

____ 'On the Sense of Loneliness.' *Envy and Gratitude and Other Works 1946–1963*. New York: The Free Press, 1984 [1963]: 300–13.

Kracauer, Siegfried. *From Caligari to Hitler: A Psychological History of the German Film*. Princeton: Princeton University Press, 1947.

Kuhn, Roland. 'The Attempted Murder of a Prostitute.' Trans. Ernest Angel. *Existence. A New Dimension in Psychiatry and Psychology*. Ed. Rollo May. New York: Basic Books, 1958: 365–425.

____ *Maskendeutungen im Rorschachschen Versuch*. Basel/New York: S. Karger, 1954.

La Bern, Arthur. *Goodbye Piccadilly, Farewell Leicester Square*. London: W. H. Allen, 1966.

Lacan, Jacques. 'Desire and the Interpretation of Desire in *Hamlet*.' *Literature and Psychoanalysis: The Question of Reading: Otherwise*. Ed. Shoshana Felman. Baltimore: Johns Hopkins University Press, 1982: 11–52.

____ 'The Mirror Stage as Formative of the *I* Function as Revealed in Psychoanalytic Experience.' *Écrits. A Selection*. Trans. Bruce Fink. New York/London: W. W. Norton & Company, 2004: 3–9.

____ 'The Purloined Letter.' *The Seminar of Jacques Lacan. Book II. The Ego in Freud's Theory and in the Technique of Psychoanalysis 1954–1955*. Ed. Jacques-Alain Miller. Trans. Sylvana Tomaselli. New York/London: W. W. Norton & Company, 1988: 191–205.

Leigh, Janet and Christopher Nickens. *Psycho. Behind the Scenes of the Classic Thriller*. New York: Harmony Books, 1995.

Leroux, Gaston. *The Phantom of the Opera*. Trans. unknown. New York: Signet Classics, 1987 [1911].

____ *The Mystery of the Yellow Room*. Trans. Terry Hale. London: Dedalus, 1997 [1907].

Libbitz, Daniel. *Gore. Die Meister des Blutes*. Hille: Medien Publikations und Werbegesellschaft GmbH, 2002.

Lindsay, Robert Bruce. *Julius Robert Mayer. Prophet of Energy*. Oxford: Pergamon Press, 1973.

Luckhurst, Roger. The Mummy's Curse: the True History of a Dark Fantasy. Oxford: Oxford University Press, 2012.

Lukacher, Ned. *Primal Scenes: Literature, Philosophy, Psychoanalysis*. Ithaca: Cornell University Press, 1988.

Mahlendorf, Ursula R. *The Wellsprings of Literary Creation*. Columbia, MD: Camden House, 1993.

Marks, Leo. *Peeping Tom*. London: Faber and Faber, 1998.

Matheson, Richard. *Hell House*. New York: Severn House, 2004 [1971].

____ *I Am Legend*. New York: ORB 1995 [1954].

____ *A Stir of Echoes*. New York: Tor Books, 2004 [1958].

McCarty, John, ed. *The Fearmakers. The Screen's Directorial Masters of Suspense and Terror*. New York: St. Martin's Press, 1994.

McCarty, John. *Psychos. Eighty Years of Mad Movies, Maniacs, and Murderous Deeds*. New York: St. Martin's Press, 1986.

McLuhan, Marshall. *Understanding Media: The Extensions of Man*. Cambridge, Mass.: The MIT Press, 1994 [1964].

Meyer, Stephenie. *Twilight*. New York: Little, Brown and Co., 2005

Moreno, J. L. *Psychodrama*. 3 Volumes. Beacon, N. Y.: Beacon House, 1980 [1946].

Mudgett, Jeff. *Bloodstains*. Gig Harbor, WA: Old Stump Productions, 2011.

Peirce, Charles Sanders. *The Philosophical Writings of Peirce*. Ed. Justus Buchler. New York: Dover, 1955.

Penley, Constance. *NASA/TREK: Popular Science and Sex in America*. London: Verso, 1997.

Poe, Edgar Allan. *The Collected Tales and Poems*. New York: The Modern Library, 1992.

Richards, Curtis. *Halloween*. New York: Bantam, 1979.

Rickels, Laurence A. *The Case of California*. Baltimore: Johns Hopkins University Press, 1991.

____ *The Devil Notebooks*. Minneapolis: University of Minnesota Press, 2008.

____ *Germany. A Science Fiction*. Fort Wayne: Anti-Oedipus Press, 2014.

____ *I Think I Am. Philip K. Dick*. Minneapolis: University of Minnesota Press, 2010.

____ *Nazi Psychoanalysis*. 3 volumes. Minneapolis: University of Minnesota Press, 2002.

____ *SPECTRE*. Fort Wayne: Anti-Oedipus Press, 2013.

____ *The Vampire Lectures*. Minneapolis: University of Minnesota Press, 1999.

Romero, George A. 'Clay.' *Modern Masters of Horror*. Ed. Frank Coffey. New York: Ace Books, 1982.

Romero, George A. and Susanna Sparrow. *Dawn of the Dead*. New York: St. Martin's Press, 1978.

____ *Martin*. New York: Day Books, 1980 [1977].

Ronell, Avital. *The Telephone Book: Technology, Schizophrenia, Electric Speech*. Lincoln: University of Nebraska Press, 1989.

____ 'Trauma TV: Twelve Steps Beyond the Pleasure Principle.' *Finitude's Score. Essays for the End of the Millennium*. Lincoln: University of Nebraska Press, 1994: 305–27.

Russo, John. *Night of the Living Dead*. New York: Pocket Books, 1981 [1974].

Sachs, Hanns. 'The Delay of the Machine Age.' *The Creative Unconscious: Studies in the Psychoanalysis of Art*. Cambridge: Sci-Art Publishers, 1942: 100–31.

Schechter, Harold. *Depraved. The Shocking True Story of America's First Serial Killer* New York: Pocket Star Books, 1996.

Schopenhauer, Arthur. 'Versuch über das Geistersehn und was damit zusammenhängt.' *Parerga und Paralipomena. Kleine philosophische Schriften*. Berlin: Verlag A. W. Hayn, 1851.

Schreber, Daniel Paul. *Denkwürdigkeiten eines Nervenkranken*. Leipzig: Mutze, 1913.

Stein, Elliott. "A Very Tender Film, a Very Nice One.' Michael Powell's 'Peeping Tom.'" *Film Comment*, 15, 5 (September/October 1979): 57–9.

Stein, Howard F. "Culture Shock' and the Inability to Mourn.' *The Psychoanalytic Study of Society*, 11 (1985): 157–72.

Stevenson, Robert Louis. 'Strange Case of Dr. Jekyll and Mr. Hyde.' *The Complete Stories of Robert Louis Stevenson*. Ed. Barry Menikoff. New York: Modern Library Paperback, 2002 [1886]: 251–324.

Stoker, Bram. *Dracula*. London: Archibald Constable, 1897.

Stoker, Dacre and Ian Holt. *Dracula The Un-Dead*. New York: Dutton, 2009.

Süskind, Patrick. *Das Parfum. Die Geschichte eines Mörders*. Zürich: Diogenes Verlag, 1985.

Suzuki, Koji. *Ring*. Trans. Robert B. Rohmer and Glynne Walley. New York: Vertical, 2003 [1991].

Theweleit, Klaus.'Sirenenschweigen, Polizistengesänge. Zu Jonathan Demmes *Das Schweigen der Lämmer*.' *Ed Gein. A Quiet Man*. Ed. Michael Farin and Hans Schmid. Munich: belleville, 1996: 323–50.

Thomson, David. *The Moment of Psycho: How Alfred Hitchcock Taught America to Love Murder*. New York: Basic Books, 2009.

Wilson, D. Harlan. *Dr. Identity*. Hyattsville, MD: Raw Dog Screaming Press, 2007.

Winnicott, D. W. 'The Antisocial Tendency.' *Deprivation and Delinquency*. Ed. Clare Winnicott, Ray Shepherd, and Madeleine Davis. London: Routledge, 2000 [1956]: 120–31.

____ 'Birth Memories, Birth Trauma, and Anxiety.' *Through Paediatrics to Psycho-Analysis. Collected Papers*. New York/London: Brunner-Routledge, 1992 [1949]: 174–93.

'The Depressive Position in Normal Emotional Development.' *Through Paediatrics to Psycho-Analysis. Collected Papers*. New York/London: Brunner-Routledge, 1992 [1954]: 262–77.

____ 'The Deprived Child and How He Can Be Compensated for Loss of Family Life.' *The Family and Individual Development*. London: Routledge, 1989 [1950]: 132–45.

____ 'Development of the Theme of the Mother's Unconscious as Discovered in Psychoanalytic Practice.' *Psychoanalytic Explorations*. Ed. Clare Winnicott, Ray Shepherd and Madeleine Davis. Cambridge, Mass.: Harvard University Press, 1989 [1969]: 247–50.

____ *Human Nature*. London: Free Association Books, 1999 [1988].

____ 'Mind and Its Relation to the Psyche-Soma.' *Through Paediatrics to Psycho-Analysis. Collected Papers*. New York/London: Brunner-Routledge, 1992 [1949]: 245–54.

____ 'Mirror-role of Mother and Family in Child Development.' *Playing and Reality*. London/New York: Routledge, 1996 [1967]: 111–18.

____ 'Mother's Madness Appearing in the Clinical Material as an Ego-Alien Factor.' *Psychoanalytic Explorations*. Ed. Clare Winnicott, Ray Shepherd and Madeleine Davis. Cambridge, Mass.: Harvard University Press, 1989 [1969]: 375–89.

____ 'Some Psychological Aspects of Juvenile Delinquency.' *Deprivation and Delinquency*. Ed. Clare Winnicott, Ray Shepherd, and Madeleine Davis. London: Routledge, 2000 [1946]: 113–19.

____ 'Struggling through the Doldrums.' *Deprivation and Delinquency*. Ed. Clare Winnicott, Ray Shepherd, and Madeleine Davis. London: Routledge, 2000 [1963]: 145–55.

____ *Therapeutic Consultations in Child Psychiatry*. New York: Basic Books, 1971.

____ 'Transitional Objects and Transitional Phenomena.' *Through Paediatrics to Psycho-Analysis. Collected Papers*. New York/London: Brunner-Routledge, 1992 [1951]: 229–42.

Woods, Paul Anthony. *Ed Gein: Psycho*. New York: St. Martin's Press, 1995.

Wünsch, Michaela. *Im inneren Außen. Der Serienkiller als Medium des Unbewussten*. Berlin: Kulturverlag Kadmos, 2010.

Index

Abbott and Costello Meet the Mummy 115
Abominable Dr. Phibes, The 212
Adorno, Theodor 3, 8, 25–6, 117
African-American 13–14, 70, 72, 96, 154, 200;
    African-American body 14–15; African-
    American president 20; African-American
    vampire 10
AIDS 10, 175
Alfred Hitchcock Presents 39
Aliens 151
American Dream 73
Amityville Horror, The 110
Anger, Kenneth 89
Antichrist 211
antisocial child 5, 28, 114, 195
Anti-War protest 69
Antonioni, Michelangelo 160
Arbus, Diane 200
Argento, Dario 115
Attali, Jacques 75, 101

Baby, The 193
Bad Seed, The 5
Bally, Gustav 25
Barker, Clive 14
Barthes, Roland 52, 119, 200
Bates Motel 30, 33, 99, 101
Bates, Norman 7, 19, 22–4, 29, 35, 39–41,
    43–5, 54–5, 57, 77, 99, 126, 158, 186, 210
B-culture 3
Bedlam 141
Belasco, Eric 104
Benjamin, Walter 3, 30, 36, 40, 48, 56, 104,
    117, 125, 136, 209
Bergman, Ingmar 109

B-film/pictures 7, 87, 89, 152–169, 211; B-film
    factories 66; vampire B-picture 163
B-genre 108, 159; B-genre consumerism 194
B-horror 12
Bildungsroman 48
Binswanger, Ludwig 78
Birds, The 34, 138, 165
Blade (trilogy) 9–10, 13–14
Blair Witch Project, The 197–200, 210
Blatty, William 211
Bloch, Robert 19, 32–3, 35, 37–40, 43–4, 55,
    101–2, 210
blockbuster 87
Blood Feast 86–7
Blood Trilogy 87–9
Blow Out 106, 163, 201
Blow Up 160, 162
Body Double 157, 160, 163, 165–6, 201
Bonaparte, Marie 207
Browning, Tod 18, 47
Bruiser 112
Bucket of Blood, A 88
Buffy the Vampire Slayer 9, 13–14, 18
Bush Jr., George W. 14–15, 62

Cabinet of Dr. Caligari, The 154
camera-killer 48
Candyman (trilogy) 13
Canetti, Elias 86, 93, 134–5, 142–3
cannibalism 32–3, 58, 68, 94–101, 104, 107,
    138, 186, 204; cannibal family 94–5, 106;
    cannibal killers 94, 108; cannibalistic
    violence 58; ex-cannibal 106
Canning, Victor 111
Capote, Truman 59–60

Carpenter, John 9, 125–7
Carrie 30–1, 153, 166
castration 49, 82–3, 157, 159
Cat People 140–1, 143
Cell, The 137
chainsaw 98–101
Chaney, Lon 117
Charley's Aunt 41
childhood 4–5, 14, 34, 48, 55, 82, 90, 95,
  113, 143, 170, 172, 195, 198, 204, 208;
  antisocial child 5, 28, 114, 195; child
  abuse 126, 168; childhood trauma 56
Chinese consumer 12
Christianity 12–14, 30, 104, 127, 131,
  146, 186, 209, 210; Christian evil 211;
  Christian Mass 146; Christian psycho
  210; Christian Right 14, 20; Christian-
  Spiritualist medium 104
Cioffi, Frank 179
Civil Rights 20
claustrophobia 163–4
Clay (story) 77, 88
Color Me Blood Red 87–8
Columbo 203
Conan Doyle, Sir Arthur 12
consumerism 15, 19, 65, 73, 194
Crane, Marion 22–4, 36, 41, 44, 72, 87, 136,
  155, 213
Craven, Wes 105–9, 172, 174, 176–9, 184–5,
  188, 201
Crawling Hand, The 81
Crazies, The 75
criminality 7, 19, 25–6, 28, 36, 43, 58, 92,
  102, 110–11, 118, 203, 207, 209–11;
  celebrity criminal 187; criminal behaviour
  185; criminal detection 1; criminal
  impulses 50; culture of real crime 188;
  normalisation of criminality 25; psycho
  criminal 6, 196
Cronenberg, David 211
Crowds and Power 86, 135, 142
CSI (Las Vegas) 202–4, 208
Curse of the Cat People, The 143
Curse of the Demon 200
Curtis, Jamie Lee 125, 165
Cutting Class 50

Danielewski, Mark Z. 197
Dawn of the Dead 71–5, 99

Day of the Dead 71, 73–5
death: get-well death 35; Hitchcock's death
  40; living death 19, 43, 76; mother's death
  32, 39, 48, 55, 107, 119, 127; undead 9–10,
  15, 17–19, 43, 77, 129; *see also* zombie
Death in Venice 196
Dead Until Dark 12
Deleuze, Gilles 205
de Lorde, André 89
Demme, Jonathan 204
Demons 31
De Palma, Brian 7, 30, 38, 40, 55–6, 121, 125,
  153, 155, 158–66, 201
depression 4, 77–8, 84, 161, 184, 190, 192–3,
  199; repressed depression 170, 193
Derrida, Jacques 96, 175, 178, 186, 207
Deus ex Machina 86
Devil 7, 9, 17, 19–20, 67, 115, 122, 125, 176,
  194, 200, 202, 205–6, 209; Devil complex
  24; Devil Dad 7, 9, 202, 206, 209, 213
Devil Notebooks, The 7, 115
Dexter 18
Diaboliques, Les 31
Dick, Philip K. 6, 62, 212
digital media 173–4
DNA 209, 211
Doppelgänger 26
Dracula (film) 18, 43
Dracula (novel) 16–17, 66, 101, 141, 148
Dracula, Count 17, 19, 67, 141
Dracula – The Un-Dead 16–17
Dressed to Kill 125, 155–60, 163, 166
Dr. Mabuse 92

Eaten Alive (aka *Death Trap*, aka *Horror Hotel*,
  aka *Starlight Slaughter*) 99
EC Comics 90
ego: auxiliary egos 42; Ego-Alien Factor 191;
  ego-control 60; ego ideal 146; cultural
  superego 2; identity of the ego 147;
  maternal superego 37; superego-style 2,
  34–5, 76, 84, 95, 115, 131
Englund, Robert 100, 115, 176, 179–80
envy 121, 188, 195; pre-Oedipal envy 147
Exorcist, The (film) 210, 212
Exorcist, The (novel) 211
Exorcist II: The Heretic 201
Eyes of Laura Mars 127
Eyes without a Face (*Les yeux sans visage*) 46

Fade to Black 67
Family Plot 110
Fantôme de l'Opéra, Le 1, 101, 115–19, 121
Fatal Attraction 146–8, 151
father: adoptive father 5; dead father 35, 69, 79, 107, 119, 127, 149, 203; father figure 53; father function 49; fatherhood 43, 62; fatherless 31, 35; father neurosis 4; founding father 148; good father 200; infernal father 206; missing father 34; Oedipal father 127; pre-Oedipal father 7, 202, 209; primal father 49, 59, 147, 202; representative of father 32
Faust/Faustian 17, 76–7, 115, 121–2, 205
Phantom of the Opera, The (1925) 7, 115, 117, 196
Phantom of the Opera (1943) 121
Phantom of the Opera, The (1998) 115
Phantom of the Opera: the Motion Picture 115
female: bodies 80; female genitals 78, 80; female identity 157; femaleness 157; female serial killer 44; female sex 80; female survivor position 168; female victim 47
Fido 75
Fincher, David 210
Fog, The 125
Forrest Gump 176
Frankenstein 29 , 141
Freddy 127, 170–7, 179, 213; see under Krueger, Freddy
Freddy's Dead 209
Freddy vs. Jason 174–5
Freaks 47
Frenzy 57–8
Freud, Sigmund 1, 3–5, 20, 26–7, 34, 47–53, 57, 63–5, 78, 82–6, 97, 104, 112, 114, 118, 136, 146, 147, 150, 155–7, 178–82, 194, 202–3, 206; Freudian psychoanalysis 4–5; post-Freudian structuralism 204
Freund, Karl 90, 115, 196
Friday the 13th 50, 101, 111, 129–31, 160, 170, 187, 210
Friday the 13th 2 129
Friday the 13th 3 130, 132
Friday the 13th Part VI: Jason Lives 112
Friedkin, William 210–11

Gdansk Man 198

Gein, Ed 2, 32–3, 57, 68, 94, 101, 127, 204
genre: B-genres 108, 160; doubling genre 112; fantasy genre 12–13; genre and media 8; genre of psychopathic criminality 211; horror film genre 1, 83, 194; new genre 67, 199; psycho horror genre 129
German cinema 1
German Expressionism 2
Gestell 38, 76–7, 88
Ghost 13
ghost 11–12, 20, 34, 45, 63, 78, 88, 103, 105, 110, 115, 118–20, 128, 143, 156, 160, 171, 180, 186–7, 189, 194, 199–200, 208, 211; friendly ghost 198; ghost-busting machine 105; ghost-effects 104; ghost face 185; ghostliness 185, 189, 192, 199; ghost memories 156; ghost movies 13; ghost of Hamlet's father 34, 51; vengeful ghost 190; see also Opera ghost
Godard, Jean-Luc 160
Gold Bug, The 53
Gone with the Wind 13
Goodbye Piccadilly, Farewell Leicester Square 59
Grand Guignol 89–91, 99, 104, 153
Green, Julian 205–6
Gothic novel 3, 101, 198
Guattari, Félix 205
Gulf War 15

Halloween 7, 38, 44, 124–31, 135, 138–9, 155, 170, 186, 208, 210
Halloween 2 125, 127–8
Halloween III: Season of the Witch 131
Halloween: H2 O 125
Hamlet 171, 207
Hamlet 32, 34, 51, 171, 208
Hand, The 84
Harris, Charlaine 12–13
Harris, Thomas 204
Heidegger, Martin 78, 84
Hello Mary Lou: Prom Night II 202
Herrmann, Bernard 153
heterograft 46, 115
Hills Have Eyes, The 106
Hills Have Eyes 2, The 106
Hilton, Conrad N. 101

Hitchcock, Alfred 1–2, 8, 19, 23, 25, 29, 31–2, 34–40, 43, 55–9, 86–7, 102, 110–11, 132, 138, 153, 160, 163–5, 173, 178, 199
Holmes, H. H. 101–3
Holmes, Sherlock 13, 118, 158
homosexuality 39, 93, 151; homosexual panic 175
Hooper, Tobe 94, 97, 99, 132
Horror Chamber of Dr. Faustus, The 46
horror cinema/films 1–2, 4, 7, 19, 30, 38, 44, 54, 64, 68, 83, 87–8, 90, 93, 100, 106–8, 112, 127, 130–2, 141–2, 169, 173, 185–6, 188, 194, 196, 200, 202, 210–11; Hollywood horror film 68, 90; horror home movies 51; low-budget horror films 161; metabolism of horror films 200; meta-horror films 47; occult horror films 142; psycho horror cinema/films 2, 4, 19, 54, 93, 100, 130, 194, 210; *see also* genre
Hostel 2
House of Leaves 197–8
House of Wax 88

I Am Legend 15, 19, 65, 71, 73, 75
If I Were You 205
I Know What You Did Last Summer 201
incest 32, 45, 68, 89, 104, 140, 151, 209
In Cold Blood 59
investigative journalism 1, 118
impotence 159, 168
Iraq War 18
Isle of the Dead 142
I Spit on Your Grave 107, 216
I Think I Am 6
I Was a Teenage Werewolf 144

Jason 14, 18, 112, 127, 129–33, 175, 187
Jaws 29
Julian, Rupert 115–17, 196
Just Before Dawn 181

Kafka, Franz 117
Kapp, Ernst 84–6
Karloff, Boris 68
Kinematik 85
King Kong 29, 141
King, Martin Luther 70
King, Stephen 199
Kittler, Friedrich 11, 16, 35, 174

Klein, Melanie 6, 21, 48, 90, 194–5, 205–7
Koch, Ilse 2, 127
Kracauer, Siegfried 1
Krueger, Freddy, 7, 108, 115, 130, 170–2, 174–5, 178, 209
Kubrick, Stanley 199–200
Kuhn, Roland 78–80, 133, 135

La Bern, Arthur 59
Lacan, Jacques 182, 184, 205, 207
Lang, Fritz 91
Last House on the Left, The 107–9, 184
LaVey, Anton 212
Leatherface 95–6, 98–9, 134, 138
Lecktor, Hannibal 204
Lecter, Hannibal 186
Legend of Hell House, The 105
Leichnam 51
Leigh, Janet 29, 39, 56, 125–6
Leopard Man, The 142
Leprechaun 13
Leroux, Gaston 1, 115–17, 119, 121
Lewis, Herschell Gordon 8, 86–90, 129
Lewton, Val 141
Lieberman, Jeff 181
lycanthrope 10; *see* werewolf

M 91, 92
Madame Butterfly 149–51
Mad Love 90, 196
madness 6, 88, 177, 191, 203
Mains d'Orlac, Les 90
Mamoulian, Rouben 83
Manhunter 204, 206–7
Maniac 124
Mann, Michael 204
Marks, Leo 53
Marnie 153, 165
Martin 75–7, 133
mask 7, 10, 45–6, 78, 86, 98–9, 112–13, 115–16, 120–2, 124–5, 127–8, 132–6, 138, 142, 173, 184, 188, 206–7; aura-mask 116; death mask 78, 115; double-mask 113; horror masks 132; mask/masque of metamorphosis 142; medical-prosthetic mask 115; pathogenic mask 136
masochism 47–8
mass culture 19, 94, 128, 167, 178
mass media 2, 4, 65, 74, 83, 162, 173, 187–8

mass murder 1, 19, 62–80; epidemic of 65, 68–9

mass psychology 13, 26, 87, 147

masturbation 34, 48, 78, 82, 127, 155; infantile masturbation 114; prohibited masturbation 177

Matheson, Richard 15, 19, 65, 71, 73, 75, 104, 156

matricide 24, 37

Mayer, Julius Robert 60

melancholia 1, 5, 7, 10, 21, 26, 32, 36, 51, 97, 211; melancholic loss 5; melancholic psychosis 76; melancholic werewolf 10; vampiric melancholia 19

Memoirs of My Nervous Illness 26, 48

mental illness 60, 204

metamorphosis 83, 133, 140, 142, 204

metaphor: anti-metaphorical 63; metaphorical/metaphysical comfort 19; metaphorical sense 63; mirrors on mirrors 49, 120

Meyer, Stephenie 10

mirror: Lacan's mirror 182, 184; mirror images 52–3, 112–13, 122, 158; mirror mask 122; mirror reflection 13, 117; mirror reflex 98; mirror relation 120, 122, 182; mirror-shield 95; mirrors of fear 49; rear-view mirror 167

mise-en-scène 207

MM 125–30, 135–6, 138–9; *see under* Myers, Michael

Monster on the Campus 142

Motel Hell 99–100

mother: absence mother 137–8; Christian-yahoo mother 31; dead mother 35, 78, 107, 126, 129; early mother 137; maternal superego 35, 37; Mirror-role of Mother 182; mother-and-child *Schauer* 130; mother as dominant 39; mother as mummy 38; mother-image 184; mother of the perfect child 5; role of mother 23

Mother's Day 192

moviegoer 1, 6, 31, 93, 121, 164, 204

multimurderer 102

mummification 38, 94, 99, 107, 138; mummy horror 115

Mummy, The 115

mutilation 89, 104

Myers, Michael 2, 124–5, 127, 172, 175, 210

mystère de la chamber jaune, Le (*The Mystery of the Yellow Room*) 118

narcissism 26, 76, 80, 150–1, 158, 174

Navidson Record, The 197–8

Navidson, Will 197–8

necromancy 13, 200

necrophilia 32, 82, 104

neurosis: father neurosis 4; immortality neurosis 202; neurosis-to-psychosis 87; neurotic analysis 27–8, 183–4; transference neurosis 4–5; traumatic neurosis 3–4, 117, 126

new media 1, 56, 118

new nihilism 200

Night of the Living Dead 7, 19, 29, 65–71, 74–5, 81, 86–7, 90, 94, 108, 138, 154, 169, 181

Nightmare on Elm Street, A 7, 44, 105, 107, 126, 167, 170–9, 186, 201

Noise 75

Norman 2, 6, 22–4, 32–43, 45, 55, 99, 129, 155; *see under* Bates, Norman

nudity 14, 34, 80

Obama, Barack 20

occultism 39

Oedipal: mother's Oedipal absence 139; Oedipal 149; Oedipal and pre-Oedipal envy 147; Oedipus complex 49, 82–3; Oedipal conflict 101, 147; Oedipal detective 101; Oedipal father 127; Oedipal film story 90; Oedipal police work 92; Oedipal prohibitions 147; pre-Oedipal blood bond 9; pre-Oedipal father 7, 56, 202, 209; pre-Oedipal mother 145, 206, 209; pre-Oedipal relationship 206; pre-Oedipal zone 127

Omega Man, The 71

Opera ghost 119–20

otherness 150

other woman 32, 144, 146–7, 190

Pabst, G. W. 56

Paranormal Activity 211

Parent Trap, The 106

Parfum, Das (*Perfume*) 116

paternal abuse 137

parental inheritance 130

Peeping Tom 8, 47–9, 51, 53–5, 57–8, 117, 127, 153–4, 160–1
Perkins, Anthony 23, 44
phantasmagoria 19, 29, 155, 174
phantom 1, 110–123, 127, 142–3, 148
phantom-like 36
Phantom of the Opera, The (1925) 7, 115, 117, 127, 196
Phantom of the Opera (1943) 121
Phantom of the Opera, The (1989) 115
Phantom of the Opera, The (1998) 115
Phantom of the Paradise 40, 121, 153, 160
Pieces 93
Poe, Edgar Allan 53–4, 112–13, 206–7
Poltergeist 13, 44
Post Card, The 207
post-9/11 15
POV 50, 54, 80, 121, 127, 135–6, 205, 207; camera POV 35, 127, 132, 138; POV as mask 78, 121, 124, 127, 132, 206; POV document 122; peeping POV 160; POV stalker 152; slasher POV 124
Powell, Michael 47–9, 53–4, 56, 83, 90, 132
pre-digital era 174
Pride and Prejudice and Zombies 12
Prom Night 201
Prom Night III 202
Prom Night IV 202
protagonist/narrator 113–14
proto-cryptological 136
Prowler, The 169
psyche-soma coexistence 20–1
Psycho (film) 1, 6–8, 24–5, 29–32, 34, 38–40, 43–4, 49, 55, 57, 59, 67–8, 89, 94, 100, 107, 125–7, 129, 135, 138, 153–5, 173, 175, 187, 189, 212; post-*Psycho* 197; pre-*Psycho* horror 196
Psycho (novel) 32–3, 55
Psycho II 23, 40–1, 43–5, 210
Psycho III 23–4, 43–4
Psycho IV:The Beginning 24
psychoanalysis 3, 11, 25–6, 112; American psychoanalysis 148, 150–1; Freudian psychoanalysis 4, 5, 179; Nazy psychoanalysis 7
psychodrama 41–3, 132
Psycho Effect 3–7, 24, 29, 31, 40, 43–4, 57, 87, 89, 92–3, 105–6, 115, 121, 126, 129, 135–6, 143, 153, 160, 172, 174–6,

186, 189, 192, 196, 198–9, 200–1, 203, 210–11; post-Psycho-Effec 186; *see also Schauer* scene
psychohistory 8, 57
psycho horror films 2, 19, 93, 210
Psycho House 33, 44, 210
psychological poverty 147, 178
psychological warfare 26
psychopathology 6, 82, 131, 198; psycho criminal 6; psychodrama 41–3, 132; psycho horror 9, 16, 19, 31, 57, 70, 89, 115, 129–32, 190, 194–213; psycho killer 4, 16, 20, 23, 33, 48, 76, 77, 92, 106, 125, 130, 132, 137–9, 142, 152, 157–9, 162, 165, 169, 172, 176, 185, 187, 190, 201, 204–5, 210; psychopathic behaviour 26; psychopathic disorders 19; psychopathic psycho 61, 202; psychopathic rage 60; psychopathological spectrum 41; psychotic delusion 67; psycho violence 1, 16, 19, 43, 93, 126, 128, 160, 181–2, 198, 200, 209; *see also* horror cinema/films
Psychopharmacology 78
Purloined Letter, The (story) 206

racism 13–15, 70, 150
Rainbird Pattern, The 111
Raising Cain 55
rape 58, 89, 108, 128, 188, 192, 209
Reagan, Ronald 13, 170
Rear Window 164
Red Dragon 204
Renard, Maurice 90
repressed memories 170, 179, 201
Return of the Living Dead 71
Richards, Curtis 127
Ring, The 200
Rollin, Jean 166
Romero, George 19, 62, 67–9, 70–7, 83, 86–8, 90, 94, 97, 109, 112
Rope 57

sadism 47–8, 80, 127
Sanders Peirce, Charles 52
Sandman, The 35, 82–3, 177, 198
Satanic movie 212
Satanism 32, 142, 210
Savini, Tom 70, 97, 169

Saw 210–12
Saw II 211–12
Saw III 212
Scary Movie 128, 189
Schauer 1, 3, 108, 112, 130, 157, 159, 175;
    Schauer scene 6–7, 22–61, 130, 141, 157,
    199; Schauer victim 86
Schizoid 152
Schopenhauer, Arthur 171
Schreber, Daniel Paul 26, 48, 77, 135, 155–7,
    163, 192, 210
science fiction 46
Scream 7, 44, 126, 138, 174, 184–92, 198,
    201
Scream 2 31, 187, 189
Scream 3 187–90
Scream 4 44, 188, 210
scream memory 49–50, 125, 163, 171
Séance on a Wet Afternoon 110
self-: self-analysis 164; self-created world 27;
    self-criticism 76; self-deprecation 45;
    self-hatred 171; self-reflection 141–2;
    self-reflexive camera 48; self-reflexivity 3,
    7, 31, 141, 162, 168, 173–4, 176, 185, 188,
    210; self-regulation 19; self-starters 42
serial killer 2, 18–19, 44, 57–8, 67, 76, 82, 92,
    101, 124, 137, 176, 194, 206
serial narrative 132
Serpent and the Rainbow, The 201
Seven 210–11
Seventh Victim, The 141
sexuality: auto-eroticism 47; genital
    sexuality 9–10, 14, 17; sexual body
    14, 52; sexual fantasy 47, 155; sexual
    repression 17, 78, 98
Shadow of a Doubt 102
Shining, The 199
Shocker 176
Shyamalan, M. Night 199–200
Silence of the Lambs, The 92, 186, 198, 204
Sisters 40, 153–6, 160
Sixth Sense, The 13, 194, 196–7, 199–200
Slumber Party Massacre, The 166
Slumber Party Massacre II 167
Slumber Party Massacre III 167
Snow White and the Seven Dwarfs 88
socio-political allegory 71
Sparrow, Susan 73–4, 76
SPECTRE 6

Spiritualism 1, 90, 103–4, 110, 117–18;
    modern Spiritualism 118–19
Star Wars 13, 127
Steinem, Gloria 179
stereotype 26, 167
Stevenson, Robert Louis 83, 112
Stir of Echoes, A 156
Stoker, Bram 16–17, 101, 148
Stoker, Dacre 16
Stone, Oliver 84
Strange Case of Dr. Jekyll and Mr. Hyde, The 83,
    112
Streiner, Russell 70
Student of Prague, The 105, 112
supernatural 12, 45, 93, 130, 142, 189, 197
Süskind, Patrick 116
Swales, Peter 179

taboo 15, 30, 63–4, 69, 194
Tales of Hoffmann, The 83, 90, 100
taxidermy 34–5, 38, 68, 87
techno-catastrophe 3–4
Texas Chainsaw Massacre, The 19, 94, 106,
    124, 135, 137–8, 186, 192
Texas Chainsaw Massacre 2, The 101
Thirty Days of Night 15
torture 2, 53–4, 88, 90, 96, 99, 103, 107,
    116–17, 128, 144, 210–11
Tourneur, Jacques 141, 200
transvestism 39, 40
trauma: menstrual trauma 31; post traumatic
    configuration 60; post-traumatic delay 1;
    post-traumatic recollection 29; post-
    traumatic returns 210; post-traumatic
    stress disorder 15, 17, 173; post-
    traumatic survival 99; trauma machine
    127; traumatic memories 199; traumatic
    neurosis 3–4, 117, 126; traumatised child
    55, 208
True Blood 9–14, 18–20
TV 8, 11, 14, 20, 25–6, 29–31, 38–40, 55–6,
    60, 68, 71, 74, 87, 101, 132, 151, 171,
    173–4, 202; TV-Führer psychology 173;
    reality TV 211; see also Adorno, Theodor
28 Days Later 15
Twilight 10–11
Two Thousand Maniacs 87–88

Underworld 10

Vampire of Düsseldorf 92
Vampires 9
vampirism 7–8, 9–21, 64–7, 71–2, 75–7,
    136, 166; African-American vampire
    10; renewal of vampirism 18; vampire
    B-picture 163; vampire film 165;
    vampire hunters 148; vampire sexuality
    10; vampire values 11; vampires as
    vegetarians 10–11, 18
Vanitas imagery 97
Van Sant, Gus 29, 37
Verdichtung 89
Vertigo 56, 153, 163–5
victim: female victim 47; psychic victims
    117; random victims 162; sacrificial
    victims 128; *Schauer* victim 86; trauma
    victim 116; undead victims 124; victims
    of war 169; vampire victim 18; victim-to-
    be 60, 130
Videodrome 211
Vietnam War 3, 68–9, 73, 99, 153, 169, 172;
    anti-Vietnam-War 170
Virgin Spring, The 109
von Trier, Lars 211
Voorhees, Jason 2, 130; *see under* Jason
voyeurism 47–8, 89, 154, 163–5

Waters, John 87
werewolf 10
Wes Craven's New Nightmare 176
Wicker Man, The 128
Williamson, Kevin 174, 185, 188, 201
William Wilson (story) 112–13, 127
Winnicott, D. W. 5–6, 8, 20–1, 25–8, 130–1,
    136–9, 182–4, 190–1, 195, 212
Wolfman, The 29
Woodstock 71
WW 113–14; *see under* William Wilson (story)
WWI 4, 48, 180
WWII 3, 19, 40, 59, 94, 127, 141, 169; post-
    WWII period 59; psychological casualty
    19

Zelig 176–9, 185, 188
Zito, Joseph 169
zombie 15–16, 19–20, 62, 69–77, 94,
    99–100, 109, 127; zombie epidemic 70,
    81; zombiefication 73; zombie hunger 62;
    zombie invasion 15; zombieism 7, 16, 71,
    76, 192; zombie projections 9, 11; zombie
    taboo 69; zombie wars 62
zombie films/movies 4, 15, 62, 201
Zombieland 15

CPSIA information can be obtained at www.ICGtesting.com
Printed in the USA
LVOW10s0128070616

491389LV00001B/1/P